FOOTPRINT... ...HE SNOW The Heroes And Heroines Of Canada

Date Due

SEP 29 1995			
SEP 26 2000			
OCT 22 2000			
DEC 21 2001			
APR 13 2004			

7673		
SEP 29 1995		
SEP 26 2000		

FOOTPRINTS

The Heroes And Heroines of Canada

LITTLE BRICK SCHOOLHOUSE / Educational Publication

IN THE SNOW

Robert Livesey

Editorial Staff: Helge Hongisto, Stan Skinner.
Design: John Zehethofer.
Office Staff: Eve Bodnar, Kim Dinsdale, Betty Green, Elizabeth Gray Livesey.

Printed in Canada by Hunter Rose Company Ltd.

Second Edition — Revised
ISBN 0-9690021-1-4

ACKNOWLEDGEMENTS
The publishers wish to thank the following persons and organizations for their aid. Every step has been taken to make the list of acknowledgements comprehensive, but in some cases all efforts to trace the owners of copyrights failed. Any errors or omissions drawn to our attention will be corrected in future editions.

ILLUSTRATIONS: Brian Gomes 2; Metropolitan Toronto Library 3, (John Ross Robertson) 19, 33, 55, 57, 65, 75, 131, 132, 137, 138, 145; Lynne Naylor 4; Hamilton Spectator 6; Public Archives Canada, (c-70239) 8, (c-3018) 17, 20 (top), 21 (c-70270) left, 24 (c-3704), 26 (c-2146), 29 (c-73712), 30 (c-70258), 35 (c-70264), 37 (c-276), 38 (c-73427), 39 (c-70229), 41 (c-70253), 47 (c-27674), 52 (c-5434), 53 (c-4782), 60 (c-21594), 62 (c-70231), 66 (c-6109), 68 (c-18737), 70 (c-73708), 101 (c-70240), 102 (c-15282), 107 (c-7797), 136 (PA-1651); 173 (c-56826), 178 (PA-37422), 178 (AC-280), 195 (z-3343-5); Peter Grau 11,12; Hudson's Bay Company 13, 20 bottom, 27, 51; Barry Ohem 15; Library of Congress. Gilbert H. Grosvenor Collection of Alexander Graham Bell Photographs, photos supplied by Bell Canada 21 right, 76, 77, 78, 79, 121, photo supplied by National Museum of Science and Technology 122; Cunard Archives 34; Provincial Archives of British Columbia 44, 71, 188; Paramount Pictures 48; Royal Army Medical College 58; Canada's Sports Hall of Fame 64, 81, 83, 112, 113, 114, 116, 125, 126, 128, 155, 157, 160, 161, 162, 163, 164, 181, 182, 186, 190, 192, 193, 194, 199, 200, 201, 203, 204; New Westminster Columbian 73; Brian Lee 80, Glenbow-Alberta Institute 86, 87, 90, 105; R.C.M.P. 88, 93; Canadian Pacific, Corporate Archives 91; Huntley Brown (captions by Walt McDayter) 94, 95, 96, 97, 141, 142, 143, 144; Archives of Ontario 99, 110, 146, 152, 168, 169, 170; Province of Manitoba Provincial Archives 100; The Toronto Star 106, 127, 140; Dr. Stuart Macdonald, son of Lucy Maud Montgomery 119, 120; Aviation & Space Division, National Museum of Science and Technology 123, 139; Ontario Government 124; Kitchener-Waterloo Record 129, 130; Miller Services 130 top, 151, 165, 205, 206; University of Toronto 148, 149, 150; Brendon Fox 158; Canada's Hockey Hall of Fame 166, 167; National Film Board of Canada 172, 174, 175, 176, 177; Bombardier Ltd. 184, 185; Vancouver Art Gallery 189; N.D.P. 196; British Columbia Sports Hall of Fame 197.

CONTENTS

Other textbooks by Robert Livesey

Incentives, 1970, Longman Canada Limited.

Faces of Myth, 1975, Longman Canada Limited.

TO THE STUDENT

This book is designed to introduce you to over a hundred personalities who have contributed to the development of Canada. You will be encouraged to read, think, discuss, and write about the people and their efforts. It is hoped that the "Topics for Discussion" will enable you to organize and state your opinions and that the "Creative Challenges" will allow you to create your own unique contributions.

You will not likely consider every person in this book a hero or heroine but you should discover some whom you admire.

GLOOSCAP

An Indian Hero

Long before the white men came to the North American continent there were stories of heroes in the history and mythology of the Indian people. Glooscap was neither a great chief nor a god, but he appears in Micmac legend at the very beginning of creation.

"He was the Master, and at his dawn he lay on his back, head to the rising sun and feet to the setting sun left hand to the south and right hand to the north."

Knowledge of all sorts was his. He brought ferocious animals under the control of his people. He cleared the rivers and lakes for navigation. Hunting and fishing were arts in which he excelled.

"After I have taught you many things, I am going to leave you. . . ." he once told the Micmacs. "One day your home will be taken away from you by palefaces. I am going to build you a new home in the North, where only you, my people, can come and live. And I will build it on mountains of gold."

The following story about Glooscap is from a book entitled, Glooscap and his Magic by Kay Hill (McClelland and Stewart Ltd.)

"We are even so far," cried Winpe. "Now for the final test!"

He brought forth two long sticks with webbing at the ends, and gave one of them to Glooscap together with a stuffed moosehide ball.

"This is a game I call tokhonon. As you see, I have set up two posts at each end of my cave. We must strike the ball back and forth, never touching it with our hands, and whoever first drives it between the other's goal posts, wins!"

Glooscap nodded his understanding, and the match began.

Ah, what a game that was! The two great heroes, each so tall and powerful, struck out with such force their sticks tore holes in the rock, and the whole cave trembled and cracked. Outside in the sea, Bootup woke with a start and heard with alarm the awesome rumbling. The black island heaved and shook, causing the waves to rise and sweep over Bootup's head.

For the space of three suns, while Noogumee and Marten watched breathlessly, the game continued without pause. Both players were by now nearly exhausted, yet neither had a single thought of giving in.

Suddenly Glooscap thought of the time that was passing. How were his people managing without him? What if Badger were up to some new tricks? The thought gave him fresh energy and, leaping high in the air, he struck the ball with such force it turned into a ball of fire and shot, burning, into Winpe's goal.

Winpe stepped back, his jaw falling with dismay.

Then slowly, he summoned up a grin and came and slapped Glooscap on the shoulder.

"You are the winner," he said

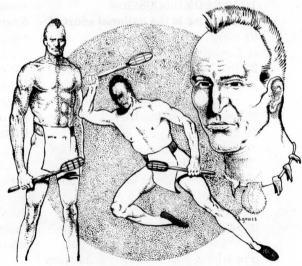

Design by student Brian Gomes.

This photograph of Indians at an 1869 lacrosse tournament was the first half-tone photograph in the world to be seen in a newspaper. The technique was developed by a Canadian, George Desbarats, and was reproduced in his paper, the Canadian Illustrated News.

heartily. "It was a good game. Now choose your prize."

Glooscap looked at Winpe's strings of pearls and sapphires and shook his head. He held out his hand for Winpe's webbed stick.

"Give me the game," he said.

Now in his time. Glooscap had given many good gifts to his people — the forests, the streams, the fish and the animals — but no gift was cherished more than the game he brought back to them from Winpe's island, the game the Indians called tokhonon, the game the white man was one day to copy and call lacrosse.

And, with this last adventure, kespeadooksit — the stories end.

TOPICS FOR DISCUSSION

1. Lacrosse is the national sport of Canada. Is it the most popular sport in Canada? Why or why not?

2. In Canada today who controls ferocious animals? Who clears the rivers and lakes for navigation? Who are the best hunters or fishermen?

3. If you had been given Glooscap's choice of prizes, would you have chosen the game as he did? Explain why or why not.

RESEARCH CHALLENGES

1. What tribe of Indians used to live where you now live? Who were their heroes?

2. Each member of the class could research an Indian tribe from a different part of Canada. Stories of the heroes discovered could be assembled in a booklet and placed in your school library. Ask your local librarian for aid in preparing this project. Who else might help you to learn more about Indian heroes? Indian organizations? Government information services? etc.

3. One explanation of the creation of the world found in the mythology of North American Indians is the story of Sky-woman. Who was Sky-woman? How did she cause the world to be created?

ETIENNE BRÛLÉ

North America's First Frontiersman

C.W. JEFFERYS

Public Archives of Canada, Ottawa   C 7 36 35

It was 1608 when fifteen-year-old Etienne Brûlé arrived in Canada with the first group of white men from Europe to set up a settlement on the banks of the St. Lawrence River. Their leader was the noble Samuel de Champlain, a visionary who had a dream of colonizing the continent of North America.

Champlain returned to civilized France, however, leaving Brûlé and a handful of other young Frenchmen to endure a miserable winter in the harsh new country. In his efforts to colonize New France, Champlain would make over twenty trips back to Europe to gain the financial support of the rich French nobility.

After two long, boring, cold winters in the confines of the tiny settlements, Brûlé, a healthy seventeen-year-old yearning for adventure, persuaded Champlain to allow him to go to live with the local Indians in their village. Champlain agreed and exchanged Brûlé for a Huron Indian of about the same age. When Champlain next returned to Paris, he showed his human prize, while Brûlé became the first white man to step into the interior of the new continent, learning at first hand the language and the customs of the Indians.

Back in France during the winter of 1610-1611, Champlain lived in royal luxury, seeking the hand of the king's secretary's daughter; eventually they were married, although he was forty-three years old and she, Helen Boulle, was only twelve. Meanwhile, in the interior of present-day Canada, Brûlé was living an isolated life in the Indian village, much to the objections of the Jesuit priests living in the religious community on the banks of the St. Lawrence.

The only records of Brûlé's activities and personality are those left by the priests, men who deplored the free and rough way of life he had adopted from his new blood brothers. If Brûlé had kept a record of his exploits, his travels, and his accomplishments, he might well be a prominent personality in Canadian history books.

Brûlé became the first white man to learn the Indian tongue; in fact, he mastered the languages of several tribes, including the Hurons, Nipissings, Martagnais, and Algonquins. He was also the first white man to travel up the Ottawa river and portage overland to Georgian Bay, then cross Georgian Bay to Lake Huron. Thus the first *coureur de bois* in New France became Ontario's first white citizen and explorer. He visited each of the five great Lakes before anyone else from Europe, and he followed Indian trails from present-day Toronto along the shores of Lake Ontario to Niagara Falls. When he returned with detailed descriptions of Lake Superior, the largest fresh water lake in the world, no one believed him.

As young Brûlé became more independent and less obedient and reliable, his relationship with Champlain deteriorated; Champlain describes Brûlé in one of his journals as "this man was recognized as being very vicious in character and much addicted to women." Nevertheless, it was Brûlé, the only one who could speak to the Indians, whom Champlain used as a guide and interpreter on his voyage up the Ottawa river and as far west into Huron territory as Georgian Bay. Without Brûlé, Champlain could never have returned to France with charts and information about the vast interior of the new continent; but Champlain's dream was to colonize the New World, and he resented Brûlé working as an interpreter for the fur traders and merchants.

About this time, the Hurons, who were friendly and helpful to the French, were being harassed by a fierce tribe known as the Andastes. Champlain offered to help by attacking the Andastes. Brûlé was supposed to scout ahead with a party of 200 Hurons and meet up with Champlain and the balance of the Huron war party in order to attack the Andaste village. Unfortunately, Champlain and the Hurons whom he commanded suffered a demoralizing defeat, because Brûlé never appeared. He and his band of Hurons got lost and they arrived two days late.

Champlain returned to Quebec, furious, while Brûlé went back with the Hurons, intending to spend the winter in their villages. Suddenly, the Hurons were attacked by the Senecas; his Indian brothers dispersed, melting into the woods, while Etienne found himself lost and starving. Unknowingly, he stumbled into a Seneca village, where he was pounced upon, the hair pulled out of his beard, his fingernails ripped out, and his body burned — he would have been tortured to a slow death if he had not outwitted his captors. Pretending to conjure up a severe thunderstorm which he saw on the horizon, he frightened the Indians into not only releasing him in the midst of the thunder and lightning, but also guiding him back to the border of Huron country.

The final break between Champlain and Brûlé came in 1629, when England and France were at war. Brûlé was sent to Tadoussac to pilot a French vessel up the St. Lawrence River. Instead, he encountered Sir David Kirke and the British fleet, and he and other *coureurs de bois* who were with him went over to the English side. They piloted Kirke's expedition up the river, where they captured Quebec and took Champlain prisoner.

After the war, New France was given back to the French by the British, and in 1633 Champlain returned as governor. Brûlé was back in the heart of Huron territory when one of the strangest events in Canadian history occurred. The Bear Tribe of Hurons, with whom Brûlé had lived for years, turned against him.

For some unknown reason, his long-time friends tortured and killed him, quartering his body, which they boiled and ate. Even the woman pregnant with his child joined in the ceremonies, along with the other members of her tribe, before they all scattered in guilt and fear of the ghost of Brûlé. The death of North America's first frontiersman in June, 1633, in the Indian village of Toanche, near the site of present-day Penetanguishene, Ontario, became North America's first unsolved murder mystery.

TOPICS FOR DISCUSSION

1. In your opinion, who was more heroic: Champlain, who devoted his life to colonizing Canada, or Brûlé, who was our first frontiersman?

2. Brûlé was Canada's first frontiersman. What could a young Canadian do today to be "first", or to match Brûlé's contribution to this country?

3. In order to communicate in the wilderness, Brûlé had to learn several different languages. Considering the change in the make-up of Canada's population since the time of Brûlé, what four languages would a Canadian be wise to learn if he or she wanted to communicate with other Canadians today?

CREATIVE CHALLENGES

1. Imagine yourself a detective. What motives can you suggest for the murder of Brûlé by his blood brothers?

2. Imagine yourself a sixteen-year-old member of a flight into space to colonize a distant planet. When you land, you encounter strange green inhabitants, who seem cruel and barbaric compared to humans. The captain of your space ship trades you for one of the space people and returns to earth with his prize. Describe your adventures among the aliens on the unknown planet.

When writing a narrative you should develop the five elements basic to all short stories: plot, character, atmosphere, setting, and theme. Which one will be most important in your story?

The Spectator, Burlington, Monday, October 31, 1977

Body of Indian may have been child of Brule's

By PAUL LEGALL
Spectator Staff

GRIMSBY — Scientists have singled out Etienne Brule — a footloose French explorer — as the man who fathered an Indian girl near Grimsby about 350 years ago.

But it's doubtful whether the evidence would stand up in a paternity suit.

Brule was fingered by Royal Ontario Museum archeologist Dr. Walter Kenyon. In analyzing material excavated from a Neutral Indian grave west of Centennial Park, Dr. Kenyon discovered a mixed-blood woman among about 370 Indian bodies.

"The story is partly fact and partly speculation," says Dr. Kenyon, who headed a six-month dig at the 325-year-old Neutral Indian burial ground.

"We know for sure that the woman was part Indian and part European, probably French, from her skull. There are traits that are distinctly European and traits that are distinctly Indian, and when you know what to look for, the distinction is as obvious as the difference between a cow and a horse's skull."

The woman, who was about 20 when she died, was the only person in the grave with European traits. All others were full-blooded Neutrals, a tribe wiped out by the Iroquois in 1650.

But who was the father at a time when white men were almost unknown to the Neutrals?

Brule, who worked for Champlain as an explorer, is the most likely candidate, Dr. Kenyon says.

Regardless who her father was, the mixed-blood woman was apparently not ostracized for her background.

It seems she rose to the coveted and prestigious position of village medicine man. She was found buried with four sucking tubes used in primitive medicine.

MARIE LATOUR
Canada's First Heroine

Fort LaTour stood on a strip of land below the high cliffs that guarded the mouth of the Saint John River. Marie LaTour, just arrived on the rugged Acadian shores, stood beside her husband Charles, who had first come as a boy in 1610 with his father, but who now, by 1640, was lieutenant-governor of the rich new land.

Charles bragged of the prosperity of his estates — of the fish which swarmed into the fish weir spread in the river, of the rich fur trade and the wild berries and sweet nuts to be gathered from the surrounding woods — as he showed Marie the living quarters for the soldiers, the woodsmen and those who worked the shore fishery. Everyone cheered her in welcome. Even in the nearby Indian village of birchbark wigwams she felt warmth and friendship. Only the black-robed Récollet friars in the tiny chapel were coldly distant when they were introduced. Unlike her "Papist" husband, Marie was a Huguenot, and under the law a Protestant was not supposed to be in the colonies of Catholic France. Once secure in the commandant's house, surrounded by expensive furniture and silver plate, she wrote home to friends in France:

"... the summer is beautiful. My Charles says the sea moderates our winters, and we have all the wood in the world, spacious fireplaces, and love to keep us warm."

But all was not peaceful. As Marie snuggled into her new Acadian home (in what is now New Brunswick), she soon became aware that she and her husband had a deadly rival — Sieur de Charnisay — across the wide Bay of Fundy at Port Royal (in what is now Nova Scotia). Charles LaTour and Charnisay were both lieutenant-governors in the new colony of Acadia, but they had conflicting land grants. Their deeds of possession overlapped; the headquarters of each was in the middle of the lands claimed by the other.

The seventeenth century was an age when women were prominent in politics and wars, as many of them held powerful positions on the thrones of Europe. Thus, when Charles was forced to travel in search of furs or supplies, it was natural for Marie to command the garrison and to rule the fort as she tended her new-born son.

Charnisay's father, René, was counsellor to Louis XIII and a relation of the powerful Cardinal Richelieu, who was the real power behind the throne of France. With Cardinal Richelieu's aid, a royal decree ordered LaTour to return to Paris to face charges of treason. Aware that many nobles with influential enemies had disappeared forever behind the solid walls of the Bastille, Charles remained in Acadia but sent agents to France to seek help to fight Charnisay. A second court order was issued, which stated that LaTour, his fort, and all its contents were to be seized. In 1643, Charnisay blocked the harbour of Fort LaTour with two large ships, four smaller ones, and a force of 500 men prepared to starve the LaTours into surrender. For a month Charnisay waited confidently

with his men and vessels, but then another ship, the *St. Clement* arrived from France, with 140 men sent by the Protestants of La Rochelle to aid the LaTours. Not wanting to risk a fight against overwhelming odds, the newcomers waited off the coast.

In a daring move, Marie and Charles finally slipped past the enemy blockade one foggy night in a tiny shallop and reached the *St. Clement,* which was at anchor beyond the harbour. They sailed immediately for Boston, where Governor John Winthrop allowed them to enlist men and ships. With an additional 144 men, four ships, and forty-eight cannons, they returned to Acadia and during a swift running sea battle chased Charnisay back to Port Royal. The angry Charnisay vowed revenge for the unexpected humiliation.

Aware that there would be more trouble, Marie agreed to return to France in the *St. Clement* to obtain further assistance from Protestant friends, while her husband stayed to maintain the fort. Charnisay was in Paris as well, and when he heard of Marie's arrival in La Rochelle, he plotted with French officials to have the queen mother place a death penalty on the head of Marie LaTour if she should attempt to return to Acadia. He also arranged that an order for her arrest be issued.

Warned by friends, Marie escaped to England, which was in the midst of a rebellion. Nevertheless, she managed to charter a ship, the *Gillyflower*. Loaded with supplies for Fort LaTour, they sailed in the

Marie LaTour's last battle.

spring of 1644, but the captain ignored Marie's demands for speed and stopped along the coast to trade, so that the voyage took six months. On one occasion, Charnisay, furious at her escape from France, even boarded the English vessel and searched for Marie, but the captain denied her presence and Marie, hiding in the hold, was not discovered.

When the *Gillyflower* arrived at Boston, Marie promptly spoke to Governor Winthrop and sued the captain for breach of charter because he had not delivered her to her destination as agreed. She received 2 000 pounds in damages, which she used to fill three ships

with supplies, and in the autumn of 1644, after a year of absence, she sailed victoriously home.

More troubles plagued Marie the following February while Charles was away on a fur trading expedition. She discovered that the two Récollet friars in the fort were trying to get her people to desert her and turn to Charnisay. Not wishing to harm the friars, she ordered them to leave the fort. They went immediately to Charnisay and reported to him that Fort LaTour, with a garrison of only forty-five men, was greatly weakened. The attack came instantly, but after a bloody battle the invaders were beaten back to Port Royal with heavy damages to

their ship. A few weeks later, however, Charnisay returned in a huge, 300 metric ton armed ship loaded with soldiers, and demanded the surrender of the fort. In defiance Marie ordered the red flag of combat to be hung out while she donned a steel breastplate and helmet.

Charnisay opened fire, and, as huge cannon balls smashed against the seaward walls of the wooden fortress, he landed his troops, which attacked in waves. Led by Marie, the inhabitants of the fort used pikes and halberds to prevent the enemy from scaling the walls. Losses were heavy on each side, but for three days and nights the defendants, outnumbered five to one, kept the enemy at bay. The fourth day of battle was Easter Sunday, and as Marie and the others knelt in prayer in the chapel, one of the guards, a Swiss mercenary secretly in the pay of Charnisay, allowed the enemy to get inside the fort.

As they poured over the unguarded walls, Marie, leading her small band of followers, charged from the church, until the attackers were forced to retreat again.

The deceitful Charnisay sent Marie an offer for her surrender. She had no hope of help from outside, and only death was certain, so she surrendered on the condition that no one else would be harmed. Charnisay agreed, but when he had control of the fort and its meagre band of defenders, he ordered all the garrison hanged except for one, who had to hang the others.

Marie, with a rope around her neck, was forced to watch her faithful followers, who had fought so valiantly and who had for years been loyal to her and Charles, go to their deaths. She was not executed immediately, but died mysteriously three weeks later. Charnisay, who had held her prisoner, claimed she died of spite after admitting her heresy, but the Acadians believed that she was poisoned by him.

TOPICS FOR DISCUSSION

1. **Did you already know about Marie LaTour? Do you believe Canadians should be aware of who she was and what happened to her? Why or why not?**
2. **When Marie married Charles, she became not only his wife and the mother of his child, but also his partner in business, politics, and war. Has woman's role in marriage changed since early settlement of this country? How? Why?**
3. **In 1640, a Protestant was not given equal rights in a Catholic colony. Is there any place in the world today where people still fight over religious differences?**
4. **Is there any place in Canada today where the government makes laws to: a) deliberately prevent Canadians from worshipping according to the religion of their choice? b) speaking the language of their choice? c) belonging to a political party of their choice?**
5. **A few years after Marie LaTour's death, Charnisay drowned in the river at Port Royal. According to the story, an Indian whom Charnisay had beaten, rescued a servant of Charnisay but left the cruel master to die. Does this seem like a just fate to you?**
6. **In 1653, Charles LaTour married** Charnisay's widow, Jeanne, but the marriage contract was like a peace treaty that established Charles as governor of all Acadia. Many waring countries eventually become friends. Give some examples from history.

CREATIVE CHALLENGES

1. **Invent a situation in Canada today where a heroine is forced to defend herself and her home against armed invaders. The first sentence of your story should attract the interest of a reader. Next, describe the situation. How will you develop the personality of the woman? Which words or phrases will best create a mood of fear, danger, or suspense? Work toward a climax in the struggle and then present a brief conclusion.**
2. **Imagine you are one of the following people and write a letter. The first sentence of the letter should state the reason you are writing, the main body of the letter should supply the facts, and the last paragraph should conclude your thoughts.**
   a. Charles LaTour writing to Marie.
   b. Marie LaTour writing to Charles.
   c. Charnisay writing to Cardinal Richelieu.

JEAN DE BRÉBEUF
The Frontier Saint

MARCH 16, 1644

News of the Iroquois attack was carried by three exhausted Hurons, who had escaped from the recently destroyed village of St. Ignace. Mixed with their tales of horror, torture and death was the warning that the fierce force of 1 000 Iroquois was close on their heels.

As the members of the Huron tribe scrambled in every direction, making plans for evacuation or defence according to their dispositions, one giant figure stood solidly in their midst. To a stranger, the white man in his long black Jesuit robe would have appeared out of place among the Indians but, towering above them at a height of 200 cm Father Brébeuf was, at fifty-six years of age, an integral part of the Huron community. He had spent twenty-three years in Huronia living with the natives in the cause to which he had devoted his life — the cause of God. During that time he had founded five missions among the Hurons. Now his Indian brothers gathered about him, begging him to flee before the Iroquois arrived.

Brébeuf knew what would happen to him if he remained. The year before, the Huron villages of St. Joseph and St. Michel had been attacked and 700 Hurons captured. The Iroquois were strict and harsh with their captives and particularly hated white missionaries, whom they considered cowards because they wore the black skirts of women. The priest's choice was clear; he would stay with the eighty warriors to resist the attackers. This was his land and these were his people, and he didn't want to leave them.

As a young man, in July of 1625, he had travelled 1290 km by canoe in order to work with the Hurons at St. Ignace (which is today the site of Midland, Ontario); the observations recorded in his diary made him one of the main chroniclers of the trail westward, which missionaries, traders and explorers would later follow. He persisted patiently in his work for six years before gaining his first adult convert to Christianity, but eventually his religious zeal impressed the Indians. Brébeuf learned the Huron language (he composed a dictionary and grammar book for his people's use), but most important, he learned that the Indians respected qualities of boldness, courage, and fortitude in suffering. When epidemics of disease carried to the continent by white people killed thousands of Indians, the priests were blamed for the disaster, and, in 1637-38, Brébeuf watched the Hurons turn against him, tear down his crosses, and even stone and torture his fellow Jesuits. He had endured it all and had won their friendship back, so he was not about to be driven away by the Iroquois enemy. If he expected the Hurons to share his God with him, he felt he would have to share in their tragedy.

Thus, Father Brébeuf, the "giant of the Huron mission", made his stand. The small force of Hurons were defeated, and he was captured by the Iroquois, who, in the cold of March, drove him with clubs and stones back to St. Ignace. There he was tied to a stake in the log church that he had constructed with his own hands. The Iroquois taunted him about his religion and his manhood. They stripped off his "woman's robes", beating and burning his naked body. Tomahawk heads were heated on the fires until they were red-hot and then hung around his neck. Even with his flesh burning, Brébeuf summoned all his courage and strength and made no cry or movement that would betray weakness.

Determined to make a special example of the stubborn priest, the Indians increased their efforts in order to break his spirit and his faith. For four hours they subjected him to tortures, which are considered the most atrocious and hideous ever suffered in the history of Christian martyrs. They peeled his skin off and made a belt of pitch and resin, which they placed around his body before setting fire to it. When Brébeuf spoke to them of God and prayed for them rather than threatening or cursing them, they cut off his lips.

With victory came death. Impressed by the bravery of Brébeuf, an Iroquois chief plunged his knife into the missionary's chest and cut out his heart. The other Iroquois joined him in saluting an enemy undefeated in torture by drinking the blood running from the priest's veins, the greatest compliment they could pay him.

The Huron mission died with Brébeuf, but as his Huron brothers dispersed to other villages with legends of the giant in black skirts and his unmatched courage, Christianity spread with them and converts reached dramatic numbers.

It was not until three centuries later, on June 29, 1930, that Brébeuf was canonized by Pope Pius XI. On October 16, 1940, he was proclaimed Patron Saint of Canada. His feast day is September 26th.

ANOTHER POINT OF VIEW

The tortures endured by Brûlé, Father Brébeuf, Radisson and many other early heroes might seem "cruel" or "uncivilized" when we first read about them but there are always two sides or viewpoints to any situation.

First, we should realize that the wars between the Hurons and the Iroquois were mainly caused by the white intruders. The English and the Dutch had made allies of the Iroquois while the French had supported the Hurons. For hundreds of years before the arrival of the whites, the Indians had respected the boundaries of each other's territory, but the whites, in their greed to monopolize the rich fur trade, encouraged and aided their respective Indian friends to attack and invade the lands of their rivals. The whites often supplied guns and leadership as we see in the story of Brûlé where Champlain leads the Huron war party against the Andastes village.

Second, it should be understood that the Indians were a very proud and strong race of people. What the whites considered "torture", the early natives saw as a "test" of a person's bravery. A boy could not become a brave or a warrior unless he was able to endure great pain without fear or cowardice. Their values might be compared to those of the ancient Greeks in the city of Sparta where the youths who wished to become warriors were trained to endure physical pain. Even in Canada today there are many sports such as hockey, lacrosse, boxing, football, etc. where it is considered admirable if a person can accept physical abuse from the opposite side without showing any

sign of fear or pain. Radisson passed the test of courage and was adopted by the Indians; Brébeuf proved that he was as brave as any Indian and was killed with honour.

Third, it should be noted that in many ways the early Indians were more enlightened than we are today. Note, for example, in the newspaper story on page six that it was possible for a woman to attain "the coveted and prestigious position of medicine man." Women in modern day Canada are still fighting for the right to hold the most coveted and prestigious positions in our society. No woman has as yet become the Prime Minister of our country.

Finally, there are examples in the history of most cultures of behaviour that seems "uncivilized". The sign of Brébeuf's faith was the cross which represented a culture that nailed its enemies to a cross and left them to die a slow death. In England and France as well as many other European cultures, people were tortured to force them to admit that they were witches and were then burnt alive at the stake. The tortures used in the Tower of London, the Bastille, or the Spanish Inquisition were as cruel as any invented by the Indians.

Try to imagine yourself 500 years in the future looking back at today's world. What present day values or behavior which we accept without thinking, might be considered as "cruel" or "uncivilized" from the point of view of a person in the future?

TOPICS FOR DISCUSSION
1. Was Jean de Brébeuf a fool not to escape when he had the opportunity?
2. Do you believe in anything so strongly that you would endure tortures like those inflicted on Brébeuf rather than betray your beliefs?
3. In your opinion, was Brébeuf a Canadian hero? An Ontario hero? A French hero? A Roman Catholic hero? A Christian hero? An Indian hero?

4. Which tells you more about Jean de Brébeuf, his behaviour during four hours of torture or his behaviour during twenty-three years in Huronia?
5. What is a martyr?

CREATIVE CHALLENGES:
1. How could you make the students in your school or the members of your community aware of the significance of the 26th of September, the feast day of the patron saint of Canada?
2. There have been many famous paintings depicting the torture of Brébeuf. If you are artistic create your own version of Brébeuf or one of the other heroes in this book.
3. Write a song or a poem about Brébeuf. Perhaps you could sing or recite it for your friends or classmates. Is there a difference between a song and a poem? Would you write a song in a different way than you would write a poem?
4. Investigate one of these two women who contributed to early settlement in Canada. Prepare a brief report on her and her achievements.
a. Marguerite Bourgeois — a nun who opened the first school in Montreal and founded the convent of the Congregation de Notre Dame de Montreal.
b. Jeanne Mance — the first nurse in North America, who founded the hospital Hôtel-Dieu in Montreal.

PIERRE RADISSON

Coureur De Bois

The three youths stood terrorized and shuddering as their clothing was ripped from their bodies by their captors and they were subjected to torture. Pierre, sixteen years old, having immigrated with his family to Trois Rivières earlier in that same year of 1651, was not familiar with the severe ordeals which the Iroquois used to test an enemy's manhood.

He looked down the long corridor between two lines of eager, screaming warriors violently waving wooden clubs, and saw their purpose almost immediately. He would have to run between the two lines while they tried to club his already exhausted body. To them it was a game; to him it meant a brutal death.

Determined not to show fear, he sprang forward, dashing, jumping, weaving, shoving his way through the violent mob. To his own amazement, he reached the other end still on his feet. Probably it was his speed, his youth, and his bravery that impressed one of the Iroquois chiefs to such an extent that he decided to adopt the white boy rather than see him killed. Pierre's two companions were not so fortunate; they were tortured and beheaded.

As the Iroquois ushered him along unfamiliar forest trails to their main village far to the south, the boy wondered if he would ever see his family again. He and his friends had been captured while they were hunting in the woods outside the settlement. For the next two years he lived the life of an Indian brave — adopted their customs,

Sketch by student Peter Grau.

The Nonsuch returns to London.

dressed like them, even stained his body as they did. The first time he tried to run away he was tracked, recaptured, and brought back to the village, where he was tortured mercilessly until again rescued by the intervention of his adopted Indian family. Undaunted, he schemed with some Dutch fur traders, who helped him escape to Fort Orange. From there, Pierre travelled to France and then directly back to Trois Rivières by March of 1654. In spite of his anxiety to return to his own family and friends, Pierre Radisson had gained an admiration for his Indian brothers and wrote of them, "I love these people well."

His two-year ordeal as a captive did not seem to have frightened Radisson, because his first decision on returning to the French settlement was to set out on a fur trading expedition. Later, during a trip into

Omondogo country in 1657-58, Radisson heroically rescued some settlers trapped in a fort by hostile Indians, by carefully arranging their evacuation and safe journey to Trois Rivières.

By 1660, Radisson had gone into partnership with his brother-in-law, Groseilliers, and the two of them planned a hazardous journey to seek furs far to the northwest. When the license they applied for was turned down, they decided to ignore the bureaucratic governor, and they set out without his permission, travelling to the Lake Superior region and beyond. Aided by friendly Cree and Sioux Indians, they returned to Montreal with 300 canoes overflowing with a wealth of furs, only to find that the conniving governor confiscated ninety per cent of their load as a penalty for trading without a license.

Furious and frustrated, Radisson and Groseilliers slipped secretly out of the colony and, in 1661, pushed further into the northwest than any white person had so far travelled. On that trip they discovered what Radisson described as "the bay to the north", which was actually Hudson Bay. Coureurs de bois had to have quick wits to survive in the dangerous fur trading business, but Radisson now combined imagination with practicality as he envisaged shipping furs in large sailing ships from the shores of Hudson Bay to Quebec or France, rather than bringing them in small canoes down rough rivers through territory held by unfriendly tribes. When he returned to Quebec to share his dream, the unimaginative officials, who were the only ones with enough money to outfit large vessels, laughed at his crazy scheme.

13

Unable to gain support in New France, Radisson and Groseilliers travelled to England to seek an alliance with King Charles II. The king referred them to his cousin Prince Rupert, who eventually, although it took four years to convince him, entrusted two ships, the *Eaglet* and the *Nonsuch,* to the daring Frenchmen. Storms at sea and other bad fortune turned them back repeatedly, but on the third attempt they reached Hudson Bay. When Groseilliers returned to England with his ship full of valuable furs, Prince Rupert and seventeen others, on May 2, 1670, were given a charter by the king, allowing them to rule and trade in the domain discovered sixty years earlier by Hudson — a territory which represented over two million square kilometres. Radisson's dream was a reality, and the Hudson's Bay Company came into existence, although its original name was "The Governor and Company of Adventurers of England Trading into Hudson Bay."

In 1676 Radisson reverted to his French allegiance and joined the French navy. For many years a fight over the possession of the territory claimed by the Hudson's Bay Company was waged, and when Radisson returned to Canada in 1682 he was commissioned to lead an expedition into Rupert's Land to gain control of the fur trade for the French. He knew the Indians so well that he successfully diverted the trade to the French, and then he captured Port Nelson, taking the English inhabitants prisoner. However, when he returned to Quebec with his captives, instead of being

given a hero's welcome, he was punished, because the French officials did not want an outright war with the English.

Discouraged and angered by the inconsistent viewpoint of the French, Radisson again changed sides, and, because of his abilities to deal with the Indians and his knowledge of the fur trade, the Hudson's Bay Company in 1684 wisely appointed him as superintendent of Port Nelson, only two years after he had captured it from them.

Eventually Radisson retired to England and lived in poverty with his English wife, supported only by the meagre pension given him by the Hudson's Bay Company. One of the bravest of the coureurs de bois, the man whose vision opened up the northwest, died penniless in England in 1710.

TOPICS FOR DISCUSSION
1. If you had spent two years in captivity like Radisson, would you return immediately to the wilderness as he did?
2. Radisson once wrote describing the feeling of the coureurs de bois, "we were Caesars, being nobody to contradict us." What does this suggest to you about his outlook on life? What is your own view or philosophy of life? How are you like, or different from, Radisson?
3. In your opinion, was Radisson justified in a) escaping from his adopted Indian father who had twice saved his life? b) leaving the fur trade of New France and going to England? c) attacking his old friends at Port Nelson? Explain the

reasons for your viewpoints.
4. After being captured and tortured, and even after seeing his friends killed, Radisson nevertheless said of the Iroquois, "I love these people well." What does this suggest to you about the nature of the Indians? What does it tell you about the personality of Pierre?
5. Pierre Radisson was one of the co-founders of the Hudson's Bay Company. What influence did the Hudson's Bay Company have on the development of Canada?

CREATIVE CHALLENGES
1. The Iroquois lived a rough and rugged life, and in their culture a man was worthy of being a warrior only if he could survive torture without showing weakness. They would force their own boys to endure torture before giving them the title of "brave" and accepting them as men into the tribe. Imagine you are an Iroquois in the year 1650, and write a description of the white people who have recently begun to settle in your land.
2. Imagine you are Pierre Radisson arriving at Trois Rivières in 1651. Write a personal diary from his point of view, including what you think might have been his emotions during each of his adventures. When you write a diary, each entry should begin with the date and should be stated clearly in the first person singular or plural. For an example of how a diary should read, examine the excerpts from the diary of Alexander Mackenzie found in the description of him in this book.

MADELEINE DE VERCHÈRES

Heroine of New France

A group of settlers worked diligently in the field along the bank of the wide St. Lawrence, thirty-two kilometres below Montreal. On the other side of the field the seigniorial fort of the Verchères stood protectively overshadowing the quiet scene. The year was 1692, during the second administration of Frontenac, and the date was October 22nd.

Young fourteen-year-old Madeleine de Verchères worked with the men and women. Her father, François Jarret de Verchères, was on military duty in Quebec, and her mother, Marie, was visiting in Montreal.

There was no warning. The Indians sprang from the woods with ferocious war whoops, their toma-

Madeleine drawn by student Barry Oehm.

hawks raised. Madeleine ran with the speed and instinct of a frightened fawn toward the fortress in which she had been born. The dying screams of her fellow workers mingled with the sound of the wind whistling past her ears. Her heart was pounding hard as she reached the entrance to the fort.

Her screams of "To arms! To arms!" were choked suddenly as a heavy tug on her shawl, which was wrapped around her shoulders, jerked her to a halt. One Indian, swifter than the others, had caught up with her and now held the other end of her streaming shawl in his firm grasp. Madeleine desperately tore herself loose from the garment and bolted inside the barricade, slamming the gate in the face of her pursuer. No one else had escaped with her. In the fields beyond, a band of forty or fifty Iroquois were scrambling among their slaughtered victims.

Securing the entrance, Madeleine turned to discover an equally disgusting sight within the walls. Two soldiers, the only men inside the fort, were preparing to blow up themselves as well as the women and children rather than risk being captured. Madeleine was furious and ashamed of their lack of courage. She had watched her mother defend the fort two years before against an Indian raid that lasted a couple of days. The vivid memory of the manner in which her mother had organized the forces returned to Madeleine, who had been only twelve years old at the time.

She ordered the two soldiers to take positions on the walls and armed the group of women along with an eighty-year-old servant and her two young brothers, aged ten and twelve. Instructing them to shoot only when the Indians appeared, she began to prepare for the siege.

Unexpectedly a cry came from one of the defenders; a small boat had landed at the dock below the fort. Peering out, Madeleine recognized the visitors, who were unaware of the Indians. She rushed from the protection of the fort, meeting them as they left the jetty, and hurried them to safety. The Iroquois, taken by surprise at this sudden action, failed to retaliate.

For eight days and eight nights the small group inside the fortress held off the Indians, until, on the ninth day, Captain La Monerie arrived from Montreal with a force of forty men to disperse the attackers and rescue the occupants of Verchères. As he examined the garrison, Captain La Monerie was highly impressed. Every preparation had been taken, the defences were as well organized as if a king's officer had been in command. He spread the story of the heroic actions of young Madeleine throughout New France, and she was awarded a Royal Pension by Frontenac.

TOPICS FOR DISCUSSION
1. Young people in the early settlements of Canada were expected to work and protect their homes. What contributions do you make to your home? What work will you expect your children to do?
2. By the age of twelve, Madeleine and her brothers had experienced an attack on their home by an enemy who wished to kill them. What is the most dangerous experience you have encountered?
3. Could a modern day fourteen-year-old take command of a situation and control it as effectively as Madeleine? Would a teen-ager today be given such an opportunity? Explain.

CREATIVE CHALLENGES
1. Invent a dialogue between the following people.
(a) Madeleine's two brothers.
(b) Two of the Indians outside the fort.
(c) The two soldiers who wanted to blow up the fort to avoid capture.
(d) Madeleine and Captain La Monerie.
If you don't know the names of the people, invent some. Present your dialogue in play form indicating the name of each speaker before his or her statement. The conversation should sound natural and should be based on the incidents in this story. Try to imagine the two people as individuals and show how they have different viewpoints from each other during their discussion. How could you end the conversation dramatically? Indicate if the speaker is laughing, crying, shouting, proud, frightened, etc. as he or she speaks. After you have completed your dialogue, choose a partner and with each of you acting one of the roles, read your dialogues to the class.

ADAM DOLLARD
The Man Who Saved Montreal

In the year 1660, waterways were the main means of transportation and travel in New France; they were the highways between the towns and settlements isolated by thick forests. Fort Ville Marie, which controlled the access to the Great Lakes, was located at the junction of three major river systems: the St. Lawrence, the Ottawa and the Richelieu. Ever since 1648, when the fierce Iroquois tribe of the Six Nations Confederation had almost obliterated the Hurons and Algonquins, who were allies of the French, the attacks on French settlements and fur traders had been increasing. When Sieur de Maisonneuve, the governor of Fort Ville Marie (which is now Montreal), received reports that Iroquois warriors were gathering on the Ottawa and Richelieu rivers, and were preparing to join forces and attack the French settlements along the St. Lawrence, starting with Fort Ville Marie, he summoned Adam Dollard des Ormeaux, his garrison commander, to discuss preparations for defending the fort.

Much to Maisonneuve's surprise, the young officer, who had arrived from France a few years earlier, had a plan of his own already worked out. He wanted to take a small contingent of men up the Ottawa River to attack the Iroquois before they poured down on the fort. He figured that an offensive attack might disrupt the organized assault of the Iroquois before it gathered strength.

As Maisonneuve pondered over Dollard's plan, memories of a rumor — a scandal back in France that had destroyed Dollard's honor — returned to haunt him. Did Dollard wish to set out on a sacrificial mission to thwart the Iroquois campaign against Montreal, or was he trying to do something brave in order to blot out the memory of that unfortunate event in France?

In the end Adam Dollard persuaded Maisonneuve that his strategy was sound. He chose sixteen unmarried youths, local farmers and artisans, and pushed up the Ottawa River to meet the gathering menace.

The fight at Long Sault painted by Aurèle de Foy Suzor-Coté.

Whispers of his mission floated through the quiet forests ahead of him, and he was soon joined by Chief Anahotaha with forty Huron braves, and Chief Mitiwemeg with four Algonquins. The Huron and Algonquin warriors were eager to seek revenge against the tribe that had massacred so many hundreds of their people, leaving them scattered and without a home. On May 1, 1660 the motley company reached an abandoned stockade at the rapids of the Long Sault, about 500 km north of Montreal (just below Hawkesbury, Ontario), and began preparations to defend it.

The first encounter was with an Iroquois scouting party. Dollard and his followers succeeded in killing all but one, and the sole survivor escaped up river to warn the others of the Frenchmen encamped at the Long Sault.

Dollard, surveying the last preparations for defence of the stockade, heard the swish of hundreds of paddles pushing through the water before he caught sight of the Iroquois. Shock and fear gripped him as a force of 300 warriors rounded the bend in the river and came at the fort like hornets whose nest has been disturbed. Never had he imagined that there would be so many Indians.

As they spread out and scrambled toward the hastily improvised fort, the Iroquois suffered heavy losses in the face of the French muskets. Twice more they attacked, but each time they were beaten back, leaving the bodies of their brothers piled high outside the stockade walls.

Then, silence! Five days of silence and confinement, with only the buzzing of flies gathering on the bloody corpses outside the walls to break the stillness. Most of the Hurons inside the fort, discontented with the little food and the muddy drinking water available, deserted, although their chief and a handful of braves remained with the seventeen whites. As the physical conditions of the defenders deteriorated because of thirst and hunger, their nerves reached the breaking point. Why did the Iroquois not attack?

At the end of the fifth day the reason for the long siege became obvious. Reinforcements of Iroquois, 800 strong, arrived from the Richelieu River. With new numbers and new courage, the Iroquois launched a full frontal assault, but the valiant group behind the flimsy wooden barricade beat them off.

The Iroquois waited another agonizing three days before risking the final attack. They came from all sides, and the sheer strength of numbers carried them to the base of the stockade, and allowed them to set fire to the walls. As his men clubbed them from the walls with their musket barrels, Dollard prepared a hastily constructed bomb of gunpowder and, after lighting it, tried to throw it over the barricade into the midst of the scrambling attackers. It fell short, bounced off the stockade walls, and blew up in the faces of the defenders. Several were killed, others burned and blinded.

Seizing on the moment of confusion, the Iroquois swarmed over the stockade, killing all but four Hurons and five Frenchmen, who suffered lingering deaths by torture.

A few days later, Pierre Radisson paddled softly toward Long Sault, returning from his escapade on Hudson Bay. As he came around the bend toward the stockade a gruesome sight met him. The bodies of the men who had defended the small fortress for over a week had been hung out on stakes by the river's edge.

When Radisson reported his odious discovery, he also reported that the river was clear of Iroquois; they had abandoned their intentions of attacking Fort Ville Marie after discovering that seventeen white men and a few Indians had killed one-third of their force. The Iroquois warriors returned home, their confidence shaken over their heavy losses, incurred while destroying a flimsy fort and overcoming a handful of young men. Thus Adam Dollard and his followers, who died on May 26, 1660, at Long Sault, are credited with saving the early settlement of Montreal and all of New France.

TOPICS FOR DISCUSSION
1. The historian T. B. Costain in *The White & the Gold,* Chapter 19, page 211 compared Dollard to a famous Greek hero.
"They held the gap long enough, even as Leonidas did at Thermapylae."
Why is this an apt comparison?
2. If Dollard disgraced himself back in France as some historians claim, does it make him any less of a Canadian hero? For how long would you continue to blame a person for antisocial behaviour? Explain.
3. Compare Davy Crockett at the Alamo with Adam Dollard at the Long Sault. How are they similar?

CREATIVE CHALLENGES
1. Have you ever seen a movie or T.V. show about Adam Dollard? Using an 8 mm camera, or video equipment, film a scene from one of the stories found in this book.
2. A simile is a direct comparison usually using "like" or "as". An example from this story would be "like hornets whose nest has been disturbed." Invent a simile which one of the following personalities in Canadian history might have used.
(a) An Indian girl about AD 1000 describing the landing of Lief Erikson, the Viking leader, at L'Anse aux Meadows.
(b) John Cabot, an Italian who sailed for the British, describing his first view of the snow-covered Labrador coastline in 1498.
(c) Henry Hudson describing the mutineers who set himself and his young son adrift on the ocean.
(d) Cartier describing his emotions when he arrived at Stadacona in 1535.
(e) A crewman on board one of Captain Cook's ships describing to his daughter back in England the natives he encountered in 1778 in Nootka Sound.

THAYENDANEGEA

War Chief of the Six Nations

Thayendanegea, also called Joseph Brant, was born in Mohawk country along the Ohio River in 1742. Like his proud ancestors, he was a warrior, and at age thirteen fought on the side of the British against the French at the Battle of Lake George, which was the first confrontation of the Seven Years War.

Unlike most of his friends, Joseph Brant wanted to learn how to read and write English. His commanding officer, Sir William Johnson, was so impressed by the boy's bravery and ambition, that he arranged for him to attend an Indian charity school at Lebanon, Connecticut, where Joseph, an excellent student, studied for two years. During those years he was converted to the Church of England.

In 1763, Pontiac, chief of the Ottawas, rebelled against the British authorities, and once again Joseph Brant joined with Johnson to defend the British cause. After the war he returned to the Mohawk Valley, where he built a home and married the daughter of an Oneida chieftain. When Guy Johnson, nephew of Sir William, became Superintendent of Indian Affairs, Brant acted as his secretary, displaying his considerable abilities as a diplomat in persuading discontent tribes to sign peace treaties. He was determined to visit England; thus, in 1775, he crossed the Atlantic and was well received in London. However, when a Turkish lord jokingly touched Brant's "funny nose", he narrowly missed being hit with a tomahawk.

When the thirteen colonies revolted against the mother country, Joseph Brant was one of the main reasons the Indians remained loyal to the British. Brant and his warriors travelled to Montreal by way of Lake Ontario and were received hospitably when they arrived, Brant receiving a commission and the rank of captain in the British army. He then led the Iroquois in devastating raids against the American rebels in the Mohawk Valley and northern Pennsylvania, where his reputation as a leader and the "war chief of the Six Nations" prompted fear and hate in rebel forces. He fought during the Saratoga campaign and, in 1778, led Indian forces against Walter Butler, who raided Cherry Valley. This massacre caused the rebel forces to place rewards on Brant's head and to launch a powerful attack against the Six Nations.

United Empire Loyalists had escaped north to territory that would

one day be Canada. Brant shifted his headquarters north as well, forming a defensive line along the border. Without his support, the north would probably have been overrun by the rebels.

In 1782, when the Revolutionary War ended, the new American states were unwilling to recognize Indian land rights. At that time many Mohawks and Senecas were encamped in what had become American territory on the Niagara River. Brant switched roles, from the fierce brave in battle to the skilled and civilized politician, earning himself once again a reputation as a diplomat. He negotiated with the British government to secure a land grant and subsidies for his people, enabling the Mohawk loyalists to settle on the banks of the Grand River, which flows into Lake Erie. The grant allotted them a strip of land 10 km wide on either side of the entire length of the Grand River (265 km). The site of the settlement became known as "Brant's Ford", and is today the city of Brantford in Ontario. Although much of the Mohawk land was later sold by the Indians to incoming white settlers, their descendants still live on the reserve near Brantford.

Joseph Brant's character then took another direction: he became a zealous Christian preacher, translating the *Book of Common Prayer* and the *Gospel of Mark* into the Mohawk tongue. With funds collected during a second visit to England in 1786, he established the first Episcopal Church in Upper Canada. Brant continued to work at improving the lot of his people, as he assisted in es-

La Vérendrye, the first white person to cross the plains and see the Rocky Mountains.

Henry Kelsey the first white person to see a buffalo.

20

tablishing Indian schools, entered enthusiastically into missionary work, built a flour mill, and organized an active sports program.

TOPICS FOR DISCUSSION
1. Which characteristics of Joseph Brant most impress you?
2. Which political leaders in Canada today look after the citizens of Canada as well as Joseph Brant looked after the interests of his people?
3. The Six Nation Reserve estab-

lished by Brant in 1782 thrives today. The life of a "reserve Indian" is different from the life of the average Canadian. What are the differences? Indicate both the advantages and disadvantages.
4. Was Joseph Brant a good chief? Was he right to accept the religion, culture, and language of the white people? Could he have helped his people better if he had not accepted the changes brought by the whites?

SUGGESTION
If possible, arrange a visit to an Indian reserve or invite an Indian to your school to describe Indian culture and viewpoints.

CREATIVE CHALLENGE
Imagine yourself to be one of the personalities below. Describe a buffalo, the Rocky Mountains, the Fraser River, or the first air flight in Canada, as if you were the person. How will you explain your unique experience? To what could you compare it?

The first flight in Canada, McCurdy flies the Silver Dart across the frozen surface of Baddeck Bay.

Simon Fraser descending the Fraser River.

MONTCALM AND WOLFE
The Heroes of the Plains of Abraham

Louis Joseph de Montcalm was born into an old and distinguished family in France on February 28, 1712. At nine years of age he entered military service as an ensign, and by seventeen he was a captain in the French army. At the age of twenty-four, he married Angelique-Louise Talon de Boulay, who was a member of a powerful family. They had two sons and three daughters.

Montcalm served in many European wars, including the war of the Polish succession, the war of the Austrian succession, and the Spanish war against the Italians. During the latter, he was defeated and taken prisoner. On October 6, 1752, after thirty-one years of service, eleven campaigns and five wounds, he petitioned for a pension and was accorded 2 000 livres. For the following seven years he lived the rich, idle life of a French aristocrat.

Then on March 11, 1756, he was appointed Major General and made the commander-in-chief of the French forces in Quebec. For this service he would receive a salary of 25 000 livres, plus 12 000 livres to cover his expenses in moving to Canada, another 16 000 livres for a living allowance while in the colony, and finally 6 000 livres in pension payable upon his return to France.

Montcalm arrived in Canada for the first time on April 3, 1756, where he displayed his courage as a leader and his intelligence in military tactics as he proceeded to win a series of battles that assured the French of control of Lake Ontario. The British fort at Oswego, New York, fell in only twelve days, and Montcalm took 16 000 prisoners. In 1757, he won another victory at Fort William Henry on Lake George. The next year at the other end of Lake George he successfully defended Fort Ticonderoga with only 3 000 men, against a British force of 16 000.

Finally, in 1759, as Montcalm waited at Quebec, an English general sailed up the St. Lawrence River to confront him.

James Wolfe was born in Westerham, Kent, on January 2, 1727, into a military family and, like his father, became an officer in the British army. As a boy he had listened to his father's stories of battles and had dreamed of military glory despite his delicate health.

At fourteen years of age he was commissioned in his father's regiment; then throughout his teen-age years he fought in European battles. He was with the 12th regiment in 1742 when they fought in Belgium, and the next year he took part in the Battle of Dettingen although he was only sixteen. In 1745, he was sent to Scotland under Cumberland to assist in crushing the rebellion in support of the Young Pretender and so was present at the Battle of Culloden.

During the Seven Years War between England and France, Wolfe was sent to North America to protect the English colonies. As a brigadier-general during the attack on Louisburg, he made military history by establishing the first "on shore" bridgehead (a position on the hostile side of a river, established by advancing troops of an attacking force, in order to protect the crossing of the main body of soldiers). Due to Wolfe's resourceful and imaginative leadership, the British captured Louisburg from the French.

Following his victory, ill health confined him to his bed for more than a month. In 1758, he wrote:

"I am in a very bad condition, both with gravel and rheumatism, but I had much rather die than decline any kind of service that is offered."

Service was offered and, ignoring his own health, Wolfe, at age thirty-two, accepted the command of the land forces that were sent to attack Quebec. In February, 1759, he left England with his army to rendezvous at Louisburg with Charles Saunders, who waited with a powerful fleet. They left together on June 1, and by the 26th had anchored off the Island of Orléans in the St. Lawrence River near Quebec.

The task confronting Wolfe seemed impossible. On a rise of land beyond the Beaufort River waited Montcalm, the ingenious French general who had defeated so many English armies. In his Quebec stronghold he was protected by natural barriers of rivers and cliffs, and he commanded an army of 16 000 men. Wolfe, with only 9 000 men, made an attempt to invade the city but was forced back. Brooding over the loss and studying the landscape, he waited three months before he decided on a daring attack strategy.

During the dark hours before

The death of Wolfe by Benjamin West. The National Gallery of Canada. Gift of the Duke of Westminster, 1918.

The death of Montcalm.

dawn on September 13th, General Wolfe led his army of only 5 000 men ashore at the base of the high cliffs, at a place known today as Wolfe's Cove. They surrounded and sealed off the area before proceeding to scale the treacherous cliff that led to the French encampment high above them. By morning they had successfully secured a position on the Plains of Abraham, which left the city of Quebec vulnerable.

The French, weakened after three months of seige, were taken entirely by surprise. Realizing the threat offered by the English troops, Montcalm attacked immediately, hoping to push them back to the river below.

Waiting until the French were only twelve meters away before he calmly gave the order for the first line to fire, Wolfe was struck in the wrist by a bullet, but he paused only to wrap his wound with a handkerchief. After twenty minutes, as the French faltered and turned to retreat in disorder, Wolfe, leading the right line of attack in pursuit, was hit in the chest by two consecutive bullets and died almost immediately, without knowing that his army went on to capture Quebec.

Montcalm, protecting the rear of his escaping troops, was also shot during the battle. Nonetheless, he mounted his black horse and was helped back to safety by his men. As he lay dying, aware of his defeat, Montcalm sent a message to the English asking them to be kind to the French wounded. He was dead by the next morning.

Thus both heroes of the Plains of Abraham died as a result of the battle. Montcalm's body was placed in a crude wooden box and buried. Today a plaque on the Plains of Abraham reads:

"The gallant, good and great Montcalm, four times deservingly victorious and at last defeated through no fault of his own."

The body of the victor, General Wolfe, was "pickled" in a barrel of rum, since there was no other means of embalming in those days, and was shipped back to England for a hero's burial.

TOPICS FOR DISCUSSION
1. Do you consider either Wolfe or Montcalm to be heroes? Explain why or why not.
2. Were Wolfe and Montcalm typical of English and French-speaking Canadians today?
3. What kind of Canada would exist today if the French had defeated the English in 1759?
4. Both Wolfe and Montcalm began their military careers at an early age. In those days there was no such concept as "teen-ager", only "boy" or "man", "girl" or "woman". How and why was such a long intermediate stage between childhood and adulthood developed? What are the advantages and disadvantages of being a teen-ager?

CREATIVE CHALLENGE
Prepare a factual essay using one of the following as your main thesis.
1. One battle on the Plains of Abraham should not have determined the subjugation of the French culture, which has lasted for more than 200 years in Canada.
2. If, after defeating the French on the Plains of Abraham, the English had not allowed them to retain their language and culture, it would have eliminated the bloodshed and antagonism that has erupted throughout 200 years of Canadian history.
3. The Battle on the Plains of Abraham and the death of both generals is symbolic of the futility of war.

The first paragraph of your exposition should state clearly your viewpoint or thesis. You should then use examples and arguments to support your thesis. The last paragraph should conclude with a restatement of your viewpoint. If you follow these instructions and state each point clearly your essay will have unity, coherence and emphasis.

ALEXANDER MACKENZIE

The First Person to Cross Canada Coast to Coast

At the beginning of the American Revolution, when Alexander was twelve years old, he was sent by his father from New York to Montreal. The boy had been born in Scotland, but after his mother's death he had moved with his father to the English colonies in North America.

In Montreal he attended school only briefly before he went to work as an apprentice with Finlay, Gregory & Co., fur traders. Bright and enthusiastic, the lean, good-looking youth was soon made a partner in the company. In 1784, his firm was absorbed into the North West Co., and he was sent to command Fort Chipewyan in Athabasca (northern Alberta today). He arrived by canoe, and as the years passed at the remote trading post, he developed a single ambition: to reach the Pacific coast by land and to see the ocean.

Such a feat would not only open a trading route, based on the expensive sea-otter pelts that were the sole domain of Russians descending from Siberia, but would also settle the territorial conflicts on the west coast of the continent. At the time Russia owned Alaska, Spain controlled California, Captain James Cook had arrived by sea to claim the entire coastline for Britain, and an American captain had sailed to the mouth of the Columbia River.

On June 3, 1789, Mackenzie, along with thirteen companions in three canoes, started north into uncharted wilderness, expecting the river they were on to turn westward and empty into the Pacific Ocean. After a voyage of 2 400 km, which took six weeks, he discovered, instead, the Arctic Ocean. Most

explorers who charted an unknown river through northern terrain would have been happy with their discovery, but Alexander was only more obsessed with unlocking the secret of the interior of the continent. He named the river he had followed "River Disappointment", which indicates his view of the unsuccessful expedition. Later it was renamed the Mackenzie River.

Realizing that he needed more than instinct and Indian legends to reach his destination, Mackenzie convinced his employers to allow him to paddle back to Montreal and to travel from there to England, where he studied for a year and a half at his own expense. When he returned in the spring of 1792, he had acquired the knowledge and the navigational instruments to accomplish his dream. On the tenth of October, he set out from Fort Chipewyan on the Peace River in an eight-meter-long birchbark shell. His second-in-command, Alexander

Mackay, six French-Canadian paddlers, and two Indian hunters accompanied him.

Around the middle of May they came to the dangerous swirling vortex of the Peace River Canyon, which was ninety meters deep and forty kilometres long. The canoe could no longer be paddled against the strong current. In his diary Mackenzie describes the adventure:

"Monday, May 20, 1793.
Now, with very much difficulty, we moved along at the bottom of a high rock. Luckily — it was not hard stone — we were able to cut steps in the rock for twenty feet. Then, at the risk of my life, I leaped onto a small rock below. There, I received upon my shoulders those who followed me along the steps. In this way the four of us passed the rock. Then we dragged up the canoe, but in doing so we broke it upon the rocks in the water. Very luckily a dry tree had fallen from the rock above us. Without it, we could not have made a fire, for there was no other wood within a mile of this place.

When we had fixed the canoe, we towed it along beside the rocks. Since we had used most of our bark to fix the canoe, two men were sent to get more bark. They soon returned with enough to last us for some time.

Then we set out again. We pushed ourselves, in the canoe, with poles. But soon we came to a part of the river where our poles would not reach bottom. Once more, men had to walk along the shore to tow the canoe along. This

was very difficult, for the men towing had to pass on the outside of the trees that grew on the edge of the cliff beside the river.

Now we had to cross the river. The water was so fast that some of my people stripped to their shirts so that they would be better prepared for swimming. They expected to be tumbled into the river and wanted to be ready when it happened. But we managed to cross without much trouble.

As we went on, the current ran faster and faster. In a distance of two miles, we had to unload the canoe four times and carry everything. Sometimes it was all we could do to keep the canoe from being dashed to pieces on the rocks.

At five o'clock, we arrived at a point where the river was one continual rapid. Here again, we took everything out of the canoe so that we could tow her along. At length, however, the water was so rough that a wave striking the canoe broke the towing line. It seemed that the canoe would be broken to pieces, and those in her would be killed. And then another wave drove the boat out of the tumbling water. At last the men could bring the canoe ashore.

Strangely, the canoe had been little damaged. But the men were in such a state that we decided not to travel any further today. For as far as we could see, the river ahead of us was one white sheet of foaming water.''

As Mackenzie's party inched its way up the Parsnip River, a hunting party of Sekanis threatened them with bows and arrows. Mackenzie told his men not to touch their weapons and, stepping from the canoe, invited the Indians to parley. They approached suspiciously, bows taut and arrows ready, but at the sight of a few trade items such as glass beads and trinkets, relaxed and spoke with Mackenzie. They

told him that to the south was another river that led to the "stinking lake" (Pacific Ocean).

The Parsnip dwindled to a labyrinth of small streams. On June 12, they took the canoe from the water, carried it about 700 m over a low-hill, and placed it in a small lake. It was an historic moment; they were the first white people to cross the Continental Divide. As they started downstream looking for the "river of the west" that would take them to the ocean, however, fierce rapids smashed their canoe against a rock, and some equipment and almost all of their ammunition was lost in the swirling waters. Soaked and mutinous, the men were ready to turn on Mackenzie, but he shamed them into obedience by talking of "the honour of conquering disasters" and the "disgrace" of returning home unsuccessfully.

By June 18, they reached a broad river that would one day be known as the Fraser, but as they proceeded west a shower of arrows sprayed them from the river bank. Mackenzie ordered his men not to shoot, and, despite the danger, he stepped ashore alone. Although they argued among themselves, some of the Indians followed him back to the canoe, where they were given knives and beads. These were the warlike Carriers, who informed Mackenzie that the river was so long and treacherous he would never reach the ocean. The chief of the Carriers then told him of a safer route to the west, which would take four days of canoeing and two days of walking. The route turned out to take two weeks, most of it struggling through dangerous wilderness on foot.

They started overland on July 4, each member of the expedition carrying a forty-kilogram pack, and as they climbed upward the weather turned cold and wet. They crossed hard-packed snow on trails high in the mountains before descending into the warmth of the Bella Coola River Valley. Along the river they

encountered a large Indian camp, where they were hospitably greeted and treated to a feast of roasted salmon freshly caught in huge traps of woven cedar roots. The chief also gave them the use of two dugout canoes, complete with crews to paddle them down to the sea on the fast-moving Bella Coola River. As soon as their party reached a coastal inlet, however, the Indians refused to go any farther and, leaving Mackenzie's party on the shore, turned back up the river.

The water in the inlet tasted salty, but twenty-nine-year-old Mackenzie was impatient to see the actual ocean shore. In a nearby Indian village he obtained a clumsy, leaking canoe, which took them into what is now Dean Channel. There they were suddenly attacked by three canoes of Indians from the Bella Bella nation. The natives overtook them, and, in the confusion, Mackenzie learned that other white men in "giant canoes at sea" had been there already and that a white chief named "Macubah" had tried to shoot the Indian chief, who now wanted revenge. The white men were ordered ashore, as ten more canoes filled with Indians appeared. As they landed on the beach, Mackenzie and his men primed their weapons and prepared for a fight, but instead of attacking, the Indians mysteriously withdrew.

The next morning Mackenzie, the first white person to reach the Pacific by crossing overland from Canada or the United States, wrote in his diary:

"I now mixed up some vermilion in melted grease and wrote in large letters, on the rock on which we had slept last night: Alexander Mackenzie, from Canada by land, the twenty-second of July, one thousand seven hundred and ninety-three."

Mackenzie at the Pacific Ocean, 1793.

TOPICS FOR DISCUSSION

1. How many Canadians a year cross Canada today? Have you seen both coasts of Canada? Should all Canadians try to cross Canada from coast to coast at least once?

2. Instead of fighting, Mackenzie offered suspicious people he met gifts and friendship. How did he benefit from his philosophy? If you encountered a hostile group of people today, could you use Mackenzie's philosophy effectively?

3. Alexander Mackenzie in later life lived in Montreal where he became a member of the Lower Canada Assembly from 1804-1808. Do you think he would make a good politician? Explain why or why not.

4. In order to achieve his goal, Mackenzie had to study navigation. What goals do you have in life? What education do you need to achieve them?

5. Mackenzie risked his life partly to obtain access to rich furs. Today many people consider the killing of animals such as seals or the slaughtering of whales at sea to be vicious and unnecessary. Who do you consider to be more heroic, people like Mackenzie or the individuals who try to prevent the harvesting of animals? Explain your viewpoint.

CREATIVE CHALLENGES

1. Plan a canoe trip for next summer that will last at least a week.

What equipment and supplies will you need? Where will you travel? Be certain that you have experienced people in your group.

2. For a month, keep a diary, as Alexander Mackenzie did, of your adventures. Afterwards, read it over. What does it reveal about yourself and your life?

3. The "white chief" whom the Bella Bella Indians called "Macubah" was obviously Captain Vancouver, who explored the western coast of British Columbia by sea. Invent a conversation among the Bella Bella Indians that explains why they never harmed Mackenzie.

DAVID THOMPSON
The One-Eyed Wizard of the Wilderness

David Thompson in the Athabaska Pass, 1810.

David, fourteen years old, stepped from the sailing ship that had carried him from England to the new land. The cool September wind of Churchill Factory welcomed him to the outpost on Hudson Bay. The year was 1784.

The boy brought with him no memory of his father, who had died when he was a baby, and few pleasant memories of the strict Grey Coast School in Westminster, where he had lived the lonely life of an orphan until the Hudson's Bay Company paid the school fifteen dollars for him. It was in this way that David found himself an apprentice at their outpost in North America. He was short for his age and, since birth, had been blind in his right eye.

David Thompson's first task as a clerk was to copy the manuscript of Samuel Hearne, a geographer and surveyor. As he sat transcribing Hearne's account of his journey to the Coppermine River, snow started floating to the ground outside. During that first winter, David saw three-metre-high snowdrifts pile up within the walls of the isolated stockade and ice build up inside the log buildings. A burning ambition inside his small frame grew and kept him warm, however; it was not the ambition for fame, or wealth, or power, but rather the desire to explore, to see rivers, lakes, and mountain passes never before seen by Europeans, and to place them on a map of the new continent for future generations.

When his outfit of clothing, which was supplied to him by the Hudson's Bay Company, arrived from England, he turned it down and asked instead for a brass sextant. This primitive instrument would allow him to "shoot" the stars and determine the positions of lakes, rivers, and trading posts. It was to earn him the name of "Stargazer" among the Indians and coureurs de bois, who came to believe that it was a magic tool. Some of them called David Thompson "the wizard of the wilderness", because

they thought that with his sextant he could "make the wind blow" and "see into the future".

From the beginning Thompson was motivated by scientific curiosity, and he wished to discover the secrets of the uncharted kilometres of rugged country. At sixteen he was sent into the western interior as clerk and writer for Mitchell Oman, who taught him much about living, travelling, and trading in Indian country. Together they travelled the Hayes River to Lake Winnipeg, then on up the Saskatchewan River. He was next sent to winter with the Piegan Indians on the shores of Bow River, at the present day site of Calgary where, from a Cree Indian friend, he learned for the first time of the country beyond the Rocky Mountains. The next winter he was confined with a broken leg to Manchester House, a post on the north branch of the Saskatchewan River; but the following year he was studying surveying, learning to use a telescope, chronometer, compass, thermometer and, of course, his sextant to make astronomical observations. In 1791, at the end of his apprenticeship, he was offered a position as surveyor and trader. The Hudson's Bay Company put him in charge of his own expedition, with orders to discover a new and shorter route to Lake Athabasca. He found one.

Fierce competition existed between the Hudson's Bay Company and its rival, the North West Company. David Thompson, known for his ability to hold listeners spellbound by tales of his wilderness adventures, was one of the main reasons the Hudson's Bay Company was gaining more control over the valuable fur trade by 1797. On the other side were men of equal reputation: Alexander Mackenzie, the Frobisher brothers, and Simon Fraser. Fraser talked Thompson into leaving the Hudson's Bay Company and joining up with the "Nor Westers" as a surveyor and mapmaker.

With the Hudson's Bay Company, Thompson had surveyed over

5 000 km of rivers and lakes, but that proved to be only the beginning of his career. He was immediately put to work by the North West Company surveying the 49th parallel west of the Lake of the Woods, the line established as the boundary between the American and Canadian west. On foot, in canoes, on snow shoes and on horseback, he travelled over 6 500 km in ten months, sometimes in blinding snowstorms and temperatures of −30°C. In total he would struggle over 80 000 km of tough terrain, recording 3 500 000 km², before he retired. His explorations included not only Canadian territory, but also Montana, Idaho, Washington and Oregon, although these areas were later given to the United States in the settlement of 1846.

While passing through the trading post at Ile à la Crosse in the summer of 1799, David saw Charlotte Small, a half Irish, half Cree girl of fourteen with long black hair. He married her immediately, and she accompanied him on his journeys into the unknown Rockies. Unlike many other fur traders and explorers, who took Métis wives and then left them and their children behind when they returned to white society, David Thompson never deserted his family, which grew to sixteen children.

David Thompson was a sensitive man of principles. He refused to use rum as a trade item when bartering with Indians, in spite of its profit. He respected the Indians, learned their codes and creeds, and was able to avoid senseless bloodshed. In 1801, when he found a pass through the Rocky Mountains and built Kootenay House, the first trading post west of the Rockies, of lodge pole pines, his small establishment was threatened by 300 Piegan warriors. In place of force, Thompson used his wits — he enticed two Piegan spies who came to the trading post into accepting a few twists of tobacco and other offers of hospitality, knowing the tribe would never break its code of honor by attacking the fort once gifts had been accepted.

When Thompson crossed the Rockies near the Banff-Yoho Park region and reached the source of the Columbia River in 1811, he and his party, including his wife and three of their very young children, knelt down to pray beside the rushing waters of the creek: "May God in His mercy give me to see where its waters flow into the ocean, and return in safety." His prayer was answered. Thompson became the first white person to travel the length of the Columbia from its source to its mouth, thus opening a valuable trading route to the Pacific.

After twenty-eight years in the northwest, Thompson left Rupert's Land and returned to Montreal on a visit; however, he never went out west again. Using the thirty-two volumes of his diary, he drew the first real map of the northwest. At last he fulfilled his dream of seeing the vast North American lands accurately charted. Most subsequent maps are based on his outlines; in fact, few modern maps are as accurate as his, in spite of the fact that he had only primitive instruments to work with. He was one of the world's best geographers.

After his retirement, he settled first in Terre Bonne, Lower Canada, and then moved to Williamstown, Upper Canada. He continued to survey until his seventieth year, but life was not to end peacefully for the man who had overcome so many obstacles for so many years. In his old age he was forgotten by the country for which he had done so much. His one good eye, with which he had viewed an entire continent, went blind, and his last ten years were spent in darkness and poverty.

He was so poor he had to pawn all of his personal possessions, including not only his coat, but also the brass sextant that he had carried for half a century over 80 000 km, and which had come to symbolize his great accomplishments. "Stargazer" died at age eighty-seven at Longueuil, near Montreal, without any public notice of his death. A river was named after him in Western Canada, but the only other tribute to the man came over a hundred years after his death — a 1957 Canadian postage stamp.

TOPICS FOR DISCUSSION
1. Which characteristics of David Thompson most impressed you? Compare your opinion with those of your classmates.
2. How could Canadians today best pay tribute to David Thompson? For example, a statue, a movie based on his life, a T.V. series about him, a popular song on the hit parade, a painting of him and his adventures, a comic book, etc.

SUGGESTIONS
1. If you know someone who is a stamp collector, take a look at the 1957 Canadian postage stamp issued to honor Thompson.
2. Find on the map of Canada the Thompson River. What waterways can you find on the same map that are named after other men mentioned in this description of David Thompson's life? i.e. — Alexander Mackenzie, Frobisher Brothers, Simon Fraser.
3. Find on the map the other rivers and lakes mentioned in this narrative. i.e. — Coppermine River, Hayes River, Saskatchewan River, etc.

CREATIVE CHALLENGE
1. In 1811 David Thompson wrote in his diary of the finding of large human-like tracks. He reported these measurements:

> Overall length — 45 cm
> width — 20 cm
> toes — 10 cm

Could this have been the first report of the mythical Sasquatch? Research other Sasquatch reports and then write a fictional description of how you and your friends encounter a Sasquatch during a camping trip in the Rocky Mountains.

Choose the adjectives and verbs that you use carefully to be certain that they are creating the mood or atmosphere that you imagine.

SAMUEL CUNARD

The Man Who Tamed the Oceans

Little Sam never went to school. He was working by the time he was twelve, but his lack of schooling never seemed to matter because he had the quick mind of a business wizard. No opportunity to make money passed him by. As a young teen-ager he was going to auctions, buying items and reselling them at a profit. During the summer he grew vegetables in his garden to sell; in the winter he knitted stockings. By the time he was seventeen years old he was running his own general store.

Born in 1787 in Halifax, Samuel Cunard was the son of a carpenter. In his late teens he convinced his father to quit his job, and the two became partners in a new ship-building firm, Abraham Cunard and Son. Europe was at war with Napoleon and the British port of Halifax prospered as a result, but no one prospered more than young Cunard. During the war of 1812, he convinced the lieutenant-governor of Nova Scotia to allow him to trade with the enemy. But he also went into the pirate business, secretly backing a Nova Scotian privateer who captured and plundered Yankee ships. Cunard's fleet of forty schooners and whaling ships, built at Dartmouth Cove, made him his first million dollars.

But Samuel Cunard was satisfied neither with the money nor with his unreliable sailing ships. He had a vision of something greater. The oceans in his day were dangerous; men, cargo and vessels often sank to watery graves in storms. The situation was dramatized by the nick-name "coffin brigs" given to the

ten gun brigs that carried the mail from Falmouth to Halifax: seven of the ships went to the bottom within ten years. Cunard's motto became "safety first and profits second." He did much to establish safety not only for his own ships, but for all who travelled the oceans. He became the first lighthouse commissioner, in an era when lighthouses and other navigational aids were almost unknown, and his system of using sailing lights (green on the starboard and red on the portside) was so successful at reducing collisions that it is used today throughout the entire world. His ships were the first to have electric lights and to utilize Marconi's wireless invention.

When Samuel spoke to his Halifax neighbours about the possibility of using steam rather than sail power, and of having an "ocean railway" so safe and reliable it could cross the seas and arrive

punctually regardless of winds or storms, they laughed at him openly. It was a revolutionary idea. However, his faith in the power of steam was confirmed when the Quebec-built *Royal William,* of which Cunard was a main shareholder, be-came, in 1833, the first ship to cross the Atlantic entirely by steam.

That was only the beginning. When the British government called for tenders for a mail service across the Atlantic in 1838, no one in Halifax would back what they con-sidered to be a foolhardy concept — delivering the mail by steamships. Cunard had to find partners in Scot-land instead. He built four steam-ships, and when the first one reached Boston, the city treated him like a hero. Later he provided the first regular service across the At-lantic with his *sixty-metre* paddle wheeler, the *Britannia,* and the people of Boston presented him with a $50,000 silver cup.

From 1854 to 1856, his fleet of ships carried troops and supplies to the Crimean War to fight against the Cossacks, and Queen Victoria made Cunard a baronet for his aid. When "Sir" Samuel died in London in 1865, his shipping line had oper-ated for twenty-five years as a pas-senger service without the loss of a single life at sea. Man at last had tamed the oceans.

The safety record of the Cunard lines continued after his death. Mark Twain once said that he, "felt himself rather safer on board a Cunard steamer than he did upon land." It wasn't until 1915, when a Cunard ship, the *Lusitania,* was torpedoed by a German submarine,

Samuel Cunard's Britannia

that the safety record was broken. That event caused the U.S.A. to declare war on Germany. In 1934, the famous *Queen Mary* was launched by the Cunard line, and, although even that great ship is now retired, the Cunard company lives on, as does the memory of the heroic Nova Scotia lad who began it all.

RESEARCH CHALLENGE
Select one of the following Canadians who, like Cunard, became a millionaire and investigate how he or she became so successful. Compare your information with that of friends or classmates who researched a different personality. Are there characteristics common to all tycoons?

1. Donald A. Smith, who started in a Labrador trading post, built the largest railroad empire in the world.

2. Elizabeth Arden, who revo- lutionized the cosmetic industry, was a truck farmer's daughter from Woodbridge, Ontario. Her original name was Florence Nightingale Graham.

3. Sam Bronfman, a Winnipeg hotel keeper, became the greatest distiller in the world.

4. Lord Thompson of Fleet, who began in Toronto as a paperboy, later became the most powerful newspaper tycoon in the world.

5. John Williamson, a Montreal geologist, went to Africa where he discovered and became the sole owner of the richest diamond mine in the world.

6. E. P. Taylor, who built an empire of farm machinery, food products, and newsprint became the biggest brewer in the world.

7. H. R. MacMillan at twenty-seven was chief forester of British Columbia but he left the public service and created the world's largest logging empire.

8. Hart Massey, from Grafton, Ontario, built one of the most lucrative businesses in farm machinery in the world.

9. Eric Harvie and Frank McMahon, who are both Calgary multimillionaires, struck it rich in the Leduc oil fields.

10. Sam McLaughlin, whose father was a pioneer in the Canadian car business, built an automotive empire, which, in 1918, amalgamated with Chevrolet to become General Motors of Canada, Ltd.

11. Gilbert LaBine lugged supplies by sled for 320 km to Great Bear Lake where he discovered a vein of pitchblende that was the beginning of Canada's prosperous radium industry.

12. Walt Disney, who developed the animation industry, was born in Ontario.

GENERAL ISAAC BROCK
The Hero of Upper Canada

On June 20, 1812, the United States declared war on Great Britain, and one of the most uneven battles in history began. The Canadian army was outnumbered ten to one, and the British, at war in Europe with Napoleon Bonaparte, couldn't spare any aid. The Americans had a dream which they called "manifest destiny": they wished to occupy all of North America.

One man more than any other was responisible for Canada's victory over the invading American armies. Isaac Brock stood 185 cm, was fair haired and blue-eyed, and was known as a hard, fist-fighting, horse-riding professional soldier. Describing how his small force defeated the overwhelming enemy numbers, he once explained, "I speak loud and look big."

When Brock was only twenty-one,

an older officer in his regiment, who was a crack shot and who had already killed several men, baited him into a pistol duel. When they arrived for the gentlemanly encounter, Brock, as the injured party, was allowed to dictate the terms of the contest. Rather than the customary twelve paces between them, Brock insisted the duel be fought at point-blank range across his handkerchief, which he laid out on the ground at his opponent's feet as he cocked his pistol. His terms meant certain death for both men; the captain refused to fight and had to resign his commission in dishonour. On another occasion, a musket ball hit him in the throat, knocking him off of his horse. A heavy muffler wrapped around his neck, however, saved his life.

Brock arrived in Canada in 1802,

sailing up the St. Lawrence with the 49th Regiment. The following year he single-handedly suppressed a dangerous conspiracy, which had been instigated by deserters from a detachment at Fort George. He had complete knowledge of the French language and grew to love the land and the people of Canada so much that he refused a post in Spain in order to remain here. By 1811 he was a major-general and had been appointed the provisional lieutenant-governor of Upper Canada.

On July 12, 1812, General Hull, with a bombastic demand that Canada surrender, led an army of 2 000 Americans into Upper Canada. Isaac Brock went into action instantly and ordered an attack on Fort Mackinac on the Huron-Michigan Strait. The easy victory by

General Brock's ride to Queenston, 1812.

the Canadians developed confidence among the Indians and fur traders of the west and sent General Hull back to the safety of his fort at Detroit. Calling a staff meeting, which included the Indian leader Tecumseh, Brock decided on an immediate assault on Detroit.

General Hull was particularly frightened of Indians, so Brock brazenly bluffed his opponent with a demand for surrender. He sent a message to the American commander which read,

"You must be aware that the numerous body of Indians who have attached themselves to my troops will be beyond control the moment the contest commences."

That night the Indians silently crossed the river and grouped in the woods behind the fort, where they began to terrify the American troops with wild whoops and signal calls. At dawn, Brock, in scarlet and gold uniform and mounted on his grey charger, Alfred, crossed the river in full view of the defenders. Tecumseh rode at his side in colourful war regalia. Brock had encouraged his scanty force of untrained militia men, rounded up from the farms and villages of Upper Canada, to march in extended order and to beg or borrow as many red uniforms as possible, in order to create the impression of a large number of professional soldiers. The Canadians had only five guns on the river opposite Detroit, whereas the American fort contained thirty-three guns. Brock's bluff worked. The first time a shell dropped inside the fort, Hull ran up the white flag and surrendered 2 500 soldiers to Brock's force of less than 800 without a fight.

On the dark, wet morning of October 13, 1812, one month after the fall of Detroit, the Americans struck again, this time along the Niagara River opposite Lewiston. The U.S. force had 6 300 men; Brock had only 1 500. During the battle the Americans scaled Queenston Heights and occupied it. Brock, realizing that whoever controlled the Heights would win the battle, gathered about ninety men for a counter-attack and, in a plumed hat and scarlet tunic, led them up the hill with his sword flashing, his cloak streaming behind him and shouting, "Push on, York volunteers!" A bullet hit his wrist, but he ignored the wound. Then an American sharpshooter took careful aim from behind a tree, and Isaac Brock fell instantly dead. The shot struck Brock in the left breast and passed straight through his body.

Even in death Brock inspired his troops. The small Canadian force, in an effort to "avenge the General", beat the Americans back across the river. The Canadians had lost only ninety-one men; they had killed or wounded 300 and had taken 958 prisoners.

By the end of the war not one metre of Canadian territory was under control of the enemy. Brock's wish "to keep the land inviolate" from American invasion was fulfilled.

TOPICS FOR DISCUSSION
1. "Isaac Brock led a dangerous, adventure-filled life. If he had survived the Battle of Queenston Heights, he probably would have met an equally violent death elsewhere." Do you agree with this statement? What would motivate a man like Brock to risk his life? Do you know people who are like Brock? Does it surprise you that Brock was forty-three years old and single when he died?
2. How would you explain the fact that so frequently during the War of 1812 small numbers of Canadians defeated and captured larger American armies?
3. When the Americans invaded Canada, they expected the people, particularly the French in Lower Canada, to welcome them as their liberators from British rule. Both French and English Canadians fought them instead. What would happen if an enemy country invaded Canada today?
4. Some people today claim that the Americans, although friendly, have invaded our country financially and culturally. Have we been overrun? What percentage of Canadian business and natural resources is controlled by Americans? What T.V. shows do you watch? Which records do you buy? Who makes the movies that you go to see? What is the difference between an American and a Canadian today?

RESEARCH CHALLENGE
1. Canada won the Battle of Queenston Heights due largely to two groups of soldiers. John Brant, eighteen-year-old son of the Mohawk leader Joseph Brant, had worked his way behind the American lines with 250 Indian scouts, and their tomahawks and war whoops terrorized the U.S. troops. The second group was Captain Robert Runchey's company of coloured men (runaway Negro slaves from Virginia), who charged the enemy, sending some of the Americans tumbling over the escarpment onto the rocks below. Do most Canadians today recognize the fact that without the aid of Indian and Negro Canadians, our country might not have survived in 1812? Prepare a survey questionnaire which asks people to identify heroic Canadians of 1812. Each member of the class could survey his or her neighbours and the total statistics could be recorded during the next class. Survey questions must be short and clearly stated. The person conducting the survey must be polite and well spoken.

Battle of Queenston, Oct. 13, 1812, by Major James B. Dennis, commander of a detachment of the 49th Regiment during the battle.

TECUMSEH
"Shooting Star"

The Shawnee chief was dead, shot by an American settler because he refused to act as a hunting guide. Wails of mourning rose from the Indian village. The chief's son Shooting Star, not yet a teen-ager, sat alone with his sorrow.

Shooting Star had been born in 1768 near Springfield, Ohio, and had grown up in the midst of warfare with white settlers. Following his father's death, Cheeseekau, his older brother, took him on a three year adventure, first hunting buffalo with the Osages and later fighting settlers with the Cherokees. By the time Cheeseekau was killed during a raid, Shooting Star had earned the reputation of a great hunter and brave warrior as well as the new name Tecumseh, which means "he moves from one spot to another".

Tecumseh also earned other reputations: as a man of mercy when he took a firm stand against the custom of burning prisoners; as an orator and leader when he and another brother, The Prophet, urged all the Indian tribes to join together to block the spread of Americans into their treaty lands; as a lover when he fell in love with Rebecca Galloway, the teen-age daughter of the white settler who introduced him to the Bible and Shakespeare; and as a politician when he bargained skillfully for Indian rights.

He became chief and, in 1808, established a village on Tippecanoe Creek, where he worked to preserve the Indian culture, based on a simple agricultural life void of the destructive liquor introduced by the white culture. While Tecumseh was travelling among other Indian tribes

General Brock meets Tecumseh.

to organize a union of peaceful resistance, in 1811 the U.S. cavalry attacked Tippecanoe and slaughtered everyone in the village, including Tecumseh's brother, The Prophet.

About this time, the American army, led by General Hull, invaded Canada as well, thinking they would free Canadians from British rule. Instead, they were astonished to discover that Canadians, both English and French, resisted their invasion. Gathering a few scattered survivors, Tecumseh moved north to aid his old allies, the British, who had granted the Indians their treaty lands before the American revolution. Although he had only thirty followers when he arrived in Canada, his reputation as a warrior drew Indians from many tribes, and their numbers grew to over one thousand. Without this support, Canada would probably be American today.

Tecumseh first met General Brock, the Canadian military leader, one evening in his camp. The two men looked each other in the eye for a moment. Then each spontaneously stepped forward, and their hands met in a warm slap that sealed a permanent friendship. Brock gave Tecumseh the rank of brigadier-general, in command of Indian allies.

Tecumseh helped to counsel the Canadian forces, advised them on their strategy, gave them the advantage of the "bush telegraph", which brought advance news of most American moves, and fought bravely at Frenchtown, Fort Meigs, and Fort Stephenson. After the surrender of Detroit, General Brock presented Tecumseh with his own silk sash and a pair of pistols in recognition of the victory, as well as awarding him a silver George III medal.

In September, 1813, the British lost control of the Great Lakes when their fleet of ships was captured, forcing the Canadians to retreat from Detroit to Moraviantown in Upper Canada. It was at Moraviantown, on October 5, 1813, that 900 Canadian soldiers led by General Proctor, plus Tecumseh's 500 Indians, met the American army of 3 500 strong.

The battle was lost before it began. Tecumseh told his braves beforehand, "Brother warriors, we enter an engagement today from which I shall not return." The Indian leader was killed during the battle as he had predicted. When the American troops went looking for Tecumseh's body after the battle,

Tecumseh at the Battle of the Thames, 1813.

they did not find it. (It was the custom for U.S. soldiers to cut strips of skin from dead Indians to make razor straps.) His Indian friends had buried their leader in an unmarked grave somewhere in southwestern Ontario.

TOPICS FOR DISCUSSION
1. Which of Tecumseh's characteristics impress you most? Do your friends and classmates agree with you?
2. Tecumseh seemed to know that he would die in battle. Would you engage in a battle if you knew you would be killed?
3. Was Tecumseh a wise leader? Compare him to other Indian chiefs described in this book such as Joseph Brant and Big Bear. Which

man would you prefer as your leader? Explain why.
4. Indian leaders such as Tecumseh fought for the survival of their race and culture. Were they successful? Compare the fears of the Indians with those of the French-speaking Canadians who see their numbers dwindling and their culture disappearing.

CREATIVE CHALLENGES
1. Invent some Indian-style names for your friends, classmates, teachers, parents, etc. The names should indicate the character, interests, or accomplishments of the individuals. For example: a teacher might be called "Brain Pounder", a track and field runner "Fleet Foot", someone who is good at mathematics "Number in the Head".

Warning: Indian names were given as an honour, not as an insult. A warrior or maiden was proud of his or her name, so those whom you name should be proud of theirs. Notice that each name begins with a capital. What is the difference between a common noun and a proper noun? What is the difference between an abstract noun and a concrete noun? What is a collective noun?
2. Invent a game based on the war of 1812. It could involve any of the following: players representing Canadians and Americans on a board, a deck of cards, a crossword puzzle, a map of North America, a dart board, etc.

LAURA SECORD

Heroine of Upper Canada

On October 13, 1812, the residents of Queenston, Upper Canada, were awakened by the roar of cannons. Alert Canadian troops spotted American soldiers attempting to row across the Niagara River under the cover of an early morning mist. In the town of Queenston, a woman rushed her five children from their home to the safety of a nearby farmhouse. Her name was Laura Secord, and her husband, James Secord, a merchant turned soldier, was fighting as a sergeant in the battle to defend Canada from the invaders.

Laura was born in 1775 in the British colony of Massachusetts, but after the American rebellion against the British, moved north with her family and settled in Upper Canada. Her father, Thomas Ingersoll, had been left with four girls when his first wife died, and Laura, at eight years of age, was the eldest. Thus the fragile and delicate Laura from an early age was expected to take much of the responsibility in the raising of her younger siblings. The expectations increased as her father remarried and the family grew larger. Thomas Ingersoll was given a land grant (which is the present site of Ingersoll, Ontario) and opened a tavern at Queenston, where Laura ran the business for her father and where she met her husband, James. The young couple were married in 1798 and, until the war broke out in 1812, life was good for them. They had five children, two servants, a pleasant frame house and a prosperous store, which carried household appliances and women's wear.

Word came to Laura that her husband lay badly wounded on the battlefield, calling her name. She rushed to the Heights, searching frantically among the corpses until she finally discovered him on the side of a cliff. He was wounded in the knee and shoulder and was unable to flee. His shoulder was bleeding badly, so Laura tore a piece of cloth from her petticoat, which she pressed against the wound in an effort to stop the flow of blood. As she worked over her husband, three American soldiers approached, killing wounded Canadians as they lay helpless on the battlefield. One of the soldiers raised his rifle butt over Jame's head, but Laura threw herself across her defenseless husband, begging the enemy soldiers to kill her instead. As the surprised soldiers hesitated, an American officer, Captain Wool, arrived and intervened, ordering the soldiers to disperse. He allowed Laura to take James back to Queenston.

Their home had been ransacked; everything of value had been looted from their store. When the Americans occupied the town in May, everyone of military age was taken prisoner, but because he was unable to walk due to the wound in his leg, James Secord was left in the care of his wife. The Secords and their children, however, were confined to the kitchen and one small bedroom in their own home, and American officers were billeted in the rest of the house.

It became the habit of the officers to sit around the dining table, after Laura had fed them their dinner, and discuss the war. On June 23rd, 1813, a special guest ate with the others — Colonel Boersteer, the commander of the American forces at Queenston. After eating, the Americans requested that they be left alone, but the Secords listened secretly as Captain Chapin convinced his commanding officer to permit him to lead a surprise attack against Lt. James FitzGibbon, who commanded the Canadian troops at Beaver Dams. A victory would give the Americans control of the entire Niagara Peninsula.

Obviously, someone had to warn FitzGibbon, and, since James was disabled, Laura resolved to carry the news herself. Shortly after 4 a.m.the next morning, before the sun rose, Laura began her journey using the pretense that she was going to St. David's to visit her sick half-brother. To avoid American sentries along the road, she was forced to travel deep into hostile forests that housed rattlesnakes, wolves and wildcats. At St. David's she was joined by her young niece, Elizabeth, and they continued together until Elizabeth, exhausted from the strenuous hike, was forced to stop; but thirty-eight-year-old Mrs. Secord, her shoes worn through and her feet cut and swollen, continued alone through the swamps with the hot summer sun beating down on her. She reached Shipman's Corners (present day St. Catherines) and started out again for De Cew House, the headquarters of FitzGibbon's militia, which was still eleven kilometres away. With dusk approaching, Laura crawled across Twelve Mile Creek on a fallen tree. But then she stopped, horrified, as she discovered herself surrounded by a tight

C. W. JEFFERYS

Laura Secord warns Colonel FitzGibbon of planned attack on Beaver Dams.

circle of Indians, whose camp she had stumbled into. Although she realized that they must be part of the Indian forces fighting with FitzGibbon against the Americans, she was still a white woman alone in the wilderness and she was terrified. The Indians, because Laura had arrived from the direction of the enemy lines, were equally suspicious that she was a spy. Only her courage and persistence convinced the chief to take her to FitzGibbon as she demanded.

Eighteen hours and almost thirty-two kilometres after she began her trek, Laura was ushered into the presence of FitzGibbon and told

him in exhausted tones of the surprise attack the Americans would be launching against Beaver Dams. FitzGibbon was later to write of his impression of Laura Secord as a woman with "a strong and persistent will", and to credit her with the victory that followed when his small force of 50 troops and 500 Mohawks ambushed and captured a larger American force at Beaver Dams, ensuring that the Niagara Peninsula remained Canadian territory. Laura returned secretly behind enemy lines to her family, without anyone knowing of her heroic journey.

In retaliation for their defeat, the

retreating American forces set fire to the towns of Queenston and St. David's on December 10, 1813. Even the churches were burned. The Canadians quickly countered by attacking Buffalo and putting it to flames.

The war ended, and twenty years of poverty passed as the Secords struggled to raise their family. In 1828, James was appointed registrar, and then judge in 1833. In 1835 he became collector of customs at Chippewa. When she was more than sixty year old Laura again displayed her courage. Her husband needed a man to help arrest some smugglers, but was unable to recruit one. Laura

41

immediately dressed in a long over-coat, pulled a cap down over her ears, and picked up a gun, with which she aided her husband to arrest two smugglers.

Unfortunately, with James' death in 1841, the termination of his income and pension left Laura destitute. Since there was no such thing as welfare, Laura turned to needle-work. She also opened a school in her cottage for children in order to make money to buy food.

Recognition of Laura Secord's role in saving the Niagara Peninsula during the war of 1812 slowly grew. A newspaper article gave her full credit for her part in the victory. FitzGibbon, by then a colonel, wrote statements verifying her actions and explaining how she had not been able to receive credit at the time because she and her family were in enemy-occupied territory. In 1860, when Laura was eighty-five, the Prince of Wales (who was later to become King Edward VII) heard of her thirty-two kilometre journey. When he returned to England from Canada he sent her a reward of one hundred pounds.

At the age of ninety-three she died. Today a plaque on the school in Queenston that bears her name has the following inscription:

LAURA SECORD MEMORIAL
IN LOVING AND HONOURED MEMORY OF
LAURA INGERSOLL SECORD
A RESIDENT OF QUEENSTON AND
A HEROINE OF UPPER CANADA WHO
SAVED HER COUNTRY FROM THE
ENEMY IN 1813

TOPICS FOR DISCUSSION
1. Are there women of thirty-eight with five children who would risk their lives to save Canada today?
2. In 1841 there was no old-age pension, no unemployment insurance and no welfare. Laura, a grandmother, had to find a means of supporting herself. Is the present-day welfare system an improvement or would Canadians be stronger individuals if they still had to depend on their own abilities to survive?
3. Does Canadian society today offer women the opportunity to be heroic? Explain why or why not.

SUGGESTION
1. Organize a thirty-two kilometre walk in your school to honour Laura Secord. Decide on a route and have all the participants obtain sponsors. Arrange for publicity through your local newspapers, radio, and T.V. Considering the character of Laura Secord, to what appropriate use should the proceeds be put?

CREATIVE CHALLENGES
Satire is defined in the Oxford dictionary as the "use of ridicule or sarcasm or irony to expose and discourage vice and folly." Write a satirical narrative, exposition, description or skit, such as you might encounter in a *National Lampoon* or *Monty Python* production, based on one of the following situations.
1. Pierre Radisson describing how he survived after being captured at the age of sixteen by Indians who killed his two companions.
2. Etienne Brûlé explaining why his blood brothers turned against him, killing and eating him.
3. Jean de Brébeuf explaining why he didn't escape before the Iroquois attacked his village as the Hurons begged him to do.
4. Madeleine de Verchères describing how she managed to defend her home against Indians with only children and old people.
5. Adam Dollard describing the fall of his fort at Long Sault after a week of fighting.
6. Laura Secord describing the most frightening aspects of her journey to warn the British troops of the American attack.
7. Paul Bunyon describing how he created the Great Lakes.
8. Louis Riel explaining why he executed Scott.

PARODY ON "THE DEVIL AND DANIEL WEBSTER"

A parody is a composition in which an author's style is ridiculed by imitation.

On the following pages are four parodies written by students about Canadian heroes and heroines which are based on a description of an American hero, found in the short story *The Devil and Daniel Webster* by Stephen Vincent Benet.

Read each parody and, if possible, the original description of Daniel Webster, then write a parody of your own based on a Canadian personality of your choice.

PAUL BUNYAN

by student Paulette Shephard

It's a ditty they tell in the lumber camps of the North, where the great rivers carry the logs downstream to the grist mills.

Yes, Paul Bunyan's dead — or at least they buried him. But every time there's an earthquake around Chibougamau, they say you can hear his thundering footsteps in the deepest gorges of the land. And they say that if you go down to his burial grounds and bellow earth-shatteringly, "Paul Bunyan! Paul Bunyan!", the continent will rumble and the forests sway. And after a while you'll hear an unfathomable voice booming, "Men, how stand the trees?" then you had better answer, "They stand ready for your axe, huge and abundant," or he's liable to rear right out of the canyon. At least that's what I was told when I was a lumberjack.

You see, he was, and always will be the strongest, cleverest giant in the world. He never got to be prime minister but he was the strongest and the cleverest. There were thousands who depended on him for his strength, and they trusted in him right next to Manitou and they told tales about him and his magnificent ox, Babe, and they were like the stories of the great woodsmen and such. They said when he swung his axe, whole forests were cleared and lakes created. And once when he accidentally breathed sawdust, he sneezed and caused the ice age. They said when he dragged his axe he created streams and that when Babe needed shoes an iron mine had to be opened in Sudbury, and when he needed a log chute to the ocean he dug the St. Lawrence River.

That was the kind of giant he was, and his big bunkhouse was so tall that the last seven storeys had to be put on hinges to let the moon go by. When Paul made his famous pancakes his griddle was so monstrous that skaters had to tie sides of bacon to their shoes to grease it. Babe was twice as big as all outdoors and playful as a hurricane, yet, she was gentle as a deer. But Paul wasn't one of your common lumberjacks. He knew all the ways of the woods and he would be up by the light of the stars to do his job.

A man with a mouth like Hudson Bay, a brow like the Canadian Shield, and eyes that twinkled like the Northern Lights — that was Paul Bunyan.

NELLIE McCLUNG

by student Diane Hill

This is a story they tell in the homes out west, where the living is quiet and change is slow.

Yes, Nellie McClung is dead — or at least they buried her. But every time there's a train rumbling past Manitou, they say you can hear her clear voice echoing across the flat prairies. They say that if you go down to her resting place and call out, "Nellie McClung, Nellie McClung!" the land will quake and the tall grass will shake, and after a while you'll hear a vivid voice asking, "Sister, how goes the struggle?" Then you had better answer, "the struggle is gaining ground, united and powerful," or she's liable to rear right out of the earth. At least, that's what I was told when I was a feminist.

You see, for a while, she was the most controversial figure in the country. She never got to be prime minister, but she was the most controversial figure.

There were thousands who believed in her right next to Parkhurst, and they told tales about her and her ally, Emily Murphy, that were like the stories of the great matriarchs and such.

They said when she made speeches, life styles were changed and loyalties made, and once she spoke against a premier and made him into a fool. They said that when she raised her pen, laws crumbled and governments capitulated, for they knew it was no use putting up a fight against her. And when she debated an issue, false chivalry was unmasked and exposed.

That was the kind of leader she was, and Mackenzie King soon recognized that.

She had so much fire and fervor that when she was burned in effigy, the flames were tremendous, and they say you can still see them glowing in the western sky at the end of the day.

But Nellie wasn't one of your faint-hearted women; she knew all the ways of the politicians, and she would be up by moonlight to see that equality was achieved.

A woman with a mouth like Athena, a brow like the Rockies, and eyes like a ray of hope — that was Nellie McClung.

Canadian actor William Shatner who created the character of Captain Kirk.

CAPTAIN KIRK

by student Carmen Stermann

It's a tale they tell out in space, where men boldly go where no men have gone before.

Yes, Captain Kirk is dead — or at least they buried him back on Earth. But everytime there's a meteor collision they say you can hear his voice booming through the vastness of outer space. And they say that if you approach Earth, where he's buried and speak loud and clear, "Captain Kirk! Captain Kirk!" the planets will shift and the stars will go out. After a while you'll hear a deep voice saying, "Scotty, how stands the Enterprise?" Then you better answer that the Enterprise stands just as he left it — at warp two — or he's bound to materialize in front of you and set his Phaser to "kill". At least that's what I was told when I worked for the fleet.

You see, for a while he was the biggest man in the universe. He never got to be Supreme Commander, but he was the biggest. There were thousands who trusted him and depended on him to protect them from the Klingons. And they told stories about him and his adventures with Spock. They said that when he beamed down to another planet, any plant life would wither under his feet, and once, when he was really angry, he picked up rocks and threw them out into space, where they made black holes in the ends of the universe. They said, when he approached enemy warships, their magnetic fields would disintegrate, for the enemies knew it was no use putting up a fight. Whenever he gave out important commands, dramatic organ music could be heard and even the evilest of the evil would bow down to him. That was the kind of man he was. His starship suited him just fine. His crew was the best and they possessed more powers than the Fantastic Four, Superman and Wonder Woman put together. Among his crew were a doctor who could produce miracle cures and a Vulcan who could paralyze victims with the touch of a finger.

But Captain Kirk wasn't one of your gentleman captains. He knew all the ways of the universe and would be up by the light of the stars, watching for Klingons. A man with a mouth like the Milky Way, a brow like the mountains of Mars, and eyes that burned bright as the North Star — that was Captain Kirk.

CAPTAIN GILBERT PIKE

by student Peter Baker

It's a story the old sailors tell, in the dim light of harbour taverns, remembering back to the days of sail.

Yes, Captain Gilbert Pike is dead — or, at least they sewed him up in canvas and scuttled him off the coast of Newfoundland. But every time the gale winds rise around Carbonear, and the dark waves toss and slam on Conception Bay, you can hear his voice in the wind as it shrieks and moans through the rigging. And they say if you climb among the rocks on the south eastern coast, and call down to the blue depths loud and clear, "Cap'n Pike! Cap'n Pike!" the wind will rise and the waves will crash and foam against the cliffs. And after a while you'll hear a deep voice saying, "How fares the wind, Mate?" Then you better answer that the wind fares as it should, fresh and from the south, strong to fill the sails and carry a ship to distant lands and adventure, or he's liable to surface right then and there. At least that's what I was told when I was a nipper.

You see, for a while he was the fiercest pirate on the Seven Seas. He never commanded a naval fleet, but he was the fiercest pirate. His crew trusted him next to God Almighty, and they told tales of him and his voyages that were like the stories of heroes and such. They said that when he took the helm, the four winds changed direction to aid him on his journey, and once he spoke against a stubborn Nor'wester and made it warm up nigh thirty degrees. They said that when he sailed north to the Arctic Ocean, the icebergs would bumb and nudge to get out of his way, for they knew it was no use putting up a fight against him and his towering ship; and when he navigated the treacherous Cape he would harness the tearing winds and sail close-hauled without losing a degree of headway. That was the kind of man he was, and his ship and crew were suitable to him.

The ship's hull was 240 cm thick and strong as iron. The keel was like a knife blade, and the masts so high they scraped the bottoms of the clouds should they venture too low. His first mate was also a sea-faring man. He could sail a ship single handed through the Panama — blindfolded. But Captain Pike wasn't one of your Sunday sailors; he knew all the ways of the sea, and he'd be on deck throughout any storm to see that his ship and crew weathered through to safety.

A man with a mouth like a bull dolphin, a brow like the prow of a great ship, and eyes like the sparkling white caps — that was Captain Pike.

WILLIAM LYON MACKENZIE

The Rebel of Upper Canada

The vandals swarmed through the smashed doorway, overturning desks, flinging papers in every direction, destroying the press. The mob was composed of angry young faces, and after demolishing the premises of the *Colonial Advocate*, a newspaper operated by William Lyon Mackenzie, they proceeded to throw the metal type into Toronto Bay.

The attack on Mackenzie's newspaper was a reaction against his verbal and written assaults on the governing clique in Upper Canada, who were known as the "Family Compact". The violence of the young men who resented Mackenzie's radical views resulted in a law suit that not only gave Mackenzie enough money in damages to build a new printing press, but also made the Scottish settler a hero of the reform movement in Upper Canada. As a result of his new popularity, Mackenzie was elected to the Legislative Assembly of Upper Canada in 1828.

In 1831, the zealous, outspoken Mackenzie was expelled from the assembly over "a libel constituting a breach of the privileges of this House". The governor of Upper Canada was appointed by the British government, and he in turn chose the Legislative Council from the wealthy and influential members of the colony. The Reformers, such as Mackenzie, could be elected to the assembly, but their decisions could be vetoed by the Legislative Council, and they had no power when it came to important decisions. The wealthy ruled, and they ruled in favor of their own business

interests. Mackenzie was re-elected by the people to the assembly five times, and each time he was expelled and even declared incapable of sitting in the assembly.

Then, in 1835, Toronto was incorporated as a city, and the people defiantly elected Mackenzie as their first mayor. In the same year he once again took his seat in the assembly, where there was now a majority of Reformers. Attempting to bring about change along constitutional lines, Mackenzie and the others presented the governor with "The Seventh Report of the Committee on Grievances (1835)". Sir Francis Bond Head dissolved the assembly in 1836 and began a personal and bitter campaign in favor of the Tories and against the Reformers. Tory election posters accused the Reformers of lying and of attempting to turn Canada into another American republic. When

the polls closed, the Tories had won the election, and even the popular Mackenzie had been defeated.

Enraged by the tactics and interference of the British governor, Mackenzie and his followers began to hold secret meetings in their homes, forming local committies. They had given up on peaceful reform; in the fields, farmers were practicing military drills. By November, Mackenzie was distributing hand bills that read:

"CANADIANS! DO YOU LOVE FREEDOM? DO YOU HATE OPPRESSION? THEN BUCKLE ON YOUR ARMOR AND PUT DOWN THE VILLAINS WHO OPPRESS AND ENSLAVE OUR COUNTRY! UP THEN, BRAVE CANADIANS! GET READY YOUR RIFLES AND MAKE SHORT WORK OF IT!"

The rebels were drilling 5 000 volunteers, but they were disorganized. The governor, Sir Francis, had sent his regular troops to help suppress the patriot uprising in Lower Canada but, with reports of rebellion in Upper Canada growing, he authorized the formation of a militia regiment under the command of a hero of the War of 1812, Colonel James FitzGibbon. The rebellion had been set for December 7, but at the last minute the date was moved ahead to Monday, December 4. The result was confusion. Rather than the expected 5 000, only 500 men gathered to attack Toronto.

On that cold December Monday, small groups of men armed with ancient rifles, pitchforks, muskets and clubs marched along Yonge Street toward Montgomery's Tavern, the headquarters of the

The battle at Montgomery's Tavern.

rebel forces, which was within five kilometres of the government buildings in Toronto. Mackenzie, so frantic with excitement that his reasoning was unbalanced, set up road blocks on Yonge Street. The first casualty of the rebellion was a government loyalist, Colonel Moodie, who was attempting to enter Toronto and warn Sir Francis. He was challenged by a guard at one of the roadblocks, and fired his pistol at the man, but was killed by the return fire.

As Mackenzie led a force of rebels toward Toronto, Alderman John Powell encountered them. Powell drew his pistol and fired point blank into Mackenzie's face. The pistol misfired and Powell was taken prisoner. Later, after killing Captain Anthony Anderson, one of the rebel leaders, Powell escaped to warn Sir Francis of the invasion.

On Tuesday evening, at the spot where Maple Leaf Gardens now stands, the rebel force of 500 was met by Sheriff Jarvis and twenty-seven men from the Queen's York Rangers. Both sides fired, but the rebels retreated back to Montgomery's Tavern, not realizing that the opposing army was so small.

By Thursday, both sides had reorganized. Like an outlaw, Mackenzie stopped and held up a mail coach, but the main battle took place south of Montgomery's Tavern. Shots were exchanged. Men died on both sides. Others lay bleeding along the roadside. Loyalist cannon shots hit the tavern and passed through it, causing the rebels to rush from the doors and scatter toward the north. In less than half an hour the rebellion was over.

Montgomery's Tavern was burned to the ground. Mackenzie, disguised in some women's clothing that had been part of the plunder from the mail coach, escaped to Buffalo. Sixty prisoners, tied to a long rope,

were marched down Yonge Street, headed by Highland pipers and guarded by 600 loyal militiamen. In the following year, over 800 people were arrested on charges of treason and insurrection, many of them being given prison terms and sent to penal colonies near Australia. Two rebel leaders, Peter Matthews and Sam Lount, were hanged.

Mackenzie, supported by 200 volunteers from the United States, occupied Navy Island, about five kilometres upstream from Niagara Falls, and declared himself Chairman of the New Republican State of Upper Canada. He even designed a flag, but within a month the British militia occupied the island and put an end to the bloody border raids that were being carried out by Mackenzie's army. The United States government arrested and imprisoned Mackenzie for a breach of the neutrality laws. After his release, he spent twelve years in the United

States writing anti-British newspaper articles, until the amnesty of 1849 when he returned to Canada and was elected to the Legislative Assembly of Canada. By this time, however, he had grown old, and the leadership of the reform movement had progressed beyond him. He retired from politics and died peacefully in Toronto on August 28, 1861.

TOPICS FOR DISCUSSION

1. Do you think William Lyon Mackenzie was a hero?
2. Do you consider any of the other men mentioned in this selection to be heroes?
3. Because of the rebellions of 1837 in Upper and Lower Canada, the British government investigated conditions in the colonies, and Lord Durham's report brought responsible government to the people of Canada. Could the same conclusion have resulted without death and bloodshed?
4. Do the wealthy, like the "Family Compact" of 1837, still rule Canada? Explain your viewpoint clearly.
5. Are there any political issues today that might cause you or others to take up arms in a rebellion? Would such violence achieve the political goals?
6. What is an amnesty? After the amnesty of 1849, the leaders of the rebellions in both Upper and Lower Canada returned to live peacefully in this country. What does this indicate to you about the nature of rebellion?
7. If you had been living in Canada in 1837, what side would you have been on, that of the Rebels or the Loyalists?
8. Mackenzie was married and had thirteen children. One of his grandsons became the Prime Minister of Canada years later. Who was the grandson? Why was he one of the most unusual Prime Ministers in the history of Canada?
9. What are the differences between the present day political systems of Canada and of the United States of America?
10. Compare the rebellions in Upper and Lower Canada. Were they caused by the same problems? Were they solved by the same means?

CREATIVE CHALLENGES

1. Along with friends or classmates who agree with you politically, draw up a list of grievances that you believe the Canadian government should solve today. Once you have stated them clearly in good English, mail the list to the Prime Minister of Canada, asking for a reply.
2. Write a short fictional story of a future rebellion in Canada. Invent a hero or heroine who leads the rebels, and a cause for which they are fighting. How do you imagine the revolt would end?

JEAN OLIVIER CHENIER
Martyr of St-Eustache

Papineau and the other political leaders who supported representative government had deserted the cause and had run for the safety of the United States before the hostility broke out. The setting was Lower Canada (present day Quebec). On one side in the small villages were the French-speaking "patriotes"; marching against them from Montreal were the British troops supporting the rich English who controlled the government of Lower Canada.

"Only Chenier remained, ranting and still unshaken, surrounded by a dwindling remnant, and keeper of the fortress now".

Chenier's "fortress' was simply the town of St-Eustache, where he and 1000 "patriotes" prepared to defend the cause with armed resistance. The thin, dark figure who moved arrogantly among the assembled resistance fighters looked about twenty-four years old, but was in fact thirty-one. He was a doctor of

medicine by profession, a rebel in the cause of representative government by passion. The sleeves of his heavy "capote" lifted and fell as he waved his rusty sword and babbled patriotic slogans.

Reports on the approach of the red-coated troops from Montreal grew, and the numbers of rebels in St-Eustache shrank. Chenier had forced many of them into service, raiding neighbouring farms in search of husbands and sons to swell his ranks, and even capturing

Rebels retreat across the ice behind the church of St-Eustache.

some as they attended church services in town. When Scott and other rebel leaders, before they themselves had fled, had told the hot-headed Chenier the cold facts, he had broken into tears, but had recovered quickly, with his sword drawn and his determination undaunted.

At 11:30 a.m. on December 14, 1837, Chenier stood, surrounded by his remaining three or four hundred "patriotes", in the square in front of the church that he had commandeered despite the protest of the priests. Distant bugles announced the approach of the redcoats. When the red horsemen were spotted across the frozen river moving along the ice, Chenier confidently called out his men and, with about a hundred following him, set out across the frozen surface of the river until they disappeared among the scattered islands. Shots were heard. Chenier and the others reappeared, on the run, firing as they retreated back to the town of St-Eustache. A file of red-coated horsemen was hot in pursuit. A field gun roared and a roundshot skidded across the ice in the midst of the scattering "patriotes".

Most of the rebel force escaped to the countryside in disorder, but Chenier was shouting above the confusion and pointing at the church, forcing the men ahead of him into it.

"We have no guns!", they screamed at him, but he answered them solemnly

"There will be dead soon, you will be able to use theirs." Thus the few who remained took shelter in their "stone trap", the church of St-Eustache.

Outside, St-Eustache was surrounded. Wetherall's brigade closed in from the north end of the town, stopping in front of the church which housed the last resistors. His cannon opened fire on the front of the church. At the same time Maitland's troops moved in from the other direction. Inside the battered

church, seventy or eighty "patriotes" remained under the leadership of Chenier. As the volunteers approached the presbytery, which was connected to the back of the church by a covered way, a few of the defenders leapt from the windows and tried to escape across the river. Out on the open ice they were pursued by the volunteers.

Young Wetherall and two other red-coated officers entered the presbytery, crept through the covered way, and battered down the back door of the church. They heard the sound of axes chopping timber as the "patriotes" in the main body of the church took refuge now in the galleries and choir loft, destroying the stairs which led up to them.

The dark interior of the church was lit only by narrow barred windows and shrouded in smoke from cannon and muskets. In ghostly silence stood the statue of St-Eustache, the Christian warrior, undamaged in the dim light. When a rain of shot showered on them from the galleries, the three officers heaped up the splintered woodwork, sprinkled the pile with gun powder and struck flint to it. As the flames leapt up, the trio escaped from the church, which was now completely ringed by a solid mass of red infantry at the front, and standing or kneeling with fixed bayonets at the rear of the church, amidst the gravestones, was the 32nd, Jock Weir's regiment.

As the dry wood of the church's interior blazed up, the screams of the trapped men inside could be heard. Some jumped out the windows, others dropped inside from the galleries only to be caught up in the flames below. Those exiting from the windows met a quicker death. As they dropped to their knees with arms upraised, guns exploded in their faces and steel bayonets drove into their bodies. The officers of the 32nd shouted at their troops to stop slaughtering the helpless survivors but they were drowned out by battle cries of

"Remember Jock Weir!"

Chenier slipped through a narrow window intending to make for a ditch behind the cemetery but a musket ball hit him in the heart and he was dead before his feet could reach the ground.

The roof of the church caved in at six o'clock that evening but the smoke continued to rise from the sad wreckage until the next morning.

TOPICS FOR DISCUSSION
1. Who was Papineau? Who were the other rebel leaders in Lower Canada in 1837?
2. Compare Chenier to other rebel leaders such as William Lyon Mackenzie and Louis Riel who are described in this book. What do they have in common? How are they different?
3. Do you consider yourself a rebel? How would you define a "rebel"? Are all young people rebels and all adults part of the establishment?
4. Jock Weir was a young officer of the 32nd regiment who had been murdered and his body mutilated by the patriotes. Does the motive of revenge justify the killing at St-Eustache?
5. Was Chenier a martyr? Explain.

CREATIVE CHALLENGE
1. Divide the class in half. Let one group imagine themselves to be "patriotes" and the other group think of themselves as members of the 32nd regiment; then have everyone write a description of the battle of St-Eustache from his or her point of view. Compare the descriptions afterwards.

When you are writing a personal description rather than a factual report, the adjectives and adverbs you use should indicate your emotions and viewpoint. Underline each adjective and each adverb in your description of the battle. Do they express the mood you wanted to create?

Front view of the church of St-Eustache.

DR. JAMES BARRY
A Man With a Secret

In 1857, Dr. James Stuart Barry was appointed Inspector-General of Hospitals for both Upper and Lower Canada. The position as chief military doctor in Canada was the highest appointment in the country's medical profession, and gave Barry authority over hospitals in Montreal, Kingston, Quebec, and Toronto.

Dr. Barry had earned the honour of such an important post. After graduating from Edinburgh University in 1812, he had served as a soldier and doctor throughout the world. In Cape Town he performed one of the first Caesarean operations in which both mother and child survived. There he had spoken out against the poor conditions in the leper colony, the jail and the lunatic asylum. Reformers were not popular; his critical statements made many enemies, who were quick to attack the doctor's personal characteristics.

He was an odd person. He strutted rather than walked and was highly effeminate in his appearance. He was only 150 cm tall, slight and fragile, and his small, delicate hands, large eyes and silky-smooth skin all caused people to gossip about him behind his back. The eccentric little redheaded doctor refused to drink with the other officers or exchange dirty stories. Lord Albemarle once wrote the following description of him.

"There was at this time at the Cape a person whose eccentricities attracted universal attention — Dr. James Barry, staff-surgeon to the garrison and the Governor's medical advisor

. . . I had heard so much of this capricious, yet privileged gentleman, that I had a great curiosity to see him. I shortly afterwards sat next to him at dinner at one of the regimental messes. In this learned Pundit I beheld a beardless lad, apparently of my own age, with an unmistakably Scotch type of countenance — reddish hair, high cheek bones. There was a certain effeminacy in his manner, which he seemed to be always striving to overcome."

However, no one dared to insult James Barry to his face, for he had already fought one duel over a personal remark made about him. His temper was quick, and on one occasion he was arrested and sent home under guard because of his aggressive behaviour.

In the Crimean war he encountered Florence Nightingale, but the famous nurse did not appreciate the

meeting. Sitting snobbishly on his horse while she stood in the sun, Dr. Barry gave her a public reprimand. Florence Nightingale later described the incident.

"He kept me standing in the midst of quite a crowd of soldiers, commissariat servants, camp followers, etc., etc. every one of whom behaved like a gentleman during the scolding I received, while he behaved like a brute. I should say he was the most hardened creature I ever met."

But everyone respected James Barry's skill as a surgeon and his knowledge of medicine.

On his arrival in Canada as inspector-general, he immediately provoked animosity and attracted attention to himself. His love of uniforms decorated with epaulets, and cocked hats with plumes, gave him an almost ludicrous appearance as he paraded around the country, dragging his sword clumsily at his side. Wrapped in musk-ox furs, he rode through the streets of Montreal in a magnificent red sleigh, complete with silver bells, a uniformed footman, coachman, a large black manservant and a small white dog.

His concern for the health and welfare of the soldiers, however, was without question. He criticized the poor food available for the troops, insisting that they be fed a diet that would include mutton and salt, as well as a roast cooked in an oven rather than "the eternal boiled beef and soup". This was despite the fact that he was a vegetarian himself, living mainly on fruit, vegetables and milk. According to

Dr. Barry, the sewage disposal and drainage in the barracks were inadequate and unhealthful.

Discovering that the married soldiers had to sleep in the barracks with their wives, he insisted they be given private married quarters. In Canada, as elsewhere, James Barry was considered autocratic and odd, although more than competent at his job.

The doctor himself became ill with bronchitis and influenza, which forced him to retire, and six years later he died during a diarrhoea epidemic. Major McKinnon, the staff surgeon who signed his death certificate, had never liked James, and so he didn't even examine the corpse. It was a char-woman, Mrs. Bishop, who discovered the secret of Dr. Barry as she was laying out his body in preparation for burial. Dr. James Barry was a woman, and, according to Mrs. Bishop, showed clear signs of once having had a baby.

In those days the chance of a woman receiving a university education or becoming a doctor was out of the question. For forty years, she had disguised herself in men's clothing to enable her to become a medical doctor. She was hurriedly buried, but the rumours and gossip spread to the newspapers. It was only then that two former associates came forward to support the story of the charwoman. In Trinidad, when Dr. Barry had lain close to death with yellow fever, the assistant-surgeon and another witness had examined her and had discovered her secret. She had regained consciousness at that moment and had sworn both of them to secrecy.

Canada's first woman doctor was in fact the world's first woman doctor.

TOPICS FOR DISCUSSION

1. Does Dr. Barry's secret explain much of the reason why she was disliked?

2. What type of a person would desire to become a doctor as strongly as Dr. Barry did?

3. Would you disguise yourself as the opposite sex for any reason? Explain why or why not.

4. Although today the descriptions of Dr. Barry seem to have been obvious indications of her real sex, no one suspected it at the time because the prejudice against women was so strong, it was assumed a female could never complete a university education or perform surgery. Does society still have prejudices against women? Are there any prejudices against men?

5. Are there any occupations in Canada today which prevent a person from participating in them because of his or her sex? Should society change its attitudes about such concepts?

6. What adjectives are used to describe women, but would be insulting if used in describing a man and vise versa? i.e. beautiful, soft, muscular, rough, etc. Should language be used to stereotype people by sex?

7. Dr. Barry was a vegetarian. Do you approve of killing animals for food? Have you ever killed an animal? Have you ever visited a slaughter house?

8. Until the emergence of modern medicine, women were traditionally the healers in society. Why would they be prevented from obtaining medical degrees?

9. Would you prefer to go to a doctor of the opposite sex or of the same sex as yourself?

10. In Russia in 1976 about 75% of the doctors were women, in Britain about 25% were women, and in Canada less than 10% were women. What do these statistics indicate to you about Canadians? Have the statistics changed since 1976?

CREATIVE CHALLENGES

1. Write an imaginative diary describing from the viewpoint of Dr. Barry the problems she must have encountered.

2. Invent an imaginary story in which a person has to live his or her life disguised as a member of the opposite sex in modern-day Canada.

3. Many people, some of them otherwise leading ordinary lives dress up on occasion in "drag" (the clothing of the opposite sex). Prepare an essay suggesting the psychological reasons for such behaviour.

4. Research and write a brief biography on one of the following Canadian women doctors.

a) Emily Stowe who was not allowed to attend a medical school in Canada but who, in 1867, obtained a degree in the U.S.A. and was finally, in 1880, given a license to practice in Canada.

b) Augusta Stowe, daughter of Emily, who in 1883 became the first woman doctor to graduate from a Canadian medical college.

c) Dr. Jennie Trout, one of Canada's first women doctors.

d) Dr. Susie Carson Rijnhart, who, while acting as a missionary in Tibet, lost her baby and her husband, who was murdered. She returned to that country to continue her work.

e) Dr. Irma Levasseur, who volunteered for active service in Serbia at the time of a typhus epidemic there.

f) Dr. Frances O. Kelsey, who went to the U.S.A. where she became chief of the New Investigational Drug Branch. Her ban on the drug thalidomide in the United States prevented babies being born with deformities in that country, such as occurred in Canada and the rest of the world.

SIR JOHN A. MACDONALD

"Old Tomorrow"

The situation was critical. Members of the colonial legislature of Canada, a union of the present day provinces of Ontario and Quebec, were deadlocked. On one side of the legislature sat "Old Tomorrow", the homely, gangling lawyer from Kingston, Ontario, so nicknamed because of his political strategy of postponement. He represented the loose union of two Canadian ethnic groups, and by his side sat George Etienne Cartier, his French-Canadian ally. On the other side of the legislature, rigid and sober, was the reformer, George Brown, who was not only a political opponent of Macdonald's, but a lifelong enemy who loathed the alcohol-addicted premier of the colony. During his political campaign, Macdonald had claimed that Canadians preferred himself drunk to George Brown sober.

The British colony of Canada, which in 1861 had been formed from the union of Upper and Lower Canada, consisted of only a few towns stretched along the St. Lawrence. The towns had muddy streets and were surrounded by half-cleared farms. Beyond that, there was only wilderness. Isolated on the Atlantic coast were the four separate colonies of Nova Scotia, New Brunswick, Prince Edward Island, and Newfoundland, which fought among themselves and considered Canada a foreign country. To the south was danger. The United States of America, fresh from a civil war, had the largest army in the world at its command. The British had openly aided the southern states during the Civil War, and now the scattered British colonies to the north were terrified that the military machine that had conquered the Confederates would be turned north against the helpless Canadians.

That was the situation confronting the colonial legislative assembly when suddenly a miracle happened. Brown and Macdonald forgot their personal and private differences, crossed the legislature and, in a

symbolic handshake amid a riot of rejoicing by their fellows, formed an agreement that caused them to co-operate in a barnstorming campaign through the Atlantic colonies. For months during 1864, they made speeches to encourage all the British colonies to unite and resist the pressures of their powerful neighbour to the south.

The turning point came at the famous Quebec Conference, where Macdonald astounded everyone with his eloquence, his knowledge of constitutional details and his sobriety during the long days of argument. During the evenings he charmed them with bawdy jokes and promises of jobs in the future government. The result was a Canadian constitution almost entirely the work of Macdonald, scribbled in his own messy handwriting and taken by him, Cartier, Brown and Galt to London to obtain the approval of the British government.

When the Canadian delegation heard that their constitution had been accepted by the British parliament, even Brown joined in the refreshments, and, arm in arm, he and Macdonald went celebrating through the streets of London. At the race track they attacked the crowds with pea shooters and bags of flour from their wobbling carriage. The new constitution of Canada was to become known as the British North America Act, and the new Dominion of Canada was proclaimed at Ottawa on July 1, 1867, accompanied by bonfires, cannon fire, and wild celebrations.

But Confederation was still shaky, and Macdonald had an uphill battle on his hands. The Atlantic colonies were already threatening to secede. On the western prairies a "Métis Nation" of buffalo hunters were revolting against the east, and beyond the Rockies the gold-rush colony of British Columbia, caught between Oregon to the south and Alaska to the north, seemed inclined to join the United States. If Macdonald's dream of a nation stretching from Atlantic to Pacific was to take

shape, he would have to lure British Columbia into the union. He did it by promising to build a railroad from the St. Lawrence to the Pacific coast, a feat that his opponents considered impossible. The railroad would have to conquer the wilds of Northern Ontario, cross the endless prairies, cut through the dangerous Rockies and continue down to the Pacific coast. Nevertheless, the project was begun.

Then came disaster. During the election of 1872, Macdonald sent a telegram to the railway syndicate in Montreal demanding money to support his campaign:

"I must have another ten thousand. Will be the last time of calling. Do not fail."

The telegram was stolen from a lawyer's safe and delivered to the opposition party in Parliament, who used it, in what became known as the "pacific scandal", to discredit and defeat the government, Macdonald, and the progress of the railroad.

The new Liberal Prime Minister, Alexander Mackenzie, thought the railroad was financial lunacy. The people of British Columbia felt betrayed and were prepared to withdraw from Confederation. Helpless, Macdonald sat in the opposition benches — a fading ghost, an historic relic — watching his vision of a nation stretching from sea to sea disintegrating. But finally in the midst of defeat and dishonour, the old warrior started to fight back.

His aged white locks and large nose were seen in every small community across the land. The legends of his parliamentary behaviour became whispered gossip. He punched one opponent who questioned his word and had to be restrained by the sergeant-at-arms in Parliament from fighting a duel of honour with another. Within five years he was seeking re-election and was once heard shouting back at a heckler in a crowd, "I can lick you as quick as hell can singe a feather." The Canadian people warmed to his convictions and re-elected him Prime Minister.

Back in power, Macdonald instituted his own national policy, which established tariffs to protect Canada's infant industries from being swallowed by the American economy — tariffs which today are still a vital economic factor in our survival. He also established a new railroad syndicate, which rapidly laid tracks across the prairies and through the Rockies until the last spike was driven on November 7, 1885. Macdonald had kept his promise to British Columbia, and he rode triumphantly through the Rockies on the cowcatcher of a locomotive.

In 1891, at age seventy-six, Macdonald ignored the advice of his doctor and fought a difficult winter election, but even as the voters elected him once again, he lay paralyzed in his home beside the Ottawa River, where he died.

TOPICS FOR DISCUSSION
1. Do you feel that Sir John A. Macdonald deserves to be called "the father of Confederation"? Explain why or why not.
2. Many other provinces have joined Canada since 1867. Do you believe Canada will expand further in the future? Do you think it could lose any of its present territory?
3. Many people talk of Canada re-organizing its provincial boundaries so that each area would be of equal size. Which of the following concepts would you favor?
(a) Reducing Canada to five provinces or areas i.e. British Columbia, the Prairies, Ontario, Quebec, and the Maritimes.
(b) Increasing Canada to more provinces by dividing Ontario and Quebec into smaller areas.
(c) Some other plan. Explain in detail.
4. Macdonald was known to have a drinking problem yet he was able to build a powerful country. Do you know of anyone who has an alcohol or drug addiction? What causes people to become addicted?
5. Although Macdonald and Brown were enemies, they forgot their personal differences in order to better their country. Do you have enemies or people whom you dislike? Would you co-operate with them to achieve a goal?
6. The "Pacific Scandal" caused Macdonald to lose an election. Are there any local, provincial or federal politicians in Canada today who have lost an election due to a scandal?
7. Although he lost the election and was no longer Prime Minister, Macdonald continued to fight for his political principles. Are you the kind of person who remains true to your convictions despite defeat? Explain.

CREATIVE CHALLENGES
1. Imagine that Canada's first female Prime Minister is elected and describe what you think she would do for the country.
2. Macdonald had to deal with a variety of individuals who are described in this book. Read the descriptions of the following people, then have members of the class play the roles as Macdonald talks with each one of them.
a) Darcy McGee
b) Joseph Howe
c) Amor de Cosmos
d) Louis Riel
e) Big Bear
3. Prepare a T.V. newscast, as it would have sounded in 1867, based on the information you have read in this book. If you find this exercise entertaining, repeat it using different dates in Canadian history.

George Brown and John A. Macdonald join forces.

THE SAINT JOHN FOUR

In 1867, only one month after Confederation, four men from Saint John, New Brunswick, represented the new nation of Canada for the first time in an international sporting event. They presented an unusual spectacle as they arrived in Paris, France, decked out in "flesh-coloured jerseys, dark cloth trousers, leather braces and bright pink caps." In contrast to the neat, conservative dress of the traditional rowing teams of Europe, the gaudy Canadian team attracted smirks and sarcasm.

Robert Fulton, George Price and Samuel Hutton were fishermen during the summer season and worked as ships' carpenters throughout the winter. The fourth, Elijah Ross, was a lighthouse keeper. Sheriff Harding of Saint John was their constant watch-dog, sent by the people of the New Brunswick town to protect their athletes in the sinful cosmopolitan centre of Europe.

Their journey to the Paris Exposition of 1867 was financed by their fellow citizens back in Saint John, who collected $4 000, and by the New Brunswick provincial government, which added another $2 000. The New Brunswick *Reporter* described the community spirit of the day:

"Although to the great International Exposition we have sent no elaborate works of art, no specimen of ingenious handicraft, no sample of the products of mine or field, we have nevertheless sent to Paris such an 'exhibit' of our energy, our hardihood and pluck as shall render us famous among all the famed at that grand international tournament."

As the Canadian team dropped their heavy, clumsy-looking vessel into the water to practice, the English reporters scoffed at them, claiming that they pulled almost entirely with their arms and that because they did not have a coxswain, they would be a menace to the other contestants due to erratic steering.

On the day of the contests, in the race for heavy in-rigged boats, the Canadians were competing against sophisticated crews from Boulogne, France, and England. An English newspaper described the race:

"The Canadians were supposed not to have a chance, and betting was strongly against them. They took the lead at a great pace, rowing some forty-six or forty-seven strokes per minute, followed by the Geslings. A determined race ensued between the Canadians and the Geslings, in which the former always led, but the Geslings pressed them very hard right up to the buoy, where the Canadians came first . . . Nearly all fouled at the buoy, including the Canadians, who, however, being without a coxswain and turning the boat themselves, were considerably benefited thereby, and passed round clear. Gesling drew up to the New Brunswick boat after the rounding, and for a time there seemed a prospect of the Parisians rowing their opponents down, but all the opposing crews had yet to learn that the New Brunswickers could row any distance."

Thus the Saint John Four won the first international athletic victory for the new nation of Canada. But it was their second feat, in the race for four-oared outrigger shells, that most shocked the spectators. Here they were matched against the most experienced rowing clubs: Oxford University, The London Rowing Club, and the Leanders of London. The Canadian boat outweighed the beautifully fashioned English shells by more than a hundred pounds and was described as "a curious old-fashioned outrigger" which looked like "a Chinese puzzle painted green . . . and curiously put together." Nevertheless, the Canadians won the race by three lengths and at the finish line were laughing and talking effortlessly in a casual manner that amazed the onlookers.

When they returned to Saint John, the city was decked with bunting, and the local brass band joined with the enthusiastic crowd of over 7 000 people who welcomed the heroes. Each rower received $500 and the freedom of the city, and they were nicknamed "the Paris Crew". The Toronto *Globe* praised their victory in patriotic terms:

"Perhaps nothing since Confederation has occurred which so thoroughly brings home to the broad mass of our people that our bold Maritime friends are now our fellow-countrymen in name and in fact. To be the first to uphold the strength, skill and pluck of our country's athletes . . . is a distinction to be proud of."

In 1871, during a world champion match against the Tyne crew, which

THE ST. JOHN CREW.—From photographs by Phelps, Dalton & Co., Boston.—

1871

was stroked by James Renforth, single sculls champion of England, over 20 000 spectators gathered at Kennebecasis. With the Saint John Four in the lead, Renforth suffered a sudden heart attack and died an hour later.

RESEARCH CHALLENGE

CANADIAN WATER SPORTS QUIZ
Who was. . .

1. The Canadian who could not afford a shell although he wanted to be a sculler, but who built instead a homemade canoe and became Canada's only singles champion in the history of the Olympics when he won a gold medal in 1936 for canoeing?

2. A seventy kilogram fisherman from the village of Herring Cove, Nova Scotia, who was a sculling champion.

3. The eighteen-year-old swimmer from Moose Jaw, Saskatchewan, who dominated the 1934 British Empire Games by taking eight titles.

4. A Canadian rowing star in 1887, who was described by Stephen Leacock in his epilogue to *Too Much College:*
"Jake was a magnificent figure of a man; he stood nicely over six feet. . . He was broad in the shoulders, straight as a lath, and till the time he died, just short of eighty, he could pick up the twenty-pound anchor of his motorboat and throw it round like a jackhammer."

5. The two men called "The Rowing Twins of Canada", who climaxed their careers by winning the Diamond Sculls.

6. The only Canadian to win an Olympic gold medal in swimming. He won two of them in 1912 at Stockholm.

7. Two men who, as a rowing team from U.B.C., won a gold medal at the Tokyo Olympics in 1964.

8. A 155 cm schoolgirl from Vancouver, who became the greatest individual woman performer in the history of the British Commonwealth Games when, at fifteen, she won four gold and three silver medals, and who was cheered by all of Canada with an enthusiastic "Wa-a-y to go, Mighty Mouse!"

9. Four British Columbia boys known as the "U.B.C. Four", who won an Olympic gold medal in 1956.

10. A father and son who were both Canadian rowing champions.

The answers to this quiz can be found along with photographs and descriptions of the people in a book called *Canada's Sporting Heroes,* by Wise and Fisher.

Renforth suffers a heart attack trying to defeat the Saint John Four.

D'ARCY McGEE
The First Canadian Politician to be Assassinated

In the year 1857, a young Irish immigrant arrived in Montreal and founded a newspaper, the *New Era*. He was short and his shoulders were stooped. His face was encompassed by a fringe of beard that ran from ear to ear and was topped with an unruly mop of hair. Despite his homely appearance, D'Arcy McGee had already proven himself to be an outstanding orator, newspaper editor and poet.

As a teen-ager, D'Arcy was a radical fighter for an independent Ireland and was very anti-British. At seventeen, he immigrated to North America and joined the staff of the Boston *Pilot;* by the time he was nineteen, he was editor of that paper. His fame as a newspaperman and lecturer spread rapidly. When he returned to Dublin to work first for the *Freeman's Journal* and later the *Nation,* he was implicated in the abortive rebellion of 1848 and escaped Ireland disguised as a priest. The rebel returned to the United States, where, in print, he blamed the Irish clergy for the rebellion's failure and signed his article "Thomas D'Arcy McGee, A Traitor to the British Government".

The D'Arcy McGee who arrived in Canada in 1857, however, was already changing in his opinion of radical rebel causes. In the United States two Irish "republicans" had challenged him to a duel over his more conservative political views as a mere "reformer". He had married in 1847 and had five daughters and one son. In Canada he began a new career, that of a politician. Within one year, he was elected to the Legislative Assembly of Canada for Montreal West, and he represented his constituency until Confederation in 1867, at which point he became their elected member in the new federal House of Commons.

McGee did much to bring about Confederation; he was present at Charlottetown and Quebec as one of the original Fathers of Confederation. The silver-tongued politician, the most brilliant orator in Canada's parliamentary history, preached "the new nationality" in passionate speeches and created a psychological basis for union.

"As fragments we shall be lost; but let us be united and we shall be as a rock."

Across the border in the United States, the Irish brotherhood known as the Fenians was led by John J. O'Neill, a self-styled general who was dedicated to the union of all Irishmen against British rule in Ireland or Canada. On June 2, 1866, he led 800 Irish-American soldiers across the Niagara River and took Fort Erie, Ontario. Loyal Canadians quickly forced him back over the border, but the U.S. government hesitated to act against the Fenian Brotherhood, which was 15 000 strong. In preparation for an invasion of the Eastern Townships of Quebec, General O'Neill amassed three million rounds of ammunition in his headquarters at Franklin, Vermont. On May 25, 1870, he tried to take Ecles Hill, but the Canadian militia beat him back again, and he was finally jailed by the U.S. government.

D'Arcy McGee had become increasingly critical of his old associates as he loyally supported the connection between Canada and Britain. Political meetings broke into open riots; he denounced the Fenian Brotherhood and defeated his opponent, Devlon, in the first election for the new House of Commons in 1867. McGee had turned his articulate abilities against the Irish extremists:

"As to Fenianism, I have strangled it when it first attempted to concentrate in Canada, and I am not going to be annoyed by its carcass," he said, and, *"I have been told that if I would let the Fenians alone, I would be let alone. But I drove the man from me. . ."*

Patrick Jones Whelan, a Fenian who had worked for McGee's opponent during the 1867 election, swore he would "blow his (McGee's) bloody brains out!"

On April 6, 1868, Whelan was seen in the House of Commons late at night, stalking up and down and shaking his fist at McGee from the visitor's gallery. After midnight, as McGee, age forty-two, stopped in front of his boarding house on Sparks Street in Ottawa to unlock the door, he was shot from behind by a 6-shot Smith & Wesson revolver owned by Whelan. Whelan insisted he was innocent, but bragged that he knew who had shot McGee. He refused to reveal the murderer, however, and was hanged for the assassination. Most authorities agree that the assassination was probably ordered by the Fenian Brotherhood.

McGee became a Canadian martyr and hero.

"The martyr McGee will take his place in history among the brightest and most noble victims ever cruelly sacrificed by ruffian hands because of devotion to their country."

Strangely enough, in a poem he had written entitled "Forewarned", McGee predicted his own assassination in a boyhood premonition:

*"In the time of my boyhood I had a strange feeling,
That I was to die in the noon of my day,
Not quietly into the silent grave stealing,
But torn like a blasted oak, suddenly away"*

TOPICS FOR DISCUSSION
1. McGee progressed from a radical anti-British rebel to a strong supporter of an alliance between Canada and Britain. Do you consider him a traitor to his former country (Ireland) or a champion of his new country (Canada)? Do you have strong ideals today on which you might reverse your opinion in the future? What do you think caused the change in McGee?
2. Are the Irish still fighting

Canadian troops fighting Fenian invasion force.

against Britain more than a hundred years later? Is there any danger of Canadians engaging in a similar type of civil warfare?
3. After McGee's death there was not another political assassination in Canada until Pierre Laporte was killed by the F.L.Q. more than a hundred years later. Are there strong politicans today who are fighting against separatism as McGee fought for federalism?
4. Have you ever had a premonition of the future such as McGee described in his poem? Do you know anyone who has? Do you believe it is possible for a person to know what will happen in the future?

5. Does political assassination ever aid a cause?

CREATIVE CHALLENGES
1. McGee was a great nationalistic orator. Have a public speaking contest to discover who in your class or school or community is the most articulate spokesperson for Canada. How could you begin your speech in a way that will attract the interest of your audience? Decide at which points in your speech you should speak slower for emphasis. At what points should you raise your voice? Can you speak emotionally for effect? Sometimes it is wise to pause for a moment after making an important statement.

Most public speakers use humour to keep their audience interested. Body language can be an important aspect of public speaking, thus you should control your movements. Your conclusion should be dramatic and should sum up your viewpoints.
2. Attempt to predict the future. Prepare a list of events that you feel might happen to you, your friends, in your school, in your home, in your city, etc. In one month check the list to see how accurate you were. What is the difference between a general prediction and a specific prediction? What type have you made?

JOSEPH HOWE

"He Fought to Bring Democratic Government to Nova Scotia"

Red-haired Joseph Howe was born in Halifax on December 13, 1804. When only thirteen years old, he had to leave school because his family was so poor, and he began to work in a printing office.

As a youth he loved all sports, particularly swimming, rowing, skating, fishing, and spearing lobsters, but he also loved reading and writing. By the age of twenty-three his interest in prose and verse led him to buy a newspaper, the *Acadian*, in partnership with a friend. By 1828 he owned his own paper, the *Nova Scotian*, which he edited until the fateful day in 1835 when he printed an anonymous letter.

At the time, Nova Scotia was governed by the dictatorial Council of Twelve, so when Howe published a letter which accused the magistrates of Halifax of "incompetence, neglect, and corruption in administering the law", he was immediately charged with criminal libel. No lawyer would defend him in court against the powerful authorities that were appointed by Britain; thus Joseph Howe was forced to argue the case for himself and for the freedom of the press in Nova Scotia.

He spoke elegantly for over six hours. The jury was moved by his words and one of its members even cried like a child. Howe concluded his defence simply:

"Yes, gentlemen, come what will, while I live, Nova Scotia shall have the blessing of an open and unshackled press."

When he was acquitted, the citizens of Halifax exploded into a spontaneous celebration, which turned into a two-day holiday of rejoicing. Howe was a hero.

His new popularity and his alliance with the Reformers brought him trouble and enemies. An enraged young member of the establishment charged his newspaper office on horseback, with sword drawn. As windows smashed onto the street, Howe physically had to wrestle the man from his mount and disarm him. He was challenged, as well, to duels. He accepted and fought two of them with pistols before announcing his refusal to continue, claiming, "A live editor is more useful than a dead hero."

Recognizing that he would have to enter politics if he wished to bring about reform, Howe ran as a representative of the legislative assembly and was elected by the people of Halifax in 1836. As the leader of the Reformers, he fought for the next eleven years to obtain responsible government. He caused the governor, Lord Falkland, to be recalled to England, and by 1847 a system of responsible government had been established. Unlike Upper and Lower Canada, there was no rebellion in Nova Scotia under the leadership of Joseph Howe. He became premier of the province from 1860 to 1863.

When his political opponent, Charles Tupper, returned to Nova Scotia with plans to join Confederation, Howe opposed the idea. He travelled to England in 1866, but failed to stop the British Government from passing the British North America Act. When he returned to Nova Scotia, however, he did succeed in turning the Easterners against the concept of Confederation. He was attempting to have the B.N.A. Act repealed when Sir John A. Macdonald and D'Arcy McGee met with him and convinced him of the advantages and necessity of Confederation. Howe then sacrificed his own reputation (because many considered him a traitor when he changed sides and supported Confederation) for what he believe would be "better terms" for Nova Scotia. In appreciation, Sir John A. Macdonald appointed him Lieutenant-Governor of Nova Scotia, but Howe never lived to enjoy the honour. He died within weeks of the appointment, on June 6, 1873.

TOPICS FOR DISCUSSION

1. Howe had to leave school due to the poverty of his family, yet he became very successful. Is it still possible to become successful without an education? Do children today have to leave school because of poverty or does everyone have an equal opportunity for education?

2. Are there still dictatorial, powerful politicians in Canada? Explain.

3. Howe's words caused tears. Have you ever cried in sympathy with something you heard, read or saw in a film? Do you remember the words that caused you or someone you know to cry? Could you create words so powerful they would make someone's eyes water? Do you know anyone who could?

4. What do you think changed Howe's political opinion about Confederation? Would you admire or reject a politician who changed his

or her opinion on a major policy? Do politicians today change drastically from one viewpoint to another?

5. Would Canadians today have to travel to England to change the B.N.A. Act? Explain how such a change would be made.

CREATIVE CHALLENGES
1. Write a letter to a newspaper complaining about or supporting your local, provincial, or federal government.

2. Invent several newspaper headlines that describe the actions of personalities in this book. Can your classmates identify the people from your headlines? Headlines often use alliteration to capture the attention of the reader. What is alliteration? Did you use alliteration in your headlines?

3. Take one incident from the selection on Joseph Howe and write a newspaper story about it such as you might have read at the time. Create a headline to go with your story. When you write a newspaper story you should begin with the most important fact and then add details until you conclude with the least important point. Examine several sample newspaper stories before writing one of your own. A good news story should include: what happened, who was involved, when it happened, how it happened, where it happened, and why it happened.

Young Joseph Howe becomes a hero in Halifax.

AMOR DE COSMOS
"Lover of The Universe"

Bill Smith was born in 1825 in Windsor, Nova Scotia, but when he was about fourteen years old his family moved to Halifax where he went to work in a grocery store.

When news of the fabulous gold discoveries in California reached the ears of the restless youth, he decided to try his luck and left to seek adventure and prosperity in the untamed west. He joined a covered-wagon train out of St. Louis, Missouri, and began a slow and dangerous trip across the wide continent, during which he had to fight Indians. He also had to fight off a group of Mormon women who, collectively, wished to become his wives. (Marriage, however, was not his goal in life; he would remain a bachelor until his death.) Rather than crossing the Rockies in winter, he remained in Utah, but continued his quest in the spring. Alone on horseback, he arrived in northern California in June of 1853.

Unsuccessful as a gold miner, he turned to a new novelty, photography, and made a living by taking pictures of miners and their claims. The lean, fiery Nova Scotian with blazing eyes and curly black beard wore twin revolvers sticking out of his boot tops as he strutted through the California gold fields. In 1854 he changed his name by legislative degree to a flamboyant combination of Latin, Greek and French — Amor De Cosmos, "Lover of the Universe". De Cosmos claimed that he changed his name as a "protest against mediocrity"; others, aware of his reputation as a drinker and carouser, suggested it should have been "Amor De Bacchus", and some

suggested he changed it only to avoid confusion at the post office. Later, enemies he made in British Columbia said he had changed it to hide some ugly incident he had been involved with in California. Amor De Cosmos, however, insisted it was chosen because it represented his love of "order, beauty, the world, and the universe".

In 1858, gold was discovered in the Fraser River, and hordes of Americans moved north to the latest fields. Since 1821, the Hudson's Bay Company had ruled the British settlements on the Pacific coast of North America with a "beneficent despotism". In 1855 there were fewer than 800 whites on Vancouver Island and only a handful of fur traders on the mainland, but the discovery of gold in 1858 brought 30 000 gold-hungry transients to the area. The rush of immigrants to the region was a threat to the fur trade and the power of the Hudson's Bay Company. The citizens of Fort Victoria were cut off from world hap-

penings and concerned mainly with local issues until, from a shipload of California adventurers, stepped a passenger who was to change the lives of the entire colony and become the most controversial figure in British Columbia. The stranger, Amor De Cosmos, was impeccably dressed in top hat, formal coat and cane as he walked arrogantly ashore.

Attempting to emulate his idol back in Nova Scotia, the crusading journalist Joseph Howe, De Cosmos founded a newspaper, the *British Columnist*, and began to fight for responsible government. The first issue of the paper claimed:

"The present constitution is radically defective and unsuited to the advanced condition of the colony. We shall counsel the introduction of responsible government."

The attacks on the Hudson's Bay Company's rule enraged the governor of Vancouver Island, James Douglas, who swore "to muzzle the meddlesome eccentric newcomer". The governor invoked an ancient British law demanding a huge licence fee of $3 000 for the newspaper, but the public saw De Cosmos as a popular hero and Douglas as a villain. Within days they raised the bond money and subscriptions to the paper multiplied, allowing it to publish three times a week rather than just once. De Cosmos accused Douglas of being "an unsuccessful statesman and a traitor to his country", and publicly opposed whatever the governor did. In return, De Cosmos was called "a self-styled reformer who wrote as though half mad". His reputation as an eccentric individualist was promoted in newspaper descriptions of the day as he attacked his opponents physically in the streets as well as verbally in the press:

> "As Mr. Robert Dunsmuir and ex-mayor Finlayson were conversing. . . they were approached by Mr. De Cosmos who applied opprobious epithets to Mr. Dunsmuir. Mr. Dunsmuir requested his insulter, who seemed to be labouring under some strong excitant, to pass on whereupon Mr. De Cosmos struck him on the side of the head with his fist. Mr. Dunsmuir retaliated by wearing out an umbrella on his assailant's head and shoulders. The combatants were then separated."

Then, in 1863, De Cosmos was elected to the Vancouver Island House of Assembly and on January 27, 1865, introduced a resolution that the island be united with the B.C. mainland. The union was achieved by 1866. De Cosmos was a visionary, and, when sent as a representative to the new Legislative Council of British Columbia, he proposed an even greater union — with a nation that was being formed far to the east called Canada. His suggestion caused turmoil. Much of the population in British Columbia was composed of American gold seekers who wanted British Columbia to become an American colony. Even London papers back in England seemed to be against De Cosmos' dream as they stated:

> "If the people of British Columbia after due reflection reject confederation as impractical and desire to join the United States, the Mother Country will in no way seek to prevent annexation."

But in 1871 he triumphed, and B.C. became the sixth Canadian province. In the following election he won a seat in the Federal House of Commons in Ottawa, as well as

one in the Provincial Assembly, and the next year became the Premier of British Columbia. As the new premier, he locked the British-appointed governor-general out of his cabinet meetings, explaining that his presence was a threat to responsible government.

In 1874, dual representation was prohibited and De Cosmos gave up his position as premier of the province so that he could remain in Ottawa, where he continued to force the Canadian government to honour its promise of a railroad to the west coast. In the agreement of union, B.C. was guaranteed that the railroad would be completed within ten years, but the Pacific Scandal had halted construction. It was De Cosmos who led the B.C. delegation to London, England, to seek repeal of the union when, by 1878, the province was threatening to withdraw from Confederation over the railroad issue. He forced the federal government to sit up and take notice of the situation in B.C., and by 1885 the transcontinental railway system was completed.

The man who had won almost all his political battles suffered his final election defeat in 1882. During the last years of his life, he became a bizarre, pitiful character, wandering the streets of Victoria, gaunt and hawklike, in his formal wardrobe. Eventually he was judged insane and locked away in a mental institution, until he died in July of 1897 unnoticed and unmourned.

His old adversary, Speaker Helmcken, was moved to write a letter to the editor which described the funeral:

> "At the graveyard some twenty or thirty saw the casket lowered. This was the mockery of honour paid to Amor De Cosmos, whom forty years ago a large proportion of the people considered a hero, a patriot, who fought for the emancipation of the people. . . Such a funeral is neither worth living or dying for. What an example to hold up to the rising generation.

> No wonder that public men nowadays should think of their own interests first and those of the country last or not at all."

TOPICS FOR DISCUSSION
1. **Do Canadians still move from one end of the country to the other to seek their fortune? What kinds of things attract them today in place of gold?**
2. **If you were going to change your name, what would you change it to that might represent your view of life?**
3. **In the 1800's, people like De Cosmos, Mackenzie, Howe, and Brown found the issue of responsible government a popular theme in their newspapers and political careers. What issues are popular with newspapers and/or politicians today?**
4. **What was the Pacific Scandal?**
5. **Does the public still forget people who were once popular? Give examples to support your view.**
6. **Do politicians today "think of their own interests first and those of the country last or not at all"? Give examples to support your view.**
7. **Does your school have a student government? What powers does it have? What issues are used by the students who are elected?**

CREATIVE CHALLENGE
If your school does not already have a school newspaper, start one. Sell enough advertising space to local businesses to cover the costs, so that you will be able to distribute the paper free of charge to each student. Invite the art students to create a design for the front page, and to prepare the advertisements. What will be the name of your paper? On the editorial page ask one parent, one teacher and one student to write expositions on your school. Include one page of poetry and creative writing submitted by students. What other material could you use in your newspaper? Who

will take the photographs? How will you decide who is the student editor? Which teachers will help you?

RESEARCH CHALLENGE
Research and write a Report on a Canadian newspaper editor of your choice. The following are suggestions only.

a) Mary Chad Carrie — a black woman who fought for integration in the newspaper she founded in Windsor, Ontario, called the *Free Man*.

b) J. W. Dafoe — editor of the *Winnipeg Free Press* who refused a knighthood because he claimed "I stoke my own furnace and shovel the snow off my own sidewalk."

c) Ma Murray — the flamboyant editor of the *Alaska Highway News* who was so notorious for her poor grammar, she would publish a paragraph of punctuation marks once a year for her readers to "sprinkle as they wished" on her writing.

Port Moody, B.C., HEAD OF HEADLINERS —Ma Murray, the outspoken retired weekly newspaper editor from Lillooet, B.C., was honoured at a special Roast Saturday night in Port Moody, the community near Vancouver where she was born. She wore a stylish hat made of newspaper names and headlines.

EMMA LAJEUNESSE

Canada's Prima Donna

In the small Quebec community of Chambly during the year 1860, an eight-year-old girl, Emma LaJeunesse, practiced rigorously for four hours a day at her music lessons. Her father, himself a musician who played harp, organ, violin and piano, encouraged her. Not even he could have suspected that his daughter was to become Canada's first international star. When Emma was fourteen, the family moved to Albany, New York, where finances and support were available to further her career, which was pointing in the direction of the opera.

Her first international debut came in 1870 in Sicily, where the beautiful eighteen-year-old French-Canadian, using her stage name Dame Emma Albani, won over the audience of Italian opera lovers. The opera critic of the *Gazetta di Messina* described the event,

> "...at one time the theatre seemed converted into a cage of mad people, such were the cries, the clapping of hands, the recalls with which Madame Albani appeared struck dumb. She burst into tears..."

She became the toast of Europe. Czar Nicholas gave her a diamond pendant. Queen Victoria invited her to tea, listened to her sing, awarded her a pearl cross, and gave her a warm personal introduction to the Empress of Austria. When Queen Victoria died, Edward VII asked Emma to sing over the coffin during a private family funeral service at Windsor Castle.

Emma was also honoured by the composers of the day. She sang Brahms' "Requiem" to him in his study, and Gounod coached her when she was to sing his music. She was best with Wagner's new operas, but Dvorak composed a role for her as well. Emma LaJeunesse was recognized throughout the world by her song, "Home Sweet Home".

TOPICS FOR DISCUSSION

1. Emma, like many Canadian performers to follow her, moved to the United States before she achieved international fame. What Canadian performers today have done the same thing? Is it necessary to leave Canada in order to be recognized?
2. The type of music that is popular at any one time in history changes, but people's reaction to music and musical stars remains the same. Compare the description of Dame Albani's debut in Sicily with a modern concert. What musicians today could excite you in the same way?
3. Do the leaders of nations today still have musical stars perform for them?
4. Do you like opera? Have you ever heard one? Would you like to hear one?
5. Do you spend four hours a day trying to perfect any of your own talents?

CREATIVE CHALLENGE

Listed below are a few of Emma LaJeunesse's experiences as she toured the world. Imagine that you were present at one of them, and write an imaginary description of the way you felt during it.
1. As she sailed out of Malta after a series of triumphant performances, Emma's ship was saluted by the entire British war squadron, which was drawn up into two lines ahead of her.
2. In Quebec, she was escorted to her hotel by a torchlit parade of snowshoe-clad Canadians in colourful sashes and tuques.
3. In Africa, after singing to an audience of mine owners and Zulus, she was presented with a large uncut diamond.
4. In India, as Emma sang "Home Sweet Home", British troops in bright red uniforms wept silent tears.
5. In Dublin, the crowds chanted below her hotel balcony window until she came out to sing "The Last Rose of Summer".

Each of the above settings is in a different part of the world. What words, phrases, and clauses can you use to indicate to your reader the location of the event?

ALEXANDER GRAHAM BELL

Inventor

Tuberculosis, an incurable disease in 1870, had already claimed the lives of Alex's older and younger brothers. When his father, who was a professor of elocution, and his mother, who was a portrait painter, had learned from the doctors that their only remaining son was also ill with the deadly disease, they had come to Canada, where they hoped the vigorous, crisp climate would help cure the youth.

Alex had a special spot he went to whenever he wanted to dream or invent. It was behind the house, overlooking the steep banks of the Grand River where stood the Mohawk Chapel. When he and his parents immigrated to Canada in 1870, they had bought the home called Tutelo Heights, which had once been part of the Six Nations Reserve three kilometres from Brantford. Alex's health did improve, and he embarked on a project with the Indians of the Six Nations. He transcribed their unwritten language into "visible speech" symbols, a code of symbols which had been developed by Alex's father and published in a book. The new system enabled the deaf to learn to speak, and his father's reputation became so well known that Miss Sarah Fuller, principal of a school for the deaf in Boston, asked him to instruct her staff in the use of "visible speech" to help them teach the deaf. Alex's father, who had other commitments, declined the offer, but sent his son in his place.

When Alexander Graham Bell returned from Boston to his home in Brantford, Ontario, in 1873, he had established for himself a consider-

able reputation as a teacher of the deaf. One of his most famous pupils, a woman who was unable to see, hear or speak when she first came to him, was Helen Keller. She once said:

"Hearing is the deepest, most humanizing sense man possesses, and lonely ones all over the world have been brought into the pleasant ways of mankind because of Dr. Bell's efforts."

But Alex was not just a teacher; he was an inventor as well. At the age of eleven he had discovered a means of removing husks from damp grain for the father of one of his playmates. His ambition in life

was to transmit sounds over wires, to "telegraph speech".

One of his early inventions was the "harmonic telegraph", which sent tones from several tuning forks over a wire and then separated the various tones at the other end. The device transmitted codes for letters, but did not carry the actual voice. He sold it to the Pacific Telegraph Company for the huge sum of $750 000, because it allowed them to transmit thirty or forty messages simultaneously. In 1875 he developed the "autograph telegraph", which made it possible to copy a picture immediately in ordinary ink or on ordinary paper.

By 1874, Alex was spending several hours every day in his special spot overlooking the Grand River, planning his newest invention — a "telephone". It was, according to Bell himself, at Tutelo Heights on August 10, 1874, that the idea of the telephone was first conceived. The first telephone in the world was tested in the laboratory shared by Alexander Graham Bell and his assistant.

Alex decided to test a long-distance transmission between his home near Brantford and the village of Mount Pleasant, which was three kilometres away. A receiver was set up in the general store of Wallis Ellis, and the historic event became a community project when a neighbour boy crawled through a culvert with the stove wire purchased by Bell, and when Alex's neighbours helped him string the wire along fence posts. There were many local people crowded into Ellis' store when Alexander re-

Alexander Bell and his student, Helen Keller, "talk" together on their hands.

ceived his uncle David's voice from Tutelo Heights reciting Hamlet's famous soliloquy, "To be or not to be", as well as several neighbours singing a variety of songs.

Next, Alex obtained the use of the Dominion Telegraph line between Brantford and Paris, Ontario. The message had to travel to Toronto and then back to Paris, making a total of ninety-three kilometres. Again the test was a success, and later in 1876, the first two-way conversation was demonstrated between Cambridgeport and Boston.

Alexander Graham Bell had only begun his exploits as an inventor with his discovery of the telephone. He later perfected Edison's phonograph into a "graphophone", which he sold for $200 000, donating the entire sum to establishing the Volta Bureau for research to aid the deaf. He also invented an electrical instrument that could locate pieces of metal embedded deep in the human body; this "surgical probe" was

used in an attempt to save President McKinley's life when he was shot in 1901. Bell made many other medical inventions but he is perhaps better known for his aeronautics inventions. He built a model helicopter in 1891, and worked with Canada's first pilots designing and building airplanes as well as hydrofoil crafts.

By 1892 he had built at Baddeck, Nova Scotia, a summer estate called "Beinn Bhreagh", which in Gaelic means "beautiful mountain". Nova Scotia reminded Alex of his native country of Scotland so much that he purchased an entire mountain there for himself, his wife, and their two daughters.

On August 2, 1922, Alexander Graham Bell died of diabetes; one year later the cure for the disease was discovered by a Canadian doctor, Frederick Banting.

TOPICS FOR DISCUSSION
1. Have you ever had a "special spot" like Alexander where you went when you wanted to be alone to think?
2. What is tuberculosis? Is it still incurable?
3. Who was Helen Keller? Have you heard of her before?
4. Have you ever tried to invent anything? If you were an inventor what would you invent?
5. To the people gathered in Ellis' store, the sound of a voice from a distance of three kilometres carried by a wire was like magic or science fiction. What inventions that might become as common as the telephone in the future would be equally astonishing to you today?
6. A year after his death, a cure was found for Bell's ailment. What diseases today are killing people? How can you help doctors find cures?

RESEARCH CHALLENGE
CANADIAN INVENTIONS QUIZ

Test your knowledge of Canadians who have aided world progress. Copy the numbers from Column A into your notebook and then write the correct name from Column B beside each number.

Column A:

1. Most people don't realize that it was a Canadian who was the inventor of radio.
2. It was a Canadian who made the world's first commercial motion picture in 1903.
3. Kerosene was developed from coal by a Canadian in 1846, thus opening the way for the development of the oil refining industry in North America.
4. The world's first submarine telegraph cable was laid between P.E.I. and New Brunswick.
5. The development, in 1908, of Marquis wheat, made Canada one of the great grain-producing nations of the world.
6. It was a Canadian who, in 1858, drilled the first commercial oil well in North America.
7. A Canadian discovered the process for the production of carbide and acetylene in the year 1892.
8. In 1927, the world's first electronic wave organ was invented by a Canadian.
9. The zipper was invented by a Canadian in 1934.
10. The first commercial electron microscope was developed by a Canadian in the late 1930's.
11. In 1925, a Canadian produced the world's first batteryless radio.
12. In 1922, the first snowmobile was a Canadian invention.
13. The world's first successful hydrofoil was developed in Canada in 1908.
14. In 1892, a Canadian was the first to cook an entire meal with electricity.
15. The game of basketball was invented by a Canadian in 1891.
16. It was a Canadian who, in the year 1878, introduced Standard Time to the world.
17. In 1869, the world's first halftone illustration appeared in "The Canadian Illustrated News".
18. In 1904, five-pin bowling was invented by a Canadian.
19. In 1929, a Canadian was responsible for the world's first commercially available frozen fish.
20. In 1906, an automobile with a water-cooled engine was invented in Canada.

Column B

Naismith
McCulloch and Boswell
Ryan
Hillier
Gesner
Fessenden
Robb
Desbarats
Gisborne
Willson
Rogers
Saunders
Ahearn
Fleming
Sifton
Bell and Baldwin
Huntsman
Williams
Bombardier
Sundback

1. If you are interested in reading more about these and other Canadian inventions, ask your librarian for a copy of one of the following books.

The Canadian Inventions Book by Janis Nostbakken and Jack Humphrey. (Greey de Pencier Publications, 1976, 59 Front Street E., Toronto)   or

The Inventors by J. J. Brown. (McClelland and Stewart, 1967)

2. Choose one of the inventions that interests you and research the details of the discovery. Present a written or oral report to the class.

The Bell-Baldwin hydrofoil HD-4 roars across Baddeck Bay.

LOUIS CYR
The Strongest Man Who Ever Lived

Legends of giants who came from the farms and lumber camps of Quebec flourished in the early years of Canada's history. Some, such as Paul Bunyan, are lost in fantasy and exaggeration, but the legend of Louis Cyr is set firmly in reality. He never backed down from a challenge and was never defeated.

Louis was born in 1863, one of seventeen children. He inherited his size from his mother, who stood 185 cm and had a mass of 121 kg. When he was twelve years old, Louis left school and became a lumberjack. At the age of seventeen, when a loaded farm wagon became stuck in the mud, Louis started to acquire a reputation when he lifted the wagon on his back.

In those days a hefty giant named David Michaud claimed to be the strongest man in Canada. Young Louis challenged him to a stone-lifting contest. Every time Michaud raised a boulder, Louis duplicated the feat, until the Canadian champion came to a 218 kg rock that he was unable to budge. Louis picked up the large stone and stripped Michaud of his title.

Louis joined the Montreal police force in 1885. He was assigned to the notorious Ste. Cunegonde district, where he kept law and order by simply walking through the streets. Everyone was afraid to take him on! One day he came across a street fight, pulled the two tough antagonists apart, tucked one under each arm, and carried them off to jail. His fame soon spread.

Richard Fox, a New York fight promoter, heard of Cyr, investigated him and signed him up as "The Strongest Man in the World", offering $5 000 to anyone who could match the Canadian's strength. The money brought challengers from around the world, but Cyr beat them all. He culminated a twenty-three month tour of England on January 19, 1889, at the Royal Aquarium Theatre in London, with the Prince of Wales as a member of the packed audience. On that day with one hand he lifted to his shoulder a barrel of cement that had a mass of 142 kg. With one hand he also lifted 124 kg to his shoulder and then above his head, and, on a platform across his back, lifted 1860 kg. Using only one finger, he lifted a 250 kg mass that day.

Cyr became as much a celebrity as movie and sports superstars are today. At a luncheon in his honour, Cyr was offered a challenge by the Marquis of Queensberry. If Cyr agreed to have one of the Marquis' driving horses hitched to each of his arms, and if he could hold the animals to a standstill as they attempted to pull his limbs from his body, the Canadian strongman could keep one of the horses. Cyr accepted the challenge, and for years afterward he drove the noble-

Sketch of Louis Cyr by student Brian Lee.

man's horse around Montreal.

It was in Boston in the year 1895 that Louis Cyr lifted the greatest mass ever lifted by one person. Using his famous back lift, on which he had built his reputation, he raised a platform on which eighteen fat men, having a total mass of 1967 kg, were sitting.

In the tavern he later operated on Notre Dame Street in Montreal, Louis would toss around 136 kg beer kegs or lift his 54 kg wife Melina on the palm of his hand. An average meal for Louis consisted of more than three kilograms of meat; this kind of overeating caused his health to deteriorate and eventually led to his early death. His funeral was one of the largest in the history of Montreal, and fans and admirers flocked to pay homage to the strongest man who ever lived.

TOPICS FOR DISCUSSION

1. Who is the strongest man or woman you have met personally?
2. Do you admire physical strength in a person? Explain why or why not.
3. What is the heaviest mass you have lifted? Who is the strongest student in your school?
4. Who is the strongest person in the world today?
5. If you had the strength of Louis Cyr, what would you do with it? How would it change your life?

CREATIVE CHALLENGES

1. The illustration of Louis Cyr tied between the two horses was drawn by a student, Brian Lee. Draw a scene from the life of Louis Cyr or one of the other personalities described in this book.
2. Exaggeration can be an imaginative and effective device when writing a description of a personality. Using exaggeration, complete the following statements:
a. Louis Cyr was so strong he. . .
b. Alexander Graham Bell was so clever he. . .
c. Laura Secord was so brave she. . .
d. Louis Cyr's mother was so large she. . .
e. Emma LaJeunesse's voice was so powerful it. . .
Invent other exaggerations using personalities from this book.
3. Louis was a superstar of his time. Write a fan letter to him or one of the other personalities in this book. How would a fan begin such a letter? What would you want to know about your idol? Explain what you admire most about the person. How would you conclude your letter? Write a humorous fan letter if you wish.

NED HANLAN
The Boy in Blue

The year is 1880, and tens of thousands jam the banks along the River Thames in England to watch the most popular sport in the English-speaking world. It's a rowing contest between Edward A. Trickett, the Australian who is champion of the world, and Ned Hanlan, "the boy in blue" from Canada. Rowing regattas always attract large crowds. Betting is heavy on the race, which will give the Sportman Challenge Cup and the championship of the world to the winner.

Ned Hanlan, a small man of only 173 cm and 70 kg, slips into his single-shell scull. His distinctive blue rowing costume, handsome features, and personal magnetism send a buzz of excitement through the crowd of onlookers. Towering above him, the Goliath-like Trickett

is 193 cm and over 91 kg. Remarking on Ned's small stature, an American reporter once observed, "The more clothes he takes off, the bigger he gets."

Ned has come a long way since he was born in Toronto, July 12, 1855. As a boy he worked in his father's hotel on Toronto Island, and he fished or rowed about the harbour in a makeshift shell he built by sharpening a twenty-centimetre plank at both ends and mounting a seat and outriggers on it. Since Confederation, he has become Canada's first national sporting hero. The unknown twenty-one-year-old youth won the single-sculls on the Schuylkill River at Philadelphia in 1876, defeating some of the best rowers on the continent. The next year he became the Canadian champion by beating Wallace Ross

of St. John, New Brunswick, on Toronto Bay. The year after that he rowed against Evan "Eph" Morris, the American sculler, on the Allegheny River near Pittsburgh to win the United States title. By 1879 he took on all comers to become the undisputed master of rowing in North America. Then he travelled to England, a colonial challenge to their traditional sport.

The race begins. The historic course, on the Thames from Putney to Mortlake, encompasses a distance of 1046 m. Ned strokes only thirty-five to the minute against Trickett's forty, yet he pulls into a two-length lead by the end of the second kilometre and begins toying with Trickett during the balance of the race. Shocking the English, who take their rowing seriously, Ned waves to the crowds in the middle

of the race, lies down in his boat until his opponent catches up to him, and then spurts ahead of him again. Ned wins the race and the world championship by three lengths, and one reporter writes "I fully expected him to stand up in his boat and dance the Highland fling."

Ned Hanlan successfully defended his title of world champion for six years. The international sporting press speculated constantly on the secret of the little athlete from Toronto.

When the press in the United States described Hanlan as "*a pure, thoroughbred American*", Ned replied, "*There's no harm in them calling me an American, but I am not an American in the sense they want to have it. I was born in Canada, and I am a Canadian, and I don't care what they say.*"

TOPICS FOR DISCUSSION

1. In 1880, rowing was the most popular sport in the world. What is the most popular sport today?

2. Although Ned was not tall or husky, he was the best rower in the world. What makes a person a world champion athlete if it is not size or strength?

3. Are there world champion athletes today who are so good they can afford to clown with their opponents?

4. If you could be the best in the world at one sport, which one would you like it to be?

CREATIVE CHALLENGES

1. Most newspapers include special columns of advice to people who request help in solving a personal problem. Imagine yourself to be one of the relatives or friends of a hero or heroine described in this book and invent a humorous problem that you have regarding the person. For example: What problem might Melina Cyr have with Louis? What advice would Louis Riel's mother request? What trouble would Emma LaJeunesse's boyfriend be concerned about? etc.

2. After you have completed your letter, exchange it with one of your classmates and write an equally humorous solution in reply to each other. There are many sources of humour such as satire, exaggeration, physical characteristics, unusual situations etc. On what type of humour is your letter based?

JERRY POTTS

Bear Child

Jerry, age sixteen, leaned casually against the counter inside the trading post at Fort Benton. His father, Andrew Potts, an Edinburgh Scotsman turned fur trader, was upstairs closing the shutters on the second floor window against the approaching cold of a prairie night. The man had a wide reputation as a square dealer among both whites and Indians in a country and at a time when few people had earned such respect. Jerry's mother, Crooked Back, a Blood Indian from the Black Elk Band, had died shortly after his birth.

Suddenly, Jerry's head jerked upward at the sharp crack of a rifle, and in the same instant he heard his father's body crashing through the upper windows before it hit the ground with a heavy thud. As the boy rushed outside and fell on his knees beside the corpse of his parent, he caught sight of an Indian pony and a Blackfoot warrier disappearing into the northern dusk. He knew instantly what had happened, and he rushed to saddle his horse.

A vagrant Blackfoot, trying to obtain goods on credit, had argued with an employee of the fur company earlier that day. To ease the situation, Mr. Potts had wisely sent the clerk away on an errand, and thus was closing the windows himself. The Indian, thinking the figure on the second floor was the post employee, had shot Jerry's father by accident.

Jerry doggedly followed the trail of the murderer both day and night until, far to the north on the Canadian prairies, he finally overtook him in the middle of a Blackfoot

camp. Ignoring the danger, the teen-aged avenger stabbed his father's killer to death. Bravery was the highest-ranking virtue in the Blackfoot code; young Jerry had added boldness, resourcefulness and courage to the good name he already possessed by being his father's son. From that moment he was welcomed into all Blackfoot camps and, among other honours, was invited to join the inner councils of the proud Blackfoot Confederacy. He never returned to the empty trading post, choosing instead to live the free life of a Blackfoot brave. He was given the name Kyi-yo-Kosee, which means Bear Child.

Many years later, in the autumn of 1870, Jerry was hunting buffalo on the Belly Plains with a large band of Blackfoot, Blood and Peigan braves when another hunting party composed of Crees, Assiniboines and Saulteux ventured into Blackfoot territory. The tribes were hereditary enemies, but the Blackfoot had been greatly reduced in a smallpox epidemic, which gave the Crees the opportunity and inclination to invade the Belly River territory.

Cree scouts, who spotted some Peigan squaws and children gathering wood along the Belly River, attacked and killed all but one boy, who escaped to warn the Blackfoot camp. Jerry Potts was just returning with a hunting party when he heard the news. He immediately led his braves against the Cree, fighting bitterly along the banks of the river for hours. When the battle ended the intruders had fled, but several

hundred lay dead. Jerry Potts returned a hero, with nineteen scalps dripping from his belt, a deep head wound, a twenty-eight-shot pellet lodged in his left earlobe and an arrow hanging from his body where it had struck. His own description of the battle was typically abrupt and to the point, for he was a man of few words who seldom spoke of his exploits. "You could fire with your eyes shut and be sure to kill a Cree."

When Assistant Commissioner MacLeod arrived with the newly formed North West Mounted Police and looked for an interpreter and guide, the logical choice was Jerry Potts, whose integrity and loyalty were never questioned by either side. In 1874, Jerry agreed to lead MacLeod to Fort Whoop Up, the stronghold of white whisky traders, to put an end to the illegal trade and to establish law on the Canadian prairies.

On October 9, the column of red-coated mounties approached the junction of the Belly and St. Mary's rivers, where Potts pointed out Fort Whoop Up. When he and MacLeod, who became known as the "Queen's Cowboy", entered the stockade, they found it empty. Only the fur trader and a few Indians remained; with the approach of the police, the liquor traders had fled south across the border.

MacLeod's orders were to build a fort in the wilderness, so Jerry Potts led him another forty-five kilometres to a broad loop of the Old Man's River, which was in the heart of Blackfoot territory. The main reason the Indians accepted the

mounties was that Jerry Potts assured them that the N.W.M.P. would bring equal justice for Indian and white. The new fort was called Fort MacLeod.

Jerry Potts continued as a scout for the N.W.M.P. for twenty-two years, during which time he became a legend. In May of 1875, he led "Bub" Walsh and the men of 'B' division 260 km east to the Cypress Hills to establish another fort there. In 1877, his role as interpreter at the signing of Treaty No. 7 at Blackfoot Crossing was one reason the mounties and Indians came to a peaceful agreement. Once, after an Indian chief had spoken for ninety minutes to the white authorities, Jerry interpreted the speech simply by saying: "He wants grub."

It was said that the short, slope-shouldered plainsman could smell water eight kilometres away and that his limbs were moulded to his saddle. He wore the skin of a wild cat under his shirt, after having had a dream that a cat skin would protect him. His ability to navigate the vast plains without losing his way caused one mountie to suggest he had "a compass in his gizzard".

Pott's uncanny ability to find his way even in the dead of night or in blinding blizzards stood him in good stead. It was during winter, the season the Blackfoot believed invoked evil, that he took a small expedition 500 km across the endless prairies. Their task was to return with a $30 000 payroll, which they did, despite temperatures that reached 55°C below zero and snow storms that blinded them. The soldiers stumbled after Potts, who found refuge from the fierce elements in a ravine. They used hunting knives to dig a cave in the snow banks and huddled there for thirty-six hours.

One day, a nineteen-year-old mountie, Marmaduke Graburn, disappeared after returning to a work site to recover a forgotten axe. When patrols could find no trace of him, Jerry Potts was put on the trail. He immediately picked up the tracks of the policeman's horse even though they were partly covered by fresh snow. He followed the tracks to a place where they were joined by those of an unshod Indian pony and discovered the prints of a second Indian horse apparently following the other tracks. Next he pointed out blood on the ground and shortly found the body of the mountie, shot from behind by the second Indian while the first held him in conversation. Although Potts tracked down the killer, Star Child, a jury of white settlers found him not guilty in fear that their farms might be burnt or their cattle slaughtered in retaliation. Star Child was set free and, ironically, in later years became a scout for the N.W.M.P., apparently serving the force well.

When Jerry Potts died in 1896 at sixty-one from cancer of the throat, he was buried at Fort MacLeod with full military honors.

TOPICS FOR DISCUSSION
1. Many of the legends of Jerry Potts contradict each other. For example, one version claims that he was only one year old when his father was killed, that he was raised by a frontier desperado, Alexander Harvey, until he was six and then by Chief Factor Andrew Dawson, who taught him English as well as several Indian languages. Which story do you think is true? Is there any way to discover the truth? What is the difference between history and legend?
2. When would you prefer to live if you had a choice, a) on the Western plains in the 1870's b) in New France in the 1650's or c) in Canada today?
3. If someone murdered a member of your family today, you could not seek them out and kill them as Jerry Potts did. Is today's society, with its civilized laws, a better sys-tem than the lawless days on the prairies? Do you think Jerry Potts recognized the advantages of law and order when he agreed to help the N.W.M.P. and convinced his brothers, the Blackfoot, to co-operate?

RESEARCH CHALLENGES
1. Lethbridge, Alberta, is the present day name of Fort Whoop Up. What other modern cities or towns have changed their original names? Make a map of Canada, placing the old names of towns and settlements on it.
2. One of Canada's most famous cowboys was big John Ware, a huge Negro who was loved and respected by all who knew him in Alberta. Prepare a short biography on him.

Big John Ware and his family.

JAMES MORROW WALSH

Sitting Bull's Friend

"Bub" Walsh could outrun, outswim and outfight any boy his size. In fact, he was good in all sports and was captain of the Prescott Lacrosse Team of 1869, acclaimed world champions after defeating all competition from Canada and the U.S.A. He was not a good student when it came to academic studies, but he graduated from the Royal Military College in Kingston, Ontario, at twenty-four. When the Fenian raiders crossed into Canada in 1866, Walsh was one of the first to join the volunteers who pushed them back across the U.S. border. His commanding officer described him as: ". . .the best drilled Canadian to graduate and one of the best anywhere in action against those wild Irishmen known as Fenians."

Although he married Mary Elizabeth Mowat, from Brockville, in 1870, and began to manage the North American Hotel in Prescott, by the autumn of 1873 he left business and family behind when he joined the North West Mounted Police force, newly established on May 20, 1873, by Sir John A. Macdonald. His personality, military training and physical strength were ideally suited for the challenge awaiting the handful of men who were to patrol and keep law and order in the vast western and northern territories. Trouble was liable to break out any time with the plains Indians; the first troops departed for the west even before they were issued with uniforms.

After training at Lower Fort Garry (present day Winnipeg), Walsh led an expedition of redcoats into the heart of the Indian and Métis land. In a broad valley close to the headwaters of Butte Creek he built a fort, which was appropriately named Fort Walsh.

As Walsh and the men in scarlet proceeded to win the trust and friendship of the Canadian Indians, south of the border an American, General Custer, was dealing harshly and violently with the Sioux Nation led by Chief Sitting Bull. It is re-

ported that before declaring war on the whites, Sitting Bull performed the sun dance to seek the approval of the Great Spirit, and gave a hundred pieces of skin, which he tore from his own body, as a sacrifice. Bleeding from these wounds, he danced continuously for one day and night before massacring Custer and 225 blue-coated U.S. Cavalry troops. One Sioux chief, Rain-In-the-Face, had vowed to eat the heart of Captain Tom Custer, younger brother of General Custer. True to his brag, he cut "Little Hair's" heart from his body after shooting him with his revolver and, tearing a piece of it between his teeth, spit it back in the face of the dead man, who was found on the battle field, slashed open, with his visceral organs protruding grotesquely. After the Little Big Horn the natural refuge for the Sioux was Canada, and the tribes ran across the border southeast of the Cypress Hills, into the territory patrolled by Superintendent Walsh and his redcoats.

Apprised of the massacre south of the border, Walsh was patrolling the plains when he encountered the first Sioux camp, that of Four Horns, a Sioux war chief. He rode boldly into the midst of the Indians, who, sensing that Walsh was tired, invited him to rest. To their amazement he accepted, stretched out on their buffalo robes and fell asleep. Never before had a white person shown such nerve; here was an enemy so fearless and trusting that he slept in a Sioux lodge. When he awoke, Walsh explained to the listening Indians the laws they would have to obey if they wished to remain in Canada. He had barely concluded when an Indian courier arrived and accused Walsh of being a "Long Knife American". Four Horns immediately distrusted Walsh. Diplomatically, Walsh announced that he and his scouts would stay in the Sioux camp overnnight and instructed Four Horns to send two or three of his young warriors to a Canadian Indian camp 100 km

away, where the Indians knew Walsh as a friend. This was done, and the next day Medicine Bear and Black Horn, accompanied by 200 braves, rode into Four Horn's camp vouching for Walsh and prepared for war if he had been injured by the Sioux.

This incident, however, was only the beginning. Almost immediately following the encounter with Four Horns, scouts reported that Sitting Bull had crossed the Missouri River and was heading for the border. Walsh, four other police officers, and a trusted Métis guide headed for Pinto Horse Butte at the bottom of Wood Mountain to intercept the band of Indians fresh from the massacre of Custer. In the valley of Frenchman's Creek they discovered Sitting Bull's camp of 5 000 Sioux.

A minor chief blocked their path at the edge of the camp, warning them that they would die. Walsh courteously enquired of the surprised Indian which teepee belonged to Sitting Bull.

"Walsh rode straight to his goal with neither halt nor change of pace. Nothing like this had ever happened before, a white man riding unannounced and apparently unafraid into the presence of the most feared native leader on the continent. The war-weary chief gazed in astonishment as this mounted man in immaculate police uniform led his little group to the tipi entrance at a bold gait."

Walsh and Sitting Bull gazed at each other. Then the red-coated soldier extended his hand. The Sioux chief responded and an historic handshake was exchanged.

"You and I must have a conversation. You know you are now on British soil," Walsh said. Looking around him at the thousands of warriors, Sitting Bull broke into a laugh at the audacity of the white man, but he called council and Walsh laid down the conditions if the Sioux were to remain in Canada:

1. They must not use Canada as a

Sitting Bull at Fort Walsh, 1878. The photographer was T. George Anderton, a North West Mounted policeman.

refuge to continue waging war with the United States.

2. They would be punished if they did not obey Canadian laws.

3. There would be no stealing of horses or cattle.

4. The North West Mounted Police would protect them.

5. If they disobeyed the law they would be jailed or forced to leave the country.

As a show of friendship Walsh and his men remained overnight in the Sioux camp.

The next morning brought trouble. Three Indians rode into camp dragging five horses behind them. The Métis guide identified the Indians as Assiniboines from Missouri, and three of the horses he recognized as belonging to a Catholic priest from the Cypress Hills. One of the arrivals, a fierce warrior named White Dog, bragged of stealing the horses. Walsh, recognizing that the moment had come to enforce the law, walked up to White Dog and ordered him arrested. White Dog, a favourite among the Sioux, was hostile and belligerent. Many of the Sioux were ready to fight for him. Walsh remained calm, but insistent, until White Dog backed down, claiming that the horses had been wandering free when he found them. Walsh wisely seized on the excuse, having forced White Dog, in front of the great Sitting Bull, to abandon his defiance of Canadian law, and allowed him to go free with only a warning.

"White Dog was disgraced in the presence of the Sioux," wrote Walsh later, "and felt his position severely, but the lesson was long remembered by Bull and his followers."

It was only three weeks after his encounter with Sitting Bull that Walsh was again required to prove the strength of the redcoats. A Canadian Indian, Chief Little Cloud, was robbed and terrorized. His village teepees were torn down, his horses shot, and his women and children threatened by a band of Assiniboines from America, who recognized no authority but their own strength. Little Cloud lodged a complaint with Walsh, who im- mediately went after the culprits and their insolent chief, Broken Arm. With twenty-five mounties he quietly entered their camp, which he discerned after a night's travel, and captured the suspects. Walsh's report stated:

"The arms of the warriors were seized. Broken Arm and twenty-five braves were captured and carried out of the camp while the alarm was being sounded."

Walsh shackled the prisoners in pairs and took shelter on a hilltop, where he built a fortress of stones while waiting for the Indian attack. As hundreds of Indians started for them, four chiefs moved to the front of the attackers and asked Walsh to explain his actions. Walsh walked forward and told them they must obey the laws of Canada. Although many argued for an immediate attack, the Indians eventually dispersed. The police quickly left for Fort Walsh, where Broken Arm was given six months in jail and where three of his warriors were also imprisoned. Walsh acted as both judge

and jury at the trial.

Among other inflictions, Walsh suffered from a skin disease, erysipelas, which was chronic and irritating. He wanted to return to the comfort and safety of home and family in the east, but another crisis erupted that prevented his immediate retirement.

A band of Indians, the Nez Percés, were being pursued across the United States and wished to enter Canada. The Sioux were in contact with the Nez Percés, and Sitting Bull was sympathetic toward them. Walsh received reports that the Sioux were preparing for war and about to go to rescue their brothers by attacking the U.S. Cavalry who were pursuing them. He hurried to the Sioux camp to have a council with Sitting Bull, where he discovered the warriors already naked and painted in readiness for battle. When Walsh stated bluntly that there would no longer be protection for them in Canada if they went on the war path, the chiefs controlled the young men, and the fight was averted. However, within a week, rumours were wild once again in the Sioux camp. White Bird, a Nez Percé war chief, had broken through the American troops and, with 200 of his people, was on his way to Canada. Sioux scouts reported to Sitting Bull that white soldiers were approaching their camp as well. Panic and outrage sent the Sioux again into preparations for war.

Walsh arrived and calmed them with the suggestion that he ride out to see who the invaders were. At first, 200 warriors joined him, but by the time he reached the U.S. border, he found himself the leader of almost 1 000 Indian braves. Instead of "Long Knives" (the U.S. Cavalry) they encountered White Bird's Nez Percés, who were befriended and taken to Wood Mountain to be nursed back to health by the Sioux.

In October of 1877, a troop of American soldiers visited Canada to try to persuade the Indians to return with them. The Sioux refused to leave. In July, 1880, Walsh was transferred back to the east, much to the dismay of Sitting Bull, who had come to trust only Walsh in the three and a half years of their friendship. Before Walsh left, Sitting Bull presented him with his most prized possession — the headdress he had worn at the Little Big Horn, which is retained to this day in the Royal Ontario Museum in Toronto.

Although he returned east, Walsh did not forget his Sioux friends. He sought assurances from the U.S. government that Sitting Bull and his people could return safely to their home south of the border without being tried for murder or hanged. Sitting Bull refused to move until Walsh sent word that it would be safe, and only when Walsh's message arrived did the Sioux return to Fort Buford in the U.S.

Walsh resigned from the N.W.M.P. on September 1, 1883. Years later, on December 20, 1890, Sitting Bull was shot to death by Indian Reservation police during an attempt to arrest him over a trumped-up charge. Walsh died in Brockville, Ontario, in 1905.

TOPICS FOR DISCUSSION
1. How would you explain the fact that Sitting Bull, who massacred Custer, lived a peaceful, law-abiding existence in Canada?
2. Which characteristics of Walsh enabled him to befriend the Indians? Which characteristics of Sitting Bull enabled him to befriend the whites?
3. Have you ever seen a movie, a T.V. show, a comic book or heard a popular song about "Bub" Walsh? If you have, try to obtain it for the classroom. If you have not, how could you encourage Canadians to pay tribute to their heroes such as Walsh?
4. In the frontier days, people like Walsh and Sam Steele acted as both judge and jury after they arrested criminals. Why does society not allow the police to have such power today?
5. Are there still R.C.M.P. heroes today? Explain.

SUGGESTIONS
1. Obtain the film, *Days of Whisky Gap* (approx. 1/2 hr.) from the National Film Board or your local library and view it in class.
2. Think of a class project that would make everyone in your school or community aware of the heroic nature of "Bub" Walsh.

Sitting Bull and "Buffalo Bill" Cody entertained audiences in a Wild West Show.

Sam Steele

BORN NEAR ORILLIA, 1849, SAMUEL STEELE AS A BOY LOVES TO RUN, RIDE AND SHOOT IN THE BACKWOODS OF UPPER CANADA. AT SIXTEEN HE'S MAN ENOUGH TO CARRY A RIFLE IN THE MILITIA, DURING THE PANIC OF THE FENIAN RAIDS!

IN 1870 HE'S A PRIVATE IN THE RED RIVER EXPEDITION. IT'S A LONG MUDDY MARCH TO MANITOBA, BUT THE TROOPS PRESS ON, SPOILING FOR A FIGHT WITH THE MÉTIS, TO AVENGE THE EXECUTION OF THOMAS SCOTT!

THE FIGHT NEVER MATERIALIZES. WHILE TROOPS ARE ENTERING FORT GARRY AT ONE GATEWAY, REBEL LEADER LOUIS RIEL IS RETREATING FROM ANOTHER! MANITOBA BECOMES A PROVINCE IN 1870, WITHOUT A BLOOD BATH.

BACK EAST, 1871, SAM STEELE JOINS 'A' BATTERY, R.C.A., FIRST UNIT OF THE CANADIAN PERMANENT FORCE, BUT TWO YEARS LATER TRANSFERS, TO WEAR THE SCARLET UNIFORM OF THE NEWLY-FORMED NORTH WEST MOUNTED POLICE!

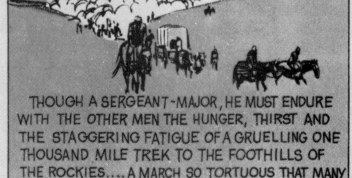

THOUGH A SERGEANT-MAJOR, HE MUST ENDURE WITH THE OTHER MEN THE HUNGER, THIRST AND THE STAGGERING FATIGUE OF A GRUELLING ONE THOUSAND MILE TREK TO THE FOOTHILLS OF THE ROCKIES.... A MARCH SO TORTUOUS THAT MANY OF THE HORSES FAIL TO SURVIVE IT.

WHEN THE MOUNTIES REACH ALBERTA, THEY FIND A LAWLESS FRONTIER RULED BY YANKEE WHISKY MERCHANTS. SO DISHONEST IS THIS BREED THAT EVEN A PILE OF WOOD SOLD TO STEELE FOR A N.W.M.P. CAMP TURNS OUT TO BE.... HOLLOW!

BUT THE GREATEST THREAT TO PEACE ON THE PLAINS COMES NOT FROM AMERICAN WHITE MEN, BUT AN INDIAN.... SITTING BULL! IN 1876, AFTER WIPING OUT CUSTER AND HIS CAVALRY AT LITTLE BIGHORN, HE SEEKS REFUGE IN CANADA.

THE MOUNTIES KEEP THE SIOUX CHIEF IN CHECK, BUT IN 1881 SITTING BULL RIDES INTO FORT QU'APPELLE, DEMANDING A RESERVATION FOR HIS WARRIORS! STEELE TELLS HIM HE'D BE WISER TO SURRENDER TO THE UNITED STATES AUTHORITIES! SHORTLY AFTER, HE DOES.

IN 1882 STEELE IS ORDERED TO ENFORCE PROHIBITION ON THE C.P.R. PRAIRIE CONSTRUCTION LINE. NO EASY TASK, FOR BOOTLEGGERS CUNNINGLY SMUGGLE THEIR ROTGUT IN EGGSHELLS, BOGUS BIBLES, EVEN IN CANNED PEACHES!

THE FOLLOWING YEAR, PROHIBITING BOOZE ON THE B.C. SECTION IS EVEN TRICKIER! HIS JURISDICTION EXTENDS ONLY OVER A TWENTY MILE BELT. BEYOND THAT, NAVVIES CAN DRINK THEIR FILL AND LAUGH AT THE LAW!

STEELE IS BEDRIDDEN WITH FEVER IN APRIL 1885 WHEN, ANGRY OVER A LONG DELAY IN THEIR SALARIES, THREE HUNDRED ARMED C.P.R. MEN MARCH ON BEAVER RIVER CAMP! EIGHT MOUNTIES FACE THEIR GUNS, AND QUELL THE RIOT!

BARELY RECOVERED FROM HIS ILLNESS, STEELE MUST RUSH TO ALBERTA TO TAKE COMMAND OF THE ALBERTA FIELD FORCE CAVALRY, TO PROTECT SETTLERS FROM INDIANS ON THE WARPATH! ...RIEL'S ALLIES IN THE 1885 REBELLION.

STEELE LEADS AN ADVANCE GUARD IN THE HUNT FOR CREE CHIEF BIG BEAR, WHOSE BRAVES MASSACRED THE SETTLERS OF FROG LAKE! SEVERAL TIMES STEELE IS ATTACKED!

BUT THE MOUNTIES GET THEIR MAN: BIG BEAR IS CAPTURED BY A N.W.M.P. SERGEANT AT FORT CARLTON. STEELE RETURNS TO BRITISH COLUMBIA, AND WITNESSES THE DRIVING OF THE LAST SPIKE AT CRAIGELLACHIE.

IN 1898, IT'S NORTH TO THE YUKON! PASSING THROUGH SKAGWAY, ALASKA, STEELE IS APPALLED AT THE GUNFIGHTS IN THE STREETS, THE ROBBERIES AND CARD CHEATING...IT'S A CRIME EMPIRE, RULED BY HOODLUM OVERLORD 'SOAPY' SMITH!

IN THE YUKON, STEELE (NOW A LIEUTENANT-COLONEL) NOT ONLY PRESERVES THE PEACE, BUT SAVES COUNTLESS LIVES, LEADING GOLD-SEEKERS OVER WHITE AND CHILKOOT PASSES, THROUGH WHITE HORSE RAPIDS. BEFORE HE ARRIVED, IN A FEW DAYS ALONE THIS HALF-MILE OF FOAM AND FURY WRECKED ONE HUNDRED FIFTY BOATS, DROWNING TEN MEN!

IN 1900 HE LEADS A CORPS OF MOUNTED RIFLE MEN ......THE LORD STRATHCONA'S HORSE.....AND THESE CANADIANS DISTINGUISH THEMSELVES, OUTRIDING AND OUTSHOOTING THE BOERS IN THE SOUTH AFRICAN WAR!

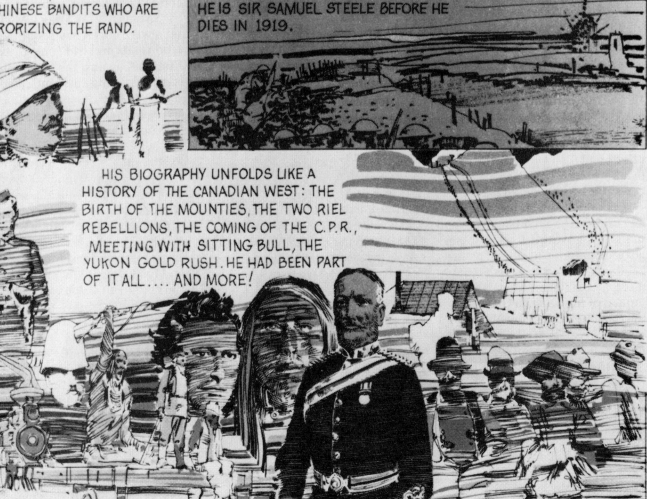

AT THE END OF THE WAR, STEELE STAYS ON TO HEAD THE TRANS-VAAL DIVISION OF THE SOUTH AFRICAN CONSTABULARY, DISARM-ING KAFFIRS, AND HELPING ROUND UP CHINESE BANDITS WHO ARE TERRORIZING THE RAND.

IN WORLD WAR I, HE RAISES AND TRAINS THE SECOND CANADIAN DIVISION, AND IN ENGLAND COMMANDS THE SHORNCLIFFE AREA OF EASTERN COMMAND. HE IS SIR SAMUEL STEELE BEFORE HE DIES IN 1919.

HIS BIOGRAPHY UNFOLDS LIKE A HISTORY OF THE CANADIAN WEST: THE BIRTH OF THE MOUNTIES, THE TWO RIEL REBELLIONS, THE COMING OF THE C.P.R., MEETING WITH SITTING BULL, THE YUKON GOLD RUSH. HE HAD BEEN PART OF IT ALL.... AND MORE!

LOUIS RIEL
The Father of Manitoba

Tuesday, November 2, 1869
The rumour ran through the nearby village of Winnipeg in advance of the invaders. Terror gripped some of the Canadians who had just arrived from the east. A Métis army was marching toward Fort Garry, the Hudson's Bay Company post at the junction of the Red and Assiniboine Rivers. The armed mob of 120 people entered the open, unguarded gates and occupied the fort without any resistance; their leader was Louis Riel.

Riel was a Métis, born on October 22, 1844 in St. Boniface; his mother, Julie Lagimodière, was the first white woman born in the West. When he was only fourteen years old the studious Louis was sent by Bishop Taché to Montreal, where he spent several years studying for the priesthood. Discovering, however, that he was not suited to a religious vocation, he returned to Manitoba.

In January of 1869, the Hudson's Bay Company sold much of its land in the north-west to the Canadian government for £300 000. The inhabitants of the Red River Settlement were not consulted or even informed of the sale. On October 1, the Canadian Government appointed William McDougall as lieutenant-governor of the colony, replacing Governor McTavish of the Hudson's Bay Company. It was out of concern for their land rights and a distrust of the new authorities that the Métis followed Louis Riel into Fort Garry and occupied it.

On November 16, "Le Comité National des Métis de la Rivière Rouge" was formed, with John Bruce as president and Louis Riel as secretary. They refused to allow McDougall inside the occupied Fort Garry because, under the Canadian government order, his duties did not officially start until December.

By November 24, "Le Comité National" issued a bill of rights for the colony. All was peaceful. Riel, the fiery orator, was elected president when John Bruce resigned. For several months Riel ruled the settlement, as he bargained with the Canadian government for Manitoba's entry into Confederation. When an Ontario settler, Thomas Scott, attempted to overthrow the provisional government, he was jailed. When he continued to defy Riel, he was executed on March 4 (he was the only casualty of the Red River Rebellion). By May, the Red River delegates sent to Ottawa had agreed to enter Confederation. Riel had successfully guaranteed the rights of the people of Manitoba in the new union with Canada, but the "Father of Manitoba" fled to the U.S.A. when Colonel Wolseley, the new governor, arrived with a few hundred aggressive troops.

Although there was a price on Riel's head, the people of Manitoba regarded him as a hero and so elected him, in 1874, to the Parliament of Canada as their representative. When he arrived in Ottawa, however, he was expelled from the House of Commons and banished from Canada for five years.

During a fifteen-year interim, Riel remained in the United States, and during that time he became a different person. He spent two years in insane asylums, changed his name to the biblical "David", was married, came to regard himself as a prophet, and waited for his people to recall him to their service.

Then one June day in 1884, while he was in the middle of mass, Riel was called from the Jesuit mission church in Montana where he was a school master. Four grim, dusty Métis, who had just ridden 1000 km from Saskatchewan, were waiting for him. Their leader was Gabriel Dumont, the "Prince of the Plains", and the delegation included English as well as French Métis who were concerned about their land rights and had come to ask Riel's aid against the Canadian government. Louis knelt and offered thanks to God; the enslaved people had sent for their David.

With a crucifix in his hand and dressed in black robes, Riel returned to attempt a peaceful negotiation. However, Ottawa ignored their demands, so a provisional government was declared by the Métis.

At Duck Lake, rebellion exploded as 200 Métis attacked a force of fifty-six North West Mounted Police and forty-one English volunteers. In the confusion of the battle, Riel, an unarmed figure in black, rode among the bullets urging his men onward. The police, under the command of Major Crozier, were forced to retreat. Twelve mounties were killed as were five Métis.

Next, the prairie Indians joined the rebellion. As Poundmaker's braves looted and burned the settlement of Battleford, Wandering Spirit, the war chief of Big Bear, attacked Frog Lake, killing nine whites and burning the community to the ground.

LOUIS RIEL, THE REBEL.
FROM A LATE PHOTOGRAPH.

Sir John A. Macdonald sent 8000 troops under General Middleton to quell the North West Rebellion of 1885. At Batoche, the Métis, outnumbered four to one, fought off the soldiers for three days until they ran out of ammunition. Following the battle, Riel wandered aimlessly through the woods for days before surrendering and standing trial.

Contrary to his lawyer's wishes, Riel refused to plead insanity when he was tried for treason in Regina. On August 1, 1885, after one hour of deliberation, the all-English jury found him guilty.

French Canada was sympathetic to Riel, and Sir John A. Macdonald was swamped with petitions begging for clemency. The issue threatened to split the country in half, but in the end Louis Riel was hanged on the gallows.

TOPICS FOR DISCUSSION

1. Was Riel a rebel? Did he deserve to die? Was he a hero?

2. How could each of the Riel uprisings have been prevented?

3. Would Riel have made a good priest?

4. After the execution of Thomas Scott at Fort Garry, Riel wrote "Me too, my life too. My life too it is taken. This will be. Oh there is blood and blood." Was Louis predicting his own execution fifteen years in the future? If he had not executed Scott, would his own life have been spared at Regina?

5. Riel deliberately surrendered rather than escaping to the U.S.A. as Dumont did, because he hoped that in a courtroom he could embarrass the government into releasing him and recognizing the Métis land rights. Was he a martyr?

6. Was Riel a capable and sane leader of his people or was he an insane religious visionary?

7. After his father's death, Louis spent ten years with his mother to keep her company, and the night before he was executed, he wrote his last letter to her. What does this suggest to you about his personality?

8. If Riel had been allowed to become a member of the Canadian Parliament in 1874 representing the Red River Settlement, do you think he would have become as famous in Canadian history?

CREATIVE CHALLENGES

1. After 1885, English Canadians wanted Riel executed, but French Canadians believed he should be spared. Pick two members of the class to represent the two viewpoints and have them debate the issue. Let the class vote on which speaker is most convincing. How will you organize the debate? How much time will each speaker have to state his or her opinions? How long will each have for a rebuttal? How will the members of the class judge the speakers fairly?

2. Write a song or a poem about the rebellions in Western Canada.

3. Draw or paint one of the scenes described in the western rebellions.

Julie Lagimodière (mother of Louis Riel) and little Jean Louis Riel (son of Louis Riel).

Violence and bloodshed were averted and the C.P.R. line was allowed through the Blackfoot reserve when Chief Crowfoot and Father Lacombe were able to negotiate in peace. Invent the conversation that you think might have taken place between the two men.

GABRIEL DUMONT

The Prince of The Plains

The man known as "The Prince of the Plains" was born in 1838 at Red River, Saskatchewan. Both his parents were Métis, so he grew up hunting buffalo on the fast ponies known as "buffalo runners".

Gabriel was already famous among his people when he became the youngest person to be elected to lead the great buffalo hunt, held twice each year in the Assiniboia country. He was a born leader, and it was said he possessed the gift of healing wounds.

As white people pushed west and the railroad invaded the prairies, the Métis saw the buffalo herds, on which they and the prairie Indians depended for food and clothing, disappearing. They also wanted legal title for their strip farms on the South Saskatchewan River. Gabriel Dumont and other Métis leaders were ignored by Ottawa, and so they travelled to Montana to urge Louis Riel, who had guaranteed the rights of the people of Manitoba in the new Canadian federation, to lead their cause. However, even Riel's negotiations failed and fighting broke out.

The first shot fired at Duck Lake killed Gabriel's younger brother, and a large bullet from a Snider rifle cut a path through Gabriel's own skull, leaving a permanent silver streak in his hair. Dumont was Riel's lieutenant-general in charge of the rebel forces during the North West Rebellion of 1885. He was a strong and powerful man, yet kind-hearted and friendly. As the enemy fled in disorder from Duck Lake, Dumont wanted to pursue them and destroy the force as it retreated in confusion. Riel objected to more bloodshed, however, and Gabriel obediently restrained his sharp-shooting buffalo hunters.

The next days were full of bloodshed. As the army of General Middleton approached Fish Creek, Dumont attacked the superior force, which was armed with cannons and gatling guns. The Métis guerrillas dug in at Batoche, where, after three days of fierce fighting against overwhelming odds, they ran out of ammunition and started shooting nails, stones and metal buttons in place of bullets. Dumont finally fled to the U.S.A. to escape capture, but there he was reduced to earning his living as a performer in Buffalo Bill Cody's Wild West Show.

TOPICS FOR DISCUSSION

1. Dumont did not wish to fight the Canadian government; he only wanted justice for the Métis. Could the North West Rebellion have been avoided? Could most rebellions be avoided?

2. What did Dumont gain by resorting to violence? What did he lose?

3. If you had been a Métis in Saskatchewan in 1885, how could you have prevented the useless bloodshed and yet ensured the rights of your people?

4. Does it seem possible to you that people such as Dumont, Sitting Bull and Annie Oakley could become circus performers?

5. In your opinion, was it a mistake to ask Louis Riel to return to Canada? Did Dumont have any other choice?

CREATIVE CHALLENGES

Invent a product or service based on the name and reputation of a Canadian hero or heroine. How would you advertise your product or service? Which personalities for example would you use to emphasize the following appeals relating to a product or service: sophistication, tradition, youth, sex, virility, strength, speed, family unity.
Prepare an advertisement for your product based on one of the following suggestions:

a. a poster campaign

b. a song (you could make a tape-recording)

c. a radio commercial.

d. a television advertisement using actors (this could be video-taped, filmed in 8 mm, or presented live to the class.

e. create a trademark or symbol.

BIG BEAR
Last of The Plains Indians

A strange dream disturbed Big Bear's sleep. In the dream a spring of water sprouted up through the ground. As the chief attempted to block the flow by placing his hands over it, the water turned to blood and squirted through his fingers. When Big Bear awoke, he felt disturbed but couldn't find the meaning of the dream. He would not realize the significance of the vision until many years later.

Big Bear was a Cree chief. He had resisted treaty money offered by the Canadian government for years, preferring to travel freely on the prairies rather than submit to life on a reserve, to be fed rations like an animal in a zoo. One of his adversaries, Commissioner Dewdney, remarked:

"I have not formed such a poor opinion of Big Bear as some appear to have done. He is of a very independent character, self-reliant, and appears to know how to make his own living without begging from the Government."

Big Bear held out as the treaty chiefs gave in because he wanted to avoid the complete subjugation of his people. For this reason, all the radical young braves gathered in his camp, and the old chief had the difficult task of dealing politically with white people at the same time as he physically restrained restless warriors eager to resort to violence.

The last Canadian buffalo hunt was held in 1879; after that the herds simply vanished, destroyed by the arrival of white settlement. In that same year the *Saskatchewan Herald* called Big Bear "the heart and soul of our Canadian Plains Indians". In 1881, the same year Sitting Bull left Canada and returned to live on a reservation in the U.S.A., the Indian commissioner described Big Bear as "a non-treaty Cree but to whom all the Cree look up to as their Chief . . . who has more influence than any Indian on the plains".

With the buffalo gone and his people facing starvation, Big Bear had no means of supporting them; finally he was forced to sign Treaty No. 6 on December 8, 1882. However, when Thomas Quinn, the Indian agent, ordered his band to settle on a reservation or have government assistance withheld, the chief ignored him and attempted to gather the scattered Indian tribes together so they could speak more strongly in unity.

When he was accused of holding secret meetings and plotting against the whites, he sent a letter to the *Saskatchewan Herald* denying the report and saying that he refused to listen to the counsel of Riel and others from across the line who were encouraging him to embarrass the government through acts of violence. Big Bear's philosophy was one of passive resistance. He knew war would result in the destruction of his people, but the hot-headed young men in his camp were difficult to control. When his braves forced surveyors to quit work on the railroad crossing the prairies, it was Big Bear who spoke for his people and settled the argument with the North West Mounted Police. When a young Indian, who was refused food by a government official, beat the white man with an axe handle, Big Bear again called for peace and the Indian was given up to the police.

However, on April 2, 1885, some warriors attacked Agent Quinn and eight other whites at Frog Lake. The aging chief rushed forward, shouting at his braves to stop the massacre, but he was too late and his vision from years before had become reality. He could not prevent the flow of blood.

What led up to and caused the Frog Lake massacre is a mystery, but one of the hostages who survived the ordeal described a scene three or four days later. Big Bear addressed sixty seated warriors, including Wandering Spirit, the war chief who had led the slaughter, and ended his speech in loud, angry tones, like the roar of a lion:

"Kias, I was a chief. Long ago we fought the Blackfoot, not a man among you could do what I did. All the South Nations – the Bloods, Peigans, Blackfoot, Crows, Sioux – knew Big Bear, that he was head chief of all the Crees. At that time, if I said anything you listened to me – you obeyed me. But now I say one thing and you do another!"

In a dramatic conclusion, Big Bear swept his arm in the faces of Wandering Spirit and the others who sat with lowered eyes, then pointed in the direction of the smouldering ruins of the post at Frog Lake. He retained his pose for a moment, his features quivering with emotion, then folded his blanket around him and strode away.

Big Bear (far right) and a group of Cree Indians.

War had come despite Big Bear's efforts. John A. Macdonald sent 4 000 troops under General Middleton to quell the uprising. The North West Mounted Police were forced to abandon Fort Pitt to the Indians. Poundmaker, Louis Riel and Gabriel Dumont had also taken up arms in the south. The North West Rebellion had begun.

It is well known that Big Bear prevented any prisoners from being killed. When Wandering Spirit tried to anger the Indians against their white prisoners, Big Bear prevented him and spoke in defence of the whites, asking the Indians to show pity to their captives. When the Indians besieged Fort Pitt, he used his influence to arrange for the evacuation of the inhabitants without the loss of their lives. Fort Pitt was burned symbolically only.

When it came to war with the white soldiers, Big Bear was more than a match for the mounties at Frenchman's Butte, but he knew he had won only a battle, not the war. He surrendered, was tried for treason, and found guilty. At his trial he spoke through an interpreter, not for himself but for his people. His powerful words moved the packed courtroom from laughter to regret.

"Now I am in chains and will be sent to prison and I have no doubt the handsome faces I ad-mire about me will be competent to govern the land (laughter from the audience). At present I am dead to my people. Many of my band are hiding in the woods, paralysed with terror. Cannot this court send them a pardon? My own children – perhaps they are starving and outcast, too, afraid to appear in the big light of day. If the government does not come to help them before the winter sets in, my band will surely perish. . . I am old and ugly but I have tried to do good. Pity the children of my tribe! Pity the old and help-less of my people! I speak with a single tongue. . .send out and pardon and give them help!"

At the conclusion of his words, the entire court remained in solemn silence.

After serving two years in Stoney Mountain Penitentiary. Big Bear was released and died almost immediately in the winter of 1887-1888.

TOPICS FOR DISCUSSION

1. Have you ever had a dream that seemed to come true? Do you believe there are people who have visions of the future?

2. Big Bear wanted to remain free and independent, but, as the buffalo disappeared, he had to give in and accept government aid. Compare his situation to that of a worker today who, because jobs are disappearing, has to accept unemployment compensaton or welfare. Is the comparison valid?

3. Play Buffy St. Marie's recording of "Now That the Buffalo's Gone" and discuss it in relation to Big Bear and his tribe. Did Canada treat the Plains Indians fairly? Give reasons for your opinion.

4. Big Bear was caught in a changing society. Is society still changing? Do you feel caught between old ideas and new ones? Do you know people who feel uncomfortable with social changes and who talk of "the good old days"? Are you prepared for changes in the future? Can you imagine what the changes will be? Have you ever heard of *future shock*?

5. Was Big Bear a good leader? Did he care for his people? Do our leaders today care for us as much?

6. Did Big Bear deserve to go to prison? Explain the reasons for your viewpoint.

7. Big Bear's young men wanted to fight. Are young people today more likely to resort to physical violence than older people?

CREATIVE CHALLENGE

1. The railroad built by John A. Macdonald across Canada antagonized the Métis and Indians on the prairies. It was built with the help of Chinese labourers under intolerable conditions. Either investigate the building of the railroad and write an exposition based on the mistreatment of the Chinese Canadians or invent a fictional Chinese hero who was present and aided his or her people.

Chief Dan George from British Columbia has adapted to the modern world by becoming a Hollywood movie star, but he uses his new role to help his people and to teach others the values of his culture.

WILFRED GRENFELL
The Good Samaritan of Labrador

In the year 1885, a young medical student wandered into a revival meeting featuring the famous American evangelists Moody and Sankey. The young Englishman, son of an Anglican clergyman, later recalled the experience,

"When I left, it was with a determination either to make religion a real effort to do what I thought Christ would do in my place as a doctor, or frankly abandon it."

On graduating, Dr. Grenfell joined a church-sponsored mission where, for five years, he ministered to fishing fleets from Iceland to the Bay of Biscay. In 1892, he crossed the Atlantic and landed on "Starvation Coast", Labrador. There he discovered 5 000 Indians, Eskimos and white "Liveyeres" spread over 1600 km of barren, subarctic tundra without any modern medicine, hospital facilities, or doctors.

The people depended on ancient superstitions. Both whites and Eskimos treated diphtheria by tying split herring around their necks. They blew sugar into children's diseased eyes in an attempt to cure them, and mixed strange potions. Diet was not sufficient either. Grenfell learned of a "Liveyere" who had killed himself and his three youngest children in order that his wife and two eldest would have enough food to survive the winter.

Dr. Grenfell immediately went on speaking tours throughout Newfoundland and Canada, collecting cash and urging his fellow doctors to bring relief to Labrador. To the natives on the bleak coast he seemed like a miracle worker, as he caused the blind to see again (with a simple cataract operation) and made the lame walk (following surgery on an ingrown toenail). He brought medical knowledge to a population where tuberculosis killed one adult in three, and where one-third of the babies died. The doctor, wrapped in Eskimo furs and sleeping on the trail in temperatures way below freezing, made his rounds on dog-sleds, ships, and snowshoes, often operating by lantern light in tents and igloos.

On Easter Sunday, 1908, word came to Grenfell that a boy was seriously ill at Brent Island. The doctor left immediately, alone in his dogsled, and took a shortcut across a frozen bay. However, he never reached the other side because his Eskimo "komatik" fell through the ice. He managed to cut his huskies free of the sinking sled and they all took refuge on a floating island of ice, frozen and nearly paralyzed by the wet ordeal. He had to kill and skin three of the dogs in order to wrap himself in their bloody furs and stay alive. As the ice float began to drift out to open sea, he curled up beside the other dogs to sleep. The next morning he waved his shirt frantically at the fading coastline, and luckily a fisherman on a cliff top looking for seals through a tele-

Sir Wilfred Grenfell.

scope saw him. Although his hands and feet were frozen, he apologized to his rescuers, "I'm sorry to put you to all this bother."

Grenfell brought more than medicine to Labrador. Local traders were giving credit to the fishermen and trappers only to claim their catches and pelts at a discount; the doctor helped to establish ten co-operative stores by lending his schooner and his money to the natives. The Catholics, Methodists, Anglicans and Salvation Army competed for students in their sectarian schools; Grenfell opened schools available to everyone and imported teachers for them. He encouraged cottage industries based on handcrafts, and he founded two orphanages. Doctors, nurses, and professional people around the world were inspired by the Labrador missionary, and volunteers came by the hundreds to help him in his struggle against disease and poverty. To aid him, the International Grenfell Association was formed in 1912. Dr. Grenfell retired from superintendent of his mission in 1937 at the age of seventy-two because he explained sadly, "I'm getting too old to drive dog-teams."

TOPICS FOR DISCUSSION
1. Do you know of anyone who, like Dr. Grenfell, devotes his or her life entirely to helping others?
2. Are there any places in Canada or the world today where people are still in need of medical help?
3. Have you ever travelled by dog-sled or slept outside in the middle of winter? Would you like to experience either of these adventures?
4. Has anyone ever had to come to your rescue or did you ever rescue anyone?
5. Do your friends or family have ancient "cures" and "prescriptions" which they use to fight ailments (i.e. to rid themselves of colds, warts, hiccups, etc.)?

CREATIVE CHALLENGE
Dr. Grenfell was a very religious person. Write an exposition in which you explain your own religion or philosophy. Do you react the same to people who are friendly, rich, hostile, lazy, weak, dishonest or poor? What do you wish to gain from life? Do you want power, happiness, money, respect, security, a family, independence, etc.?

Organize your thoughts clearly. Your basic theme should be obvious, each statement should logically relate to the whole, and your opinion or attitude should be emphasized through arrangement or literary devices.

TEKAHIONWAKE

The Mohawk Poet-Princess

Tekahionwake was born on the Six Nations Indian Reserve on the Grand River, which had been established by the great hero Joseph Brant. Her father was head chief of her tribe, and her mother was an English woman. As a child Tekahionwake loved poetry. She would often make up jingles about her pet dogs and cats and would easily memorize poems that were read to her. When a friend of her family was taking a trip to a distant city and asked the four-year-old child what she would like as a present, she replied instantly, "Verses, please."

Although she never went to high school or college, by twelve years of age the Mohawk princess was writing poetry and had read every line of Scott and Longfellow, and most of Byron and Shakespeare. She grew up on the Indian Reserve enjoying poetry and canoeing. As a canoeist her love of adventure and nature caused her to run strange rivers, cross lonely lakes, and camp alone in the wilderness of Canada. Once she traveled 1300 km up the Caribou trail to the gold fields. When she was still young her father was tragically murdered, beaten to death by bootleggers he had exposed.

Then one evening in 1892 she was invited to a poetic reading in Toronto. The evening of poets dragged until the Indian poet-princess was introduced.

"She glided rather than walked and her sinewy form was the essence of gracefulness. . .then she gave her first rendition of her "Cry from an Indian Wife" (a poem which shows the Indian's side of the North-West Rebellion). Thrilling was the effect, dramatic the appeal of this dark-hued girl who seemed to personify her race."

She was greeted with tremendous applause from the audience and was the only poet to receive an encore that evening. The Toronto papers demanded to hear more and so she gave a recital two weeks later, for which she wrote her best known poem, "The Song my Paddle Sings".

She was a natural entertainer and for the next twenty years displayed her passion, pride and intensity to captivated audiences in Europe and North America. During the first season she covered fifty towns and cities, giving over one hundred and twenty-five performances. By 1906, when she travelled again to England, she carried letters of introduction from Sir Wilfrid Laurier, Prime Minister of Canada.

As a platform performer, she would appear in a scarlet blanket, wearing silver Mohawk brooches, a necklace of cinnamon bear claws, a buckskin dress and a dagger, which was used as a prop in one of her passionate love poems.

Although most Canadians remember her today as Pauline Johnson, she liked to be called by her Indian name. She once explained:

"There are those who think they pay me a compliment by saying I am just like a white woman. I am an Indian and my aim, my joy and my pride is to sing the glories of my own people. Ours was the race that gave the world its measure of heroism, its standard of physical prowess. Ours was the race that taught the world that avarice veiled by any other name is a crime and ours was the faith that taught men to love without greed and to die without fear."

Tekahionwake, in the tradition of her people, died without fear in the city of her chosen retirement, Vancouver, B.C. For two years she heroically fought a losing battle against the pains of cancer and, when told by her doctor that she would die, wrote a poem entitled, "And He Said Fight On", in which she says:

*"Time and its ally, dark disarmament have compassed me about;
Have massed their armies and on battle bent
My forces put to rout,
But though I fight alone, and fall and die,
Talk terms of Peace? Not I."*

At her funeral, a large crowd of people silently lined Georgia Street, in Vancouver, standing all through the service until the funeral cortege had passed on its way to Stanley Park, where a simple stone surrounded by rustic palings marked her grave. On the stone was carved simply, "Pauline".

Her biographer, Marcus Van Steen, described her contribution to Canada.

"Miss Johnson swept into those remote communities like a vigorous and refreshing wind from civilization, bringing not only entertainment but a vision of

Canada stretching from sea to sea. She preached the gospel of a united Canada at a time when the concepts of Canada had still not encompassed the separate and rival concept of Ontario, British Columbia, Nova Scotia or even more limited regions. . ."

TOPICS FOR DISCUSSION
1. Pauline Johnson objected to people saying she was just like a white woman. Are there Canadians today whom you would insult by such a statement?
2. What statements do people make, intending to be considerate or complimentary to you, which you find insulting?
3. If you were told by your doctor that you were going to die, how would you react?
4. Tekahionwake's two greatest pleasures were poetry and canoeing. Which one would you prefer? Why?
5. Has Canada outgrown the need for someone like Pauline Johnson, who "preached the gospel of a united Canada"?
6. If Pauline Johnson lived today, she would have the use of records, radio, T.V., movies, etc. Compare her to Buffy St. Marie. Play some records of Buffy's and compare them with the poems of Pauline. What are the similarities? What are the differences?

CREATIVE CHALLENGES
1. If there are some good actresses in your class, have them dress in Indian style like Tekahionwake and read one of her poems, as she would, with passion.
2. Write a poem of your own that indicates your own pride in Canada or in your racial origins and read it dramatically to the class.

JAMES NAISMITH

The Inventor of Basketball

In 1870, at the age of nine, James Naismith and his older brother became orphans suddenly when their parents died of typhoid. They were left alone on the family farm in Lanark County, three kilometres from Almonte, Ontario, where they lived a rugged pioneer life in the bush with a Scottish Presbyterian atmosphere surrounding them. Although their uncle, Peter Young, took the boys in, James had to quit Almonte High School for three years to help support the family.

By the time James returned to complete his high school education, he had made the decision that the only real satisfaction he would ever derive from life was to help his fellow beings. For this reason he went on to McGill University and graduated in 1890 in theology. While studying to be a minister, he played centre for McGill's football team and participated in gymnastics, wrestling and, his favorite game, lacrosse. His unique talents for athletics and theology caused him to join the Y.M.C.A. and attend their training school in Springfield.

In the fall of 1891, he was working under Dr. Luther Halsey Gulick, an American pioneer in the field of physical education, who gave Naismith the assignment of inventing an indoor sport that would fill the time between the football and baseball seasons.

Naismith decided his game should use a large light ball. He wished to abolish rough physical contact, so he labelled such behavior as a "foul". Running with the ball would encourage tackling, so he decided the ball would be advanced by passing it (dribbling would be introduced later). If the goal were horizontal instead of vertical, he concluded, the players would be compelled to throw the ball in an arc; and force, which made for roughness, would be of no value. He decided to use a box at each end of the floor and to raise it above the player's heads to prevent them from physically blocking it with their bodies.

The first game was played in December, 1891, by Naismith's students and might have ended up being called "box ball" except that the janitor couldn't find any boxes. They substituted two baskets instead. The enthusiastic students wanted to name it "Naismith Ball", but the modest inventor only laughed and told them that that name would kill any game.

The game of "basketball" reflects the desire of a country boy to eliminate unnecessary injury in sports and to encourage brotherly co-operation among the participants rather than rivalry and hate. In his own words:

"If men will not be gentlemanly in their play, it is our place to encourage them to games that may be played by gentlemen in a manly way, and show them that science is superior to brute force. . ."

TOPICS FOR DISCUSSION

1. **What causes people like James Naismith to devote their lives to helping other human beings and worshipping God? Do you know such a person?**
2. **Naismith invented Basketball as a game that would eliminate brute force and encourage co-operation and skill. Do basketball players today play the sport in the spirit in which it was invented?**
3. **What do you think Naismith would say about professional basketball if he was alive today?**

CREATIVE CHALLENGE

Invent a new game of your own. Describe the equipment. Write out the rules and provide a diagram of the playing area, which includes the dimensions. Give some thought to the main objectives of your game and to which physical skills it aids. If possible, try playing the game with your friends or classmates. You must be careful to state your rules and objectives clearly.

An early game of basketball using an old peach basket.

GEORGE DIXON

"Little Chocolate"

George Dixon was only sixteen when he knocked out Young Johnson in the third round during a fight in his home town of Halifax. By the time he was seventeen, he had gone to Boston to become a professional boxer.

In 1890, he was matched against a well-known New Yorker, Cal McCarthy, at Washington Hall in Boston. The two men, wearing fifty-seven gram gloves, fought seventy rounds in four hours forty minutes to end in a draw, but "Little Chocolate" became known as a result of the bout. The next year in England he knocked out Nunc Wallace in the eighteenth round, to earn the world bantamweight title, and thus became the first black to win a world boxing championship.

Then, on July 8th, 1891, he moved up to the featherweight division when he knocked out Australia's Abe Attell in only five rounds, becoming the world champion in the heavier weight class. He fought off all challengers to his second world title successfully for six years, until he lost it in October of 1897. But he won it back the next year and held onto it until 1900.

Nat Fleisher, the dean of boxing, rated Dixon as the number-one bantam weight champion in the entire history of the sport, calling him "the greatest little fighter the black race has ever produced."

CANADIAN BOXING QUIZ

Match the names of the following Canadian boxers with their descriptions:

1. **Larry Gains**	a. A French-speaking Canadian nicknamed "Frenchy" from Toronto's Cabbagetown who became the world's flyweight champion.
2. **Lou Brouillard**	b. A tough 57 kg featherweight of Italian background who came out of Hamilton, Ontario, to win the National Boxing Association Championship.
3. **Johnny Coulon**	c. A Quebec-born boxer who won world titles in both the welterweight and middleweight divisions.
4. **Jackie Callura**	d. Although less than 152 cm tall and weighing only 50 kg, he won the world bantamweight championship and defended it for four years.
5. **Albert Belanger**	e. A Toronto heavyweight who won the British Empire Championship but was never able to contest the championship of the British Isles because he was black.
6. **Sam Langford**	f. Nicknamed "Lefty", this little boxer who used to be a jockey won a gold medal for Canada in bantamweight boxing during the 1932 Olympics.
7. **Jimmy McLarnin**	g. A Canadian heavyweight boxer from Nova Scotia called the "Boston Tar Baby" classified as one of the best ten heavyweights in the history of boxing, yet he died blind and in poverty.
8. **Jack Delany**	h. An Irishman from Vancouver who earned about a half million dollars during fifteen years of boxing as well as winning the welterweight title twice before he retired at age twenty-nine.
9. **Horace Gwynne**	i. A Canadian light heavyweight who won the world Championship in 1926.

RESEARCH CHALLENGE
Most Canadians don't realize how many boxing champions came from Canada. Can you discover the answers to the above quiz?

SUGGESTION
If you would like to read more about these or other Canadian athletes and also see photographs of them, look for a book entitled

Canada's Sporting Heroes, by Wise and Fisher, in your school or local library or order a copy from the General Publishing Company, Ltd. in Don Mills, Ontario.

TOMMY BURNS
Canada's Heavyweight Champion of the World

Noah, born in 1881 in a log cabin farm house near Hanover, Ontario, was the twelfth of thirteen children. His parents, Frederick and Sofa Brusso, were devout German Methodists, but despite their efforts to control him, Noah loved to fight. His ability with his fists earned him a legendary reputation in the small schoolyard, and he was particularly successful in Canada's two most rugged sports: hockey and lacrosse.

At an early age Noah shipped out on a passenger boat and, in the middle of Lake Erie, found himself in trouble with a burly second mate, whom the youngster beat into the deck. Two things were immediately obvious to the youth: first, he would have to get off the ship and, second, he should enter professional fighting, where his aggressive instincts could profit him. When they reached Detroit, he jumped ship and joined the Detroit Athletic Club, where he began his early training as a boxer.

For six months he exercised, bashing at heavy bags, boxing with his shadow, and skipping rope, until one fateful night he and his friends went to watch Jack Cowan, a local fighter. As Cowan arrived at ringside, he waved to his fans, leaped eagerly over the ropes and collapsed in a painful heap with a sprained ankle. Nineteen-year-old Noah was pushed by his comrades into the ring to take Cowan's place: he knocked out his first professional opponent in the fifth round. Five fights and five knockouts later he was middleweight champion of Michigan.

Because his choice of a career

upset his mother, Noah changed his name to the Irish-sounding Tommy Burns. Following one fight, Tommy and his seconds were kept in jail on charges of assault for three days while Ben O'Grady, Tommy's opponent, remained unconscious from the severe punishment he had received from Tommy's fists. With his growing reputation for brutality it was difficult to obtain a fight for the middleweight championship; his opponents were too timid. Then, in 1905, James Jeffries, the heavyweight champion of the world, retired, and his title was passed on to Marvin Hart, who looked around for an easy fight the first time he defended his title. Underestimating the young Canadian in the lighter weight class, he agreed to a title fight in Los Angeles.

As they met in the ring in February of 1906, Tommy Burns deliberately insulted and taunted Hart, until the big man lost his temper and chased wildly after his elusive antagonist while Tommy kept landing powerful and damaging punches. By the end of twenty-five rounds a Canadian was the new heavyweight champ, even though he had a mass of a mere 79 kg and stood only 170 cm. There also emerged a new boxing tactic — psychology — as Tommy's verbal attacks on his opponents became as famous as his fists.

Determined to prove he deserved the title despite the fact he is still to this day the shortest man in boxing history to hold the heavyweight crown, Burns went on a world tour to defend it. In San Diego he met two challengers on the same night

and beat both of them. Next he met Jim Flynn who was a solid puncher and who outweighed Tommy by fourteen kilograms, but he was knocked unconscious in the fifteenth round. Burns then beat the light heavyweight champion, Jack O'Brien, and knocked out Australia's Bill Squires in two minutes and twenty-eight seconds.

The flamboyant Tommy Burns headed for Europe, taking with him his overt self-confidence and his sharply critical tongue. The Marquis of Queensbury described the Canadian boxer:

"Burns was prepared to tell anyone who would listen that he was in a class by himself. As champion he was arrogance itself during the preliminaries leading up to his fight with Gunner Moir, the best English heavyweight available at that time. . . In view of his offensive conduct, it is not strange that for once the National Sporting Club members permitted partisanship to sway them. It was not so much a case of plumping for Moir as it was a devout hope that the braggart and mannerless visitor should be taught a salutary lesson. Unhappily, the Gunner was not equal to the task; Burns was too good for him, scoring a knockout in the tenth round."

Another English fighter, Jim Palmer, was knocked unconscious by the fourth round, and Tommy humiliated the Irish champion, Jim Roche, in a match that is still the shortest heavyweight title defence on record — the Irishman went down early in the first round in front of a home-town Dublin crowd. In Paris, Burns won twice again with knockouts. During two years and nine months, Burns defended his world crown ten times, more than any other champion for such a short space of time. In a career of sixty fights he lost only four.

It was a giant American Negro who took the little Canadian's title away from him. Jack Johnson, who stood 183 cm and weighed 93 kg, followed Tommy Burns to Australia and met him in the ring. By the fourteenth round the police stopped the fight, because Tommy refused to collapse under the powerful blows of the challenger even though it was obvious to all that he had finally met his match.

In later years Tommy Burns became an evangelist, reverting to the religious instruction of his youth, and it was during a tour that he died of a heart attack in Vancouver, B.C., at seventy-three years of age.

TOPICS FOR DISCUSSION
1. Although Tommy Burns was one of the most vicious and insulting boxers in history, he reverted to God and religion in later years. How would you explain this contradiction in his personality?
2. Should the brutal sport of boxing be banned in a civilized society?
3. Are there boxers or athletes today who taunt and jeer their opponents in order to unsettle them psychologically? Is this the way a good sportsperson should behave?
4. Would it be possible for a Canadian boxer to become heavyweight champion today? Explain.

CREATIVE CHALLENGES
1. Every sport has a jargon or slang language used to describe it.
a. What nouns are used to describe the various blows or types of punches in a boxing match?
b. What verbs are used by sports writers to indicate that one team defeated another?
c. List several sports and then indicate which phrases or expressions are associated with each one.
2. Write a satirical play by play description of a sports event where the announcer confuses the traditional language used to describe it.
3. Write a description of a sports event being played on another planet. Invent a name for the unusual game and also imaginative and original expressions to describe it.

LUCY MAUD MONTGOMERY
The Island Girl

Lucy was born in 1874 on the North Shore of Prince Edward Island. Twenty-one months after her birth, her mother died, and her father left her in the care of her grandparents while he set out for Western Canada.

The young girl grew up in the sheltered, Island community of Cavendish, but her imagination and ambitions knew no limits. By the age of eleven she was sending her first manuscript to an American magazine. It was rejected, but she continued to write and send her material to magazines and newspapers until a verse-narrative reworking of a P.E.I. legend, was published when she was fourteen years old.

During the early years she received only five or ten dollars for her articles, but she was determined to make a living as a writer. She became a teacher, and every morning, from six to seven, she would write by lamplight in the old farmhouse where she boarded, sitting on her feet to keep them warm. When her grandfather died, she stayed with her grandmother for thirteen years, writing to support them both. Only after the old woman died did she feel free to marry.

In 1904, she wrote *Anne of Green Gables,* a novel that still captures the imagination and emotions of young people. The central character of this book, a red-haired, freckled orphan girl, was to become Canada's greatest fictional heroine. The dreams and anxieties of adolescent girls are personified in Anne, and "the Island" setting is a mythical world of the soul. Although the

Maud Montgomery, a young woman of twenty-five.

now-famous novel was at first rejected by publishing companies, in 1906 it was put into print and became an immediate success. The readers and fans of *Anne of Green Gables* demanded more, and Lucy Maud Montgomery spent the rest of her life writing sequel after sequel to satisfy them.

Many plays and Hollywood movies have been produced based on the Prince Edward Island girl and her adventures, which symbolize so perfectly the pleasures and pains of growing up. Although Lucy died in 1942 and was buried in Cavendish, the people of P.E.I., Canada, and the world have never forgotten her nor her fictional creations.

Maud Montgomery at fourteen.

TOPICS FOR DISCUSSION
1. Only after her grandmother died did Lucy marry and raise a family. Would you wait thirteen years to marry because of family obligations? Explain why or why not.

2. What do you think was the main reason that Lucy became a world-famous novelist? Do your friends and classmates agree with you?
3. Today on Prince Edward Island, the old "Green Gables" house is a tourist attraction, a statue of Lucy stands in memory and plays based on her famous novels are performed as part of an Island festival. Have you ever visited P.E.I.? Would you like to see it one day?
4. Who is the best Canadian author today? Explain clearly the reasons for your choice.

RESEARCH CHALLENGES
1. Read one of the books written by Lucy Maud Montgomery and then write a book report on it.
2. The first novel in Canada was written by a woman, Frances Brooke, between 1763 and 1768. It was called *The History of Emily Montague.* What can you discover about the book and the novelist?
3. Mazo De La Roche is another famous Canadian author. Her books were translated into fourteen languages and sold more than twelve million copies. Read one and write an explanation of why you believe it was so popular.

J. A. D. McCURDY AND "CASEY" BALDWIN
Canada's First Pilots

Canadian aviation was born in the hills of Cape Breton. There, in the small town of Baddeck, Nova Scotia, lived the famous Alexander Graham Bell, who had invented the telephone in 1876 and who has been called "the father of aviation in Canada".

In the year 1906, the white-bearded Bell could be seen flying strange, honeycomb-shaped kites on the hillsides. His "tetrahedral" kites (meaning they had four triangular faces) were highly stable in the air. When young John McCurdy, nineteen-year-old son of a local newspaper editor, introduced his fellow engineering graduate from the University of Toronto, "Casey" Baldwin, to Bell, both the young men became intrigued by the kite experiments. By the summer of 1907, they were aiding the old inventor, with their engineering knowledge, to place a gasoline engine in one of his kites for a powered flight.

One evening as they sat comfortably around the fireplace discussing the problems of aviation with Glenn Curtiss, a motorcycle racer and manufacturer from New York who had built an engine for Bell, and with Lieut. Thomas Selfridge, an American army officer, Mrs. Bell offered to finance an association to develop a flying machine. Thus, at the suggestion of Alexander's wife, the Aerial Experiment Association was formed and registered at Halifax on October 1, 1907. Its objective was "the construction of a practical aeroplane or flying machine driven through the air by its own power, and carrying a man."

Their first accomplishment was on Bras d'or Lake on December 6,

The AEA: Glenn Curtiss, Casey Baldwin, Dr. Bell, Thomas Selfridge, and J.A.D. McCurdy.

J.A.D. McCurdy in the Silver Dart, February, 1909.

1907, when Bell's tetrahedral cell kite, with Selfridge in it, was pulled behind a steamer and rose fifty-one metres above the water. Next they built a small box-kite biplane glider out of bamboo and muslin, which was balanced by the pilot swinging his arms through a section in the middle of the bottom wing. A total of fifty flights were made, always landing softly on snow-covered countryside to cushion the impact. Then they decided to build real airplanes; each member of the A.E.A. would design his own.

The "Red Wing" was the first, designed by Selfridge with an engine built by Curtiss from motorcycle cylinders. It had runners rather than wheels, and when Baldwin flew it over the frozen surface of nearby Lake Keula on March 12, 1908, he became the first Canadian to fly an airplane. Five days later due to lack of lateral control, it crashed during a second flight.

Baldwin climbed from the wreck and designed his own plane. His "White Wing" included four small wings, or ailerons, hinged to the leading edge of the wing tips and controlled with connecting wires to a shoulder yoke fitted on the pilot, which gave it lateral control. If the machine tipped, the pilot could simply lean to the high side. This would move the hinged flaps, to change the angle that the wind struck the wing surface, thus altering the "lift" effect to allow level flight again. The White Wing was the first flying machine to have ailerons for lateral control, and on May 18, 1908, Baldwin flew it a distance of eighty-five metres at a height of three metres. Curtiss and McCurdy also flew for the first time in the White Wing.

The *Scientific American* Trophy was offered to the first airplane to fly a distance of one kilometre. Curtiss designed the "June Bug", and on July 4, 1908, he flew almost two kilometres at a speed of fifty-five kilometres an hour to win the prize.

Finally came McCurdy's invention, the "Silver Dart", which was completed in December, 1908. The other planes had been flown in the United States, but now for the first time in Canada, at Baddeck, Nova Scotia, a plane would fly through the air. On February 23, 1909, the residents of the tiny community flocked onto the frozen bay, many on skates, to observe the unusual and historic spectacle. McCurdy, in a knitted woollen helmet, slipped into the Silver Dart and began to

Baldwin and McCurdy in later years.

warm up its fifty-horsepower engine. Slowly the machine moved across the ice surface, rose gracefully, flew for one kilometre at a height of three to ten metres, and dropped to a controlled stop. It was the first flight in Canada and the first flight in the British Commonwealth.

Shortly after the flight of the Silver Dart, the A.E.A. was disbanded. In 1908, Selfridge had been called back to the U.S.A. to be a military observer at the flying trials of Orville Wright, and he became the first victim to die in an airplane disaster when Wright's plane crashed. Curtiss also returned to the U.S.A., where he became a famous airplane builder.

The Canadians, Baldwin and McCurdy, formed Canada's first aircraft plant. Bell lent them the

money and gave them the space to open their factory. Baldwin and McCurdy flew together to complete the first passenger flight in Canada at Camp Petawawa, and they established many early aviation records.

When McCurdy left to go barnstorming in the U.S.A., Baldwin settled down to spend the rest of his life at Baddeck, where he and Bell worked as a team until Bell's death in 1922. They experimented with hydrofoils for boats and by 1919 built a craft that set a world's water speed record of 114.04 km/hr. In Nova Scotia, Baldwin became a well-respected figure and eventually a member of the legislature.

McCurdy, who was successful as an aircraft manufacturer, was also honored by his country. He was appointed as assistant director general

of aircraft production in the federal Department of Munitions and Supply during World War II, and was lieutenant-governor of Nova Scotia from 1947 to 1952.

TOPICS FOR DISCUSSION
1. Between the late fall of 1909 and the spring of 1911, thirty-five early aviators crashed to their deaths in primitive flying machines. What activities today would be equally dangerous?
2. Have you ever flown in an airplane? Have you ridden in a helicopter? Have you experienced the thrill of gliding? Have you parachuted or sky-dived? If you have not tried any of the above, is it because you don't want to or because you haven't had the opportunity yet?

3. J. A. D. McCurdy and "Casey" Baldwin tried to convince Canada's Militia Minister Sam Hughes of the military value of the airplane, but they were told it was "an invention of the devil" with no place in a nation's defence. Is there any military weapon today that you would consider an invention of the devil?

CREATIVE CHALLENGES
1. Try to build and fly a tetrahedral kite, similar to the one used by Alexander Graham Bell and his associates during their early experiments.

2. Write a short science fiction story describing the first Canadian to fly to another planet or galaxy.
3. The members of the Aerial Experiment Association were not the only ones in Canada experimenting with the concept of air travel, although they were the most successful. Below are some other Canadians who were attempting to fly in those early years. Prepare a brief research essay on one of them.
a) Three Underwood brothers on their farm near Stettler, Alberta.
b) William Gibson of Balgonie, Saskatchewan.

c) Two brothers, William and Winston Templeton, and their cousin William McMullen, in British Columbia.
d) Another brother team, George and "Ace" Pepper, at Davidson, Saskatchewan.
e) William Straith of Brandon, Manitoba.
4. Nova Scotia honoured McCurdy by appointing him to the position of lieutenant-governor of the province. Who is the lieutenant-governor of your province today? What does a lieutenant-governor do?

Pauline McGibbon was the first woman to become Lieutenant-Governor of Ontario.

TOM LONGBOAT
The World's Best Distance Runner

Two years after the 1885 rebellion in western Canada, an Onandaga Indian boy was born on the Six Nations Indian Reserve in Ontario that had been founded by Joseph Brant.

His mother, speaking through an interpreter, described his early interest in running:

"Tommy practiced running for two years on the reservation. He run every morning. He run every night. He run down to the Long House and get beaten. He come back and run some more. Soon he run five miles easy in 23½ minutes. Next time we have five-mile race here, Tommy win by nearly quarter of mile."

The "five-mile race" described by Tom's mother was the annual twenty-fourth of May race at the Caledonia Fair on the edge of the reserve. By 1906 he was out-running a horse around a nineteen kilometre course.

In 1906, Tom Longboat, a lanky nineteen-year-old, stood in a baggy bathing suit and dirty sneakers at the starting line of the Hamilton Round-the-Bay Race, suffering abuse and ridicule from the onlookers who were amused at his comical appearance. As the race began, Tom's running style appeared slow. His feet kicked awkwardly to the side and he held his arms in an odd position. After following the experienced English marathoner, John Marsh, for a long stretch, the Indian suddenly "cut loose and left Marsh as if he had been standing" to win the race by three minutes.

Recognizing the potential for making money, opportunists persuaded Tommy to live at Toronto's West End Y.M.C.A. and train for the 1907 Boston Marathon. In 1906, he won the twenty-four kilometre marathon at the C.N.E. against a field of sixty-two. The next year he raced on the tough, hilly course of the Boston Marathon against 125 opponents, battling snow, rain and slush to set a record time of 2:24:24 hours, a record never beaten until the course was made easier. On his return to Toronto, gigantic crowds turned out at Union Station to escort Tom in a torchlight procession to City Hall, where he was given a gold medal and was the subject of a speech by the mayor.

The Indian hero was out of his environment. He had difficulty maintaining his emotional balance. Discovered drinking and smoking, he was suspended from the Y.M.C.A. Tom Flanagan and Jim O'Rourke, two Toronto Irishmen who owned the Grand Central Hotel, took him in and began to

train him. But in November, 1907, Tom Longboat was declared a professional by the president of the U.S. Amateur Athletic Union, who said he "has been a professional from the time he began his athletic career. He has always been in the hands of a manager . . . he is taken from town to town . . . with bands and carriages and silk hats . . . He ran all kinds of races at country fairs for money."

The Canadian public immediately rebelled in an anti-American sentiment. The Irish-Canadian Athletic Club, formed by Flanagan and O'Rourke, named Tom Longboat the owner of a cigar store on King Street in Toronto to retain his amateur status. As a result, he was allowed to run in the Olympic games of 1908. When the popular Canadian runner slowed down and came to a halt without finishing the race, speculation ran high that he had been doped or that Flanagan and the other Irishman who were managing him had collected $100 000 on bets against him. Meanwhile, inside the stadium at the finish line, Dorando Pietri of Italy was disqualified when well-meaning officials aided him over the finish line, and the race was given to Johnny Hayes of the U.S.

The fiasco at the Olympics sent loud demands from around the world for a rematch. Dorando and Hayes turned professional and staged a re-run at Madison Square Garden in New York. Dorando won. Public interest in racing was high. Tom Longboat had continued to win amateur events, including his third consecutive win in the Ward Marathon against 153 competitors. Then he turned professional and was matched against Dorando Pietri of Italy in Madison Square Garden on December 15, 1908. Longboat won. Two weeks after the victory, he married Lauretta Maracle and was given a wedding reception by his Toronto fans on the stage of Massey Hall. Alfie Shrubb, an English professional, challenged Longboat to a race. Immediately, one of the most famous rivalries in sporting history began to develop, and it culminated in "the race of the century" at Madison Square Garden. Longboat was accompanied by Indian Chiefs in traditional dress and a uniformed mountie as he arrived to race against Alfie Shrubb. At twenty-four kilometres the Englishman was seventy-two metres ahead, but Longboat began to close the distance until he passed him at the thirty-ninth kilometre. Shrubb immediately collapsed and the Onandagan completed the race victorious, to be acknowledged as the world's best distance runner.

Then, to Tom's humiliation and distress, Flanagan sold his contract to an American promoter for $2 000.

"He sold me just like a racehorse!" complained Tom.

"He refuses to train properly and just generally went prima donna on me," countered Flanagan.

At twenty-one, when most people are just starting out in life, Tom was beginning his decline. Within a few months he was re-sold for $700. There followed a series of exciting contests against Shrubb, and Tom set a new twenty-four kilometre record on Toronto Island. But in 1911 in Toronto, he was given a suspended sentence for drunkenness and rumours of his drinking grew.

When Tom enlisted in the Canadian Army and served overseas during the First World War, he was falsely reported killed. He returned home to find that his wife had remarried. His racing money had long disappeared; he drifted from job to job, until, in 1927, he was a helper on a Toronto garbage wagon.

Tom Longboat died in 1949, back on the Six Nations Reserve.

TOPICS FOR DISCUSSION
1. Tom Longboat has been described as "a victim of his own talents, the rapaciousness of promotors, the short-lived worship of the public, and his vulnerability to the corruptions of white society". Do you agree with all or any of

these observations? Do you have any opinions of your own about the life of Tom Longboat?

2. Like many athletes, Tom had to accept a role as a non-hero after being the pride of a nation. What effect could this drastic change have on an individual? How would you deal with it yourself? Is it possible for a person to accept a change from an active life to an inactive one? Is this the same change a senior citizen must accept?

CREATIVE CHALLENGES

1. Tom Longboat was a Canadian superstar. Is it a national disgrace that his country allowed him to end up as a garbage collector? Should Canada give special treatment to people who become famous or should they be left to survive on their own like everyone else? Write an exposition in which you indicate what responsibility a country has to its heroes and heroines.

2. There is a style of writing — "stream of consciousness" — in which there is a constant flow of thoughts presented to the reader in no organized fashion. They represent the wandering thoughts of a character in a narrative while he or she is engaged in an activity. Write down what you imagine to be the thoughts of Tom Longboat as he runs a race or collects the garbage.

3. The following four Canadians also became world famous runners. Investigate one of them or a current Canadian track star whom you admire. Write a poem about the person. What type of poem would best suit the person? — a narrative poem? — a descriptive lyric? — a reflective lyric? — a sonnet?

Percy Williams.

Johnny Miles.

William J. Sherring.

Harry Jerome.

JOE BOYLE

"The Uncrowned King of Rumania"

Joe, a Confederation-year baby, grew up in Woodstock, Ontario, where, as a boy, he rode his father's thoroughbred racing horses and enjoyed working around the stables more than going to school. Then, at the age of seventeen, he suddenly disappeared, leaving behind him his school, his home, and a hurriedly scrawled note: "I have gone to sea. Don't worry about me. Joe."

When he eventually returned from his escapades at sea, he was twenty-one years old. He met an attractive divorcee from New York and married her three days later.

Within less than five years he was a successful horse-feed merchant, owned a home in the country and was the father of four children. Most men would have been content with a prosperous business and with watching the children ride their ponies, but not Joe Boyle. At thirty years of age he left his wealth to his family and disappeared again, this time to the gold fields in Canada's frozen north.

Dawson City in 1898 was a wide open town. Joe, who arrived with only fifty cents in his pocket, first earned a meagre grubstake as sparring partner to "The Sydney Cornstalk", Frank Slavin, the Australian heavyweight champion of the British Empire.

Looking around him, Joe noticed that every Klondike sourdough had an equal-sized claim on which he panned for gold, and that each creekbed claim had a frontage of 150 m. Travelling to Ottawa with his Siwash guide, a team of huskies, a poke of gold nuggets and a plan to build the largest gold dredges in the

world, Boyle talked the government into granting him a huge downstream lease covering ninety-seven square kilometres of the Klondike River Valley, with a frontage thirteen kilometres long. It was the greatest mining coup of the day and Joe financed it with Rothschild money.

By 1914, when war broke out in Europe, Joe was a millionaire, but, at the age of forty-seven, he was too old for military service. Undaunted, he created his own private army, which he personally financed and called "Boyle's Yukon Machine Gun Battery". Each of the fifty men stood over one hundred and eighty-three centimetres tall and were crack shots. In London Boyle was named an honorary lieutenant-colonel, but no one knew what to do with the unorthodox Canadian soldier of for-

tune, who definitely didn't fit into the Canadian military establishment. Then the British Transport Mission found the perfect challenge for a man to whom nothing was impossible.

Russia's railroad system had broken down. The ally country was in the midst of both winter and revolution. Because the trains couldn't move, supplies and food needed desperately on the Eastern front were sitting dormant. Colonel Boyle accepted the challenge and with the talent that caused his daughter, Flora, to describe him as a "man with a positive genius for getting things done," he mobilized the Russian trains.

Fate led Joe Boyle to Rumania, a small, starving country squashed between German and Russian troops. The royal court had fled from Bucharest to Jassy, and it was at Jassy that Joe met English-born Queen Marie, struggling to survive against the hardships of war. From that moment he dedicated the rest of his life to helping Rumania and its queen.

It was now late in 1917, and the Bolsheviks had seized power. In Moscow, Boyle commandeered a train and set out to return the Rumanian treasury and crown jewels to Jassy, where Queen Marie waited. Bolshevik guerillas frightened the engineer and fireman into deserting, so Joe was forced to drive the locomotive himself, aided only by an English spy who shovelled coal into the fire-box. The gigantic Canadian, with badges of Klondike gold on his khaki uniform and wearing cavalry boots,

Rumania's Queen Marie at her coronation.

brought the royal fortune home to Queen Marie and arranged a peace treaty between Royalist Rumania and Leninist Russia.

Because he was attached to no army unit, Joe Boyle issued his own orders and followed his own independent course of action. During one adventure, he sailed across the Black Sea, risking his freedom and safety to rescue fifty Rumanian hostages. On another occasion he went to Ekaterinburg to visit the imprisoned Czar Nicholas II. Boyle offered to arrange an escape for the Russian royal family, but the Czar refused to leave his homeland, and within six months he and his entire family were executed by the Communist rebels.

When World War I ended, Joe Boyle stayed in Rumania, where he became the constant companion of Queen Marie. The chivalrous Canadian colonel, who had once been a bouncer in Swiftwater Bill Gates' famous Monte Carlo Saloon, was now the talk of Europe as whispers of his romantic attachment with the Queen gained him the title of "the uncrowned king of Rumania".

Joe Boyle's newest interests were the rich Rumanian oil fields at

Ploesti, and it was during a business trip on a flight across Europe that he suffered a stroke that left him paralyzed. Forced to live the life of an invalid, he retired to the home of an old Yukon friend in England. In his absence from Canada his gold industry had collapsed, so when he died in 1923, he was penniless.

Queen Marie designed the headstone for his grave. On it was carved her name, "Marie", and two lines from Robert Service's famous poem,

"A man with the heart of a Viking
And the simple faith of a child."

TOPICS FOR DISCUSSION
1. Would it still be possible for someone to leave school and home as Joe Boyle did, and become a millionaire?
2. By the age of thirty, Joe had accomplished most people's dreams. Why do you think he left his family and fortune to go to the Klondike?
3. If you were forty-seven years old, a millionaire, and too old for military service, would you form your own army? Explain why or why not.
4. What is your personal opinion of Joe Boyle? Would you wish to be

his friend? Explain.
5. Which incidents in this story suggest that, although Joe became a millionaire, he was not interested in money?

CREATIVE CHALLENGES
1. Invent a conversation between the following people. Develop the conversation so that it ends in a dramatic emotional moment.
a) Joe Boyle and his parents before Joe ran off to sea.
b) Joe Boyle and his wife before Joe left for the Klondike.
c) Joe Boyle and the recruiting officer who refused to let him join the regular army.
d) Joe Boyle and Queen Marie before Joe retired to England.
e) Two gossips discussing "the uncrowned king".
2. Robert Service created in his poetry some of the most famous fictional personalities in Canadian literature. Read the poems *The Shooting of Dan McGrew* and *The Cremation of Sam McGee* and then:
a) Choose members of the class to dramatize scenes from them.
b) Draw a cartoon figure representing either Dan McGrew or Sam McGee.
c) Write a poem of your own in which you create a fictional hero or heroine as Robert Service did.

Joe Boyle's grave.

MARY PICKFORD

America's Sweetheart

The name of the Toronto play production was "Silver King", and a five-year-old actress in golden ringlets stole the show. She was Gladys Smith, and she grew up in the rough slum area around University Avenue in Toronto. At age ten, the poor, fatherless girl, who had had only one year of education at Louisa Public School, left Toronto for a career on the stage.

Her dream was to act on Broadway, and at thirteen years of age, she waited outside stage-producer David Belasco's office until he gave her an interview, a part in a play, and a new stage name, Mary Pickford.

In 1909, Mary's mother tried to convince her daughter to leave the New York stage for the new media, called "flickers", which was just starting on the west coast of the United States. Mary at first was uncertain but, when her mother allowed her to have her first pair of silk stockings and high-heeled shoes, she agreed to talk with D. W. Griffith at Biograph Studio. Griffith told her that she was too short and too fat, but he offered her five dollars per day to make her first two-day film. Mary refused the offer, demanded ten dollars per day and got it. She continued to have constant conflicts with Griffith, who called her a "hellcat". After one of his insulting criticisms in the midst of a film production, Mary attacked and bit him.

Owen Moore, her leading man, fell in love with Mary, who was only seventeen, and the two were secretly married. The young girl found herself burdened with an

alcoholic husband while trying to build her own future. She became the first silent screen star to show, through facial close-ups, her inward emotions rather than by flinging her arms in the air. However, the film backers objected and told Griffith that they were paying to see a whole body on the screen.

By the time she was nineteen, Mary Pickford was billed as "America's Sweetheart", and a myth was born. The poverty she had experienced in her youth left a scar, and she demanded increasingly higher salaries as her popularity soared. In January of 1914, she was earning $500 per week at Famous Players. By February, her salary had doubled to $1000 per week, and a year later had climbed to $4000. Then, in June of 1916, she signed a contract for $10 000 per week payable on Mondays. Still not content, she switched studios, going to First National a year later, where she received $350 000 per picture. It was originally the girl from the slums of Toronto who created the aura of luxury and wealth in the fast developing Hollywood dream factory.

During World War I, Mary, along with Charlie Chaplin and Douglas Fairbanks Sr., toured the United States raising money for war bonds, and in one single day in Pittsburgh raised five million dollars for the war effort. After the war the eccentric trio joined up with Griffith and formed United Artists movie company. Most observers at the time were skeptical and one remarked, "The asylum is now in the hands of the maniacs."

When Mary Pickford divorced Owen Moore to marry Douglas Fair-banks, North American fans were shocked and outraged, but during their European honeymoon they were cheered and greeted as "the perfect couple". When they returned, North American fans had also accepted the "marriage of god and goddess", and the couple built a Hollywood shrine that they called "Pick Fair" mansion.

Mary's wealth and fame did not bring her happiness. Her new husband found another woman who was more attractive than she, and death claimed Mary's mother, brother and sister within a few short years. In 1929, she played in her first talking picture, "Coquette", and won an Academy Award, but she soon afterward divorced Fairbanks and retired from motion pictures. When she left the screen, she bought the rights to all her old silent movies and refused to release them. Most people today have no memory of Mary Pickford, because she, in her well-guarded retirement, was the only one who had access to the films that made her one of Hollywood's most famous actresses. She died in 1979.

TOPICS FOR DISCUSSION
1. Do you ever daydream of becoming a famous actress or actor? Do most people have such fantasies?
2. Is it still possible for a Canadian to become a film star? Are there any Canadians who are film stars today?
3. If you were earning $4 000 per week, what would you do with the money?
4. Why do you think Mary Pickford kept her old films for herself only? If you were in her place,

would you have done the same?
5. In the first four years that the Academy Awards existed, three Canadian women won the prize as "Best Actress". Who were the other Canadian actresses who won academy awards in those early years?
6. What type of person becomes an actress or actor? Are you a good actress or actor?
7. Why do people enjoy watching films, plays, television, etc.? Do the viewers gain anything of value from the experience?
8. Should students today study films and television as seriously as plays and novels? Explain the reasons for your opinion.

CREATIVE CHALLENGES
1. Imagine you have won an Academy Award. Describe the moments before they announce your name, your acceptance of the award and your feelings afterward.
2. Make your own short silent movie using 8 mm film. Plan how you can tell the story without the use of dialogue.
3. Obtain a short film from your local library or use a T.V. show. Play the film or television show without the sound track and invent your own dialogue and plot for the actors and actresses.
4. Visit with some senior citizens and ask them about their memories of Mary Pickford.
5. Write a description of your favourite actress or actor today. Explain clearly what qualities they have that you admire.

THE BRAVEST SOLDIERS IN THE EMPIRE

The Victoria Cross is the most prestigious award given by Britain to its heroes; ninety-four Canadians have been awarded it.

Lieutenant Alexander Dunn, from York, Upper Canada, was the first Canadian to earn the Victoria Cross. During the famous charge of the Light Brigade in the Crimean War he urged his horse forward and, with slashing sabre and smoking pistol, killed a dozen Russian soldiers.

Another Canadian who wore the decoration was George Richardson, who was born in 1831 in Ireland but came to Canada to serve with the government forces during the Fenian raids. On April 27, 1859 at Cawnpore in India, with his arm broken by a rifle bullet and his leg ripped open by an enemy sabre, he saved the life of his officer, who was being attacked by six natives. Richardson killed five despite his crippled condition, and the sixth fled. He was also recommended for the Victoria Cross on three other oc-casions while serving with the 34th Border Regiment of the line in India. When Richardson was more than eighty years of age, he was indignant when his offer to fight in World War I was refused.

In September, 1918, while serving as a private in the Seventh (British Columbia) Battalion, Captain I. Rayfield, VC, charged ahead of his company into a strongly-manned German trench. He bayoneted two of the enemy soldiers and took ten prisoners. Later, a sniper began killing off the Canadians one by one. Under heavy fire, Rayfield rushed the trench from which the sniper was shooting, killed him, and captured thirty more German prisoners single-handedly.

TOPICS FOR DISCUSSION

1. **Women rarely are given the opportunity to become war heroes. Should they fight, kill, and die for their country during a war?**
2. **Most countries against which Canadians have fought in the past are now friendly allies. What causes a war between countries? How can you explain people killing each other and then their countries becoming friends a few years later?**

RESEARCH CHALLENGES

1. **Many new Canadians became heroes and were awarded the Victoria Cross. Have each member of the class investigate and write a brief description of the bravery shown by the following Canadians who were born outside this country. A class booklet could be prepared and placed in your school library.**

Almost half (forty-two) of Canada's Victoria Cross winners were born outside of this country. The following list indicates their birthplaces:

The Victoria Cross.

ENGLAND 17

Bourke	Knight	Osborn	A. H. L. Richardson
Cairns	Lyall	Pattison	Spall
Coppins	McKean	Pearkes	Young
Flowerdew	Merrifield	Rayfield	Wilkinson
Hobson			

SCOTLAND 11

Barron	Kinross	Milne	Strachan
Clark-Kennedy	MacGregor	J. Richardson	Tait
Combe	MacKenzie	Shankland	

IRELAND 7

De Wind	Hanna	Nunney	O'Rourke
F. W. Hall	Harvey	O'Leary	

UNITED STATES OF AMERICA 4

Hutcheson	Metcalf	Mullin	Zengel

DENMARK 1

Dineson

INDIA 1

Bellew

RUSSIA 1

Konowal

2. Below are the native born Canadians who received the Victoria Cross. The list is arranged according to the province in which each was born. Have each member of the class investigate the heroic actions of a different personality and afterwards present an oral report to the group.

Fifty-two winners of the Victoria Cross were born in the following provinces of Canada:

ONTARIO 20

Algie	Cockburn	Holland	Reade
Bishop	Cosens	Honey	Rutherford
Brown	Dunn	Hornell	Sifton
Campbell	Fisher	G. F. Kerr	Tilston
Clarke	Foote	Miner	Topham

QUEBEC 9

Brillant	Kaeble	MacDowell	Triquet
Douglas	Learmonth	Scrimger	Turner
Holmes			

MANITOBA 6

Barker	McLeod	Mynarski	O'Kelly
Brereton	Mitchell		

BRITISH COLUMBIA 5

Gray	Mahony	Merritt	Smith
Hoey			

NOVA SCOTIA 4

Bent	W. Hall	J. C. Kerr	Robertson

NEW BRUNSWICK 3

Good	Gregg	Peck

NEWFOUNDLAND 2

Ricketts

SASKATCHEWAN 1

Currie

PRINCE EDWARD ISLAND 1

Peters

ALBERTA 1

Bazalgette	Croak

Billy Bishop beside his plane.

BILLY BISHOP
The Greatest Fighter Pilot of the British Commonwealth

When he was a boy in Owen Sound, Ontario, Billy Bishop would practice with his rifle in the woods near his home. His skill at hitting moving targets, developed early in his life, would one day make him the greatest fighter pilot of the British Commonwealth.

At the outbreak of World War I, he joined the Canadian Expeditionary Force, but, once in England, he quickly transferred to the British air forces. Since Canada had no active air force, that was the only way a Canadian could become a pilot during the first world war.

On March 25, 1917, in a *Nieuport Scout,* he flew for the first time to the front line and shot down his first German plane. Two weeks later he was awarded the Military Cross for destroying a German observation balloon and fighter plane. By April 20, he had earned the official title of "ace", which meant he had five enemy "kills" to his credit.

Then, on May 2, 1917, as he flew high in the clouds over the front lines, he spotted five German planes below him, descended on them, shot down two and chased the others away. That was only one of a dozen flights he made that day. Below in the trenches, the infantry would watch the "dog fights" in the sky above them. The pilots wore no parachutes; if their planes caught

fire or crashed, they fell with them. The term "eyeballing" came into use, exemplifying the close relationship between the pilots on opposite sides. As a plane was hit, the pilot would fly past his falling adversary, "eyeballing" him with a steady stare of victory before the unfortunate opponent crashed in flames. For his exploits on May 2, Billy Bishop received the Distinguished Service Order, an unusual

honour for a junior officer.

Billy awoke before dawn on June 2, and climbed into his flimsy craft, and flew, alone, twenty kilometres into enemy territory where he attacked an aerodrome. Three German planes rose to stop him, but he shot down all of them. The Commonwealth gave him its highest award, The Victoria Cross, for his bravery on that day.

By August, his score had mounted to forty-seven confirmed "kills"; he was promoted to major and given the safe job of instructor at a flying school in England. However, since Billy was restless for the excitement and danger of the front, he returned to the war in the spring of 1918, in command of his own squadron at only twenty-four years of age. Within twelve days he shot down twenty-five German planes and was awarded the Distinguished Flying Cross. The French government also presented him with the Legion of Honour and the Croix de Guerre.

By the end of World War I, Billy Bishop had created, along with other outstanding Canadian fighter pilots, a tradition that was to inspire many R.C.A.F. pilots twenty-five years later in World War II. His total victories gave him a record seventy-two enemies destroyed, five of them on his last day at the front.

BILLY BARKER
One Against Sixty

Billy Barker learned to ride and shoot on the Canadian prairies near his home town of Dauphin, Manitoba. As a boy he learned to "lead" his target, and he became proficient at shooting birds "on the wing".

Having mastered the use of machine-guns as a corporal in the Canadian Mounted Rifles, he soon proved his skill with a Lewis gun when he transferred to the British air force early in 1916. He began as and observer in a two-seater aircraft, but quickly became a gunner; and then, after only two dual-instruction flights, he qualified as a fighter pilot and found himself in command of a flight with the rank of captain.

Above the hills of Italy, the Austrian air force ruled the skies from the Alps to the plains of Lombardy — until late 1917, when Barker led the British pilots in their *Sopwith Camels* to establish complete control of the air. Disobeying orders against penetrating too deep into Austrian-held territory, he led a Christmas-Day sneak attack on an Austrian airfield, bombing mess halls, pulverizing planes that sat unmanned on the runways, skimming down, until his wheels bounced across the ground, to send volleys of bullets through open hangar doors. During another raid he sprayed machine-gun fire on the Austrian army headquarters. He also dropped leaflets by the thousands, daring the Austrian aces to come up and duel. By September, 1918, he was a legendary figure, with forty destroyed enemy aircraft to his credit.

When, at age twenty-four, Bill

Barker received orders to report back to England to fill an instructor's post, he was unhappy. Nevertheless, he was returning to England in his *Sopwith Snipe* on the morning of October 27, 1918, when he spotted a larger German reconnaissance plane high above him. With the instinct of a hunter, he stalked his prey and fired a burst from his machine gun, which exploded the enemy in mid-air. As he veered his plane to continue his homeward voyage, explosive bullets tore into the side of his cockpit and shattered his right thigh.

A German *Fokker* had caught Bill off guard, but, with the skill of a veteran, he sent it down in flames after a short "dog fight". While he watched the second enemy falling from the sky in a cloud of dark

smoke, bullets showered his *Snipe* from all sides; he was caught in the midst of three squadrons of German fighters stacked up in the air above him, sixty *Fokkers* in all. Another *Spandau* bullet penetrated his left thigh, leaving both legs useless.

Ridiculously outnumbered, he fought back, but he lost consciousness and his plane went into a death spin. The Germans followed him down, determined to finish him off. However, the gust of fresh air into the open cockpit brought the falling Canadian pilot back to consciousness. He regained control of his craft, picked up an enemy in his sights, and fired off a hail of bullets that sent the antagonist down in flames. However, the German pilot had also got off a few rounds, and Billy's throttle arm was shattered at the left elbow. With only one arm, he operated his control stick and firing button, shooting down a fourth enemy before turning to escape. Directly in front of him, blocking his exit, was another German formation. He fought off the new attackers and managed to crash-land behind British lines. Bleeding and dazed, he crawled from the bullet-riddled *Sopwith* that lay upside-down in the mud, knowing he had shot down five of the sixty enemy planes.

Barker lived to fly again and to bring his number of "kills" to a total score of fifty. He received, all told, the Victoria Cross, the Distinguished Service Order, the Military Cross, the Croix de Guerre from France, and the Silver Medal for Valour from Italy.

Bill Barker in a captured German plane.

TOPICS FOR DISCUSSION

1. Would you risk your life for your country? Explain.

2. There is one day set aside every year on which Canadians are asked to remember the people who fought for their country. What day is it? Should there be such a day? What do you think about on that day?

3. Do you believe Canada will one day go to war again? Explain why or why not.

4. In her song, *The Universal Soldier,* Buffy St. Marie suggests that war could be prevented if the people in every country refused to become soldiers. Listen to the song. Would her suggestion work? Explain your viewpoint clearly.

CREATIVE CHALLENGES

1. Investigate the type of aircraft used in the First World War. Build a model of one.

2. Write a description of an imaginary "Dog Fight".

3. Write a science-fiction narrative about a Canadian space pilot in the year 2001.

4. Write an exposition in which you argue either for or against the idea of women becoming fighter pilots.

The choices above involve three different types of writing: description, narrative, exposition. What is the difference between each?

SUGGESTION

Invite a war veteran into your class to discuss the experiences he or she recalls.

Buffy St. Marie, Canadian singer and song writer.

"Wop" May

WAR IS RAGING IN EUROPE IN 1916 WHEN WILFRED 'WOP' MAY OF CARBERRY, MANITOBA, PARTLY OUT OF PATRIOTISM, BUT MOSTLY OUT OF THE RESTLESSNESS OF YOUTH, ENLISTS IN THE CANADIAN ARMY!

HE WEARS THE UNIFORM OF THE INFANTRY, BUT HE LONGS TO BE A FIGHTER PILOT. HE DECIDES TO TRANSFER TO THE ROYAL FLYING CORPS, HOPING TO FIND ADVENTURE ABOVE THE MUDDY TRENCHES OF FRANCE!

HE FINDS IT! ON HIS FIRST COMBAT FLIGHT ON APRIL 21, 1918... HIS GUNS JAM! A RED FOKKER ZEROES IN, GUNS RATTLING, EAGER FOR AN EASY KILL!

BEHIND THE GERMAN GUNS SITS BARON VON RICHTHOFEN, THE RED KNIGHT.... EIGHTY KILLS TO HIS CREDIT, THE GREATEST ACE OF THE WAR! IT LOOKS AS THOUGH 'WOP' MAY'S FIRST DOGFIGHT WOULD BE HIS LAST!

FROM OUT OF THE SUN COMES ANOTHER CANADIAN ...ROY BROWN, FROM EDMONTON.... AND HE BLASTS THE RED KNIGHT OUT OF THE SKY!

RICHTHOFEN IS DEAD. A NARROW ESCAPE FOR A ROOKIE PILOT, BUT 'WOP' MAY GOES ON TO GUN DOWN THIRTEEN ENEMY AIR-PLANES, AND WINS THE DIS-TINGUISHED FLYING CROSS!

WHEN THE WAR ENDS,'WOP' MAY GIVES UP FIGHTING BUT NOT FLYING! HE FORMS AN AVIATION COMPANY IN EDMONTON, AND IN THE YEARS AHEAD, BLAZES MANY SKY TRAILS, CARRYING MEN, MAIL AND MACHINES INTO THE ONCE INACCESSIBLE NORTH!

IN THE ZANY ERA OF CANADIAN BARN-STORMING, FEW FLYERS CAN MATCH 'WOP' MAY! IN AUTUMN, 1919, HE SWOOPS TEN FEET ABOVE A BASEBALL DIAMOND, TO PERMIT THE EDMONTON MAYOR TO PITCH THE FIRST BALL FROM THE AIR!

BUT ON NEW YEARS DAY, 1929, A CARGO MORE PRECIOUS THAN A BASEBALL. HE VOLUNTEERS TO FLY ANTITOXIN TO FORT VERMILION, TO AVERT A DIPHTHERIA EPIDEMIC AT LITTLE RED RIVER. HE AND HIS PARTNER, VIC HORNER.....

... BRAVE A BLINDING BLIZZARD...LASHED BY ICY GALES AND SNOW, TEMPERATURE FORTY DEGREES BELOW ZERO....IN AN OPEN COCKPIT!

FORCED DOWN, THEY MIRACULOUSLY LAND WITHOUT SKI GEAR ON THE ICY SURFACE OF ROUND LAKE AT McLENNAN! TO TAKE-OFF LATER, THEY MUST HEAT THEIR ENGINE OIL ON A PRIMUS STOVE, AND THAW OUT THE ENGINE WITH A BLOW TORCH!

....DESPITE ALL ODDS, THEY REACH FORT VERMILION, AND SAVE A SETTLEMENT! WINGS BACK TO EDMONTON FOR A HERO'S WELCOME....

THAT SAME YEAR 'WOP' MAY MAKES HISTORY WHEN HE LANDS AT AKLAVIK ON DECEMBER 30... ...THE FIRST TIME OFFICIAL MAIL HAS BEEN DELIVERED TO THE ARCTIC COAST!

IN 1932, FROM POSTMAN TO POLICEWORK! THE R.C.M.P. ASK FOR THE FLYER'S AID IN TRACKING DOWN MOUNTIE-KILLER ALBERT JOHNSON....THE MAD TRAPPER OF RAT RIVER!

AS THE MOUNTIES CLOSE IN ON THE CRAZED DESPERADO RACING FOR THE ALASKA BORDER, 'WOP' FERRIES IN SUPPLIES...TEAR GAS BOMBS, AMMUNITION, FOOD..... AND SCANS THE NORTHERN WILDERNESS FOR THE KILLER'S TRACKS!

AFTER ONE OF THE MOST FANTASTIC MANHUNTS IN CANADIAN HISTORY, THE MOUNTIES CORNER JOHNSON....THE MAD TRAPPER TRIES TO SHOOT IT OUT! A SHOWER OF LEAD ENDS HIS REIGN OF TERROR!

...AT A HIGH COST TO THE MOUNTIES....KILLING ONE... WOUNDING TWO!

'WOP' MAY'S PLANE CHEATS THE KILLER OF HIS LAST VICTIM. HE RUSHES A CRITICALLY WOUNDED CONSTABLE TO AKLAVIK!

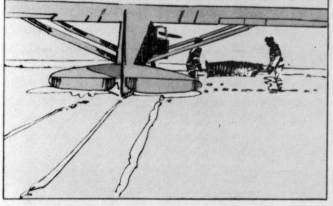

IN RECOGNITION OF HIS RESCUE FLIGHTS AND PIONEERING OF AVIATION IN CANADA, IN 1935 KING GEORGE V AWARDS WILFRED 'WOP' MAY THE ORDER OF THE BRITISH EMPIRE!

HE DIED IN 1952, BUT HIS NAME IS WRITTEN INDELIBLY INTO CANADIAN HISTORY! HE AND BUSH PILOTS LIKE 'PUNCH' DICKINS AND 'DOC' OAKS HAVE BECOME A NEW BREED OF HERO ...WINGED PATHFINDERS WHO UNLOCKED THE TREASURE CHEST OF THE NORTH!

RESEARCH CHALLENGES

After the first world war came the era of the "bush pilots", who risked their lives flying over Canada's unmapped wilderness. Research and report back to the class on one of the following.

1. Bush pilot Hector Dougall and mechanic Frank Ellis, who, in 1920, made the first commercial flight into Canada's northland when they flew from Winnipeg to The Pas.

2. "Doc" Oaks, who established an air service from Sioux Lookout, Ontario, to the Red Lake gold fields, founded the Western Canada Airways, and was the first winner of the McKee Trophy in 1927.

3. "Punch" Dickins, who was the first pilot to cross the "circle" in the western Arctic, and who chalked up 1 200 000 km as a bush pilot.

4. Fred Stevenson, who initiated freighting by air on a big scale.

5. Matt Berry, who found two lost flyers near Fort Reliance on the eastern shore of Great Slave Lake in 1936.

6. Tom Lamb and his six sons, who were known as the "Flying Lambs" and began their northern adventures with a trading post at Moose Lake.

7. Dick and Lorna de Blicquy, who were a husband and wife team with Atlas Aviation Ltd. at Resolute Bay on Cornwallis Island.

8. Robert Gauchie, who survived a record fifty-eight days after running out of fuel in the −52°C weather sixty-five kilometres south of the Arctic Circle in 1967.

A Sopwith Camel.

AGNES CAMPBELL MACPHAIL

The First Woman Elected to Canada's Parliament

When Canadian men went overseas to fight in World War I, women took over their jobs and roles at home. They worked the farms, ran the businesses and laboured in the factories. Before the end of the war, they had proved themselves to be the equal of men, and they started demanding that they be allowed to vote.

In 1916, the Western provinces allowed women the right to vote, and in 1917, two women were elected to the Alberta legislature. Ontario followed the lead of the west, and by 1918 the federal government extended the franchise to all women already on provincial voters' lists.

"Aggie", born in a log farmhouse, was the eldest of her family and, like her two younger sisters, was educated in a small rural school. At sixteen, she had to argue with her parents to convince them that she should be allowed to attend high school in Owen Sound, Ontario. In those days, when girls were seldom educated beyond public school, she wanted to work and be independent rather than marry and raise a farmer's family. By the age of eighteen, Aggie had completed high school and was working as a teacher.

She became a highly respected member of the western Ontario farming community where she lived and worked. She joined the new political party known as the United Farmers of Ontario, where she became a strong supporter of farming issues. By the election of 1921, the Ontario farmers joined with the farmers of the west to form the

Progressive Party of Canada. Up until this time there had been only two political parties, the Liberals and the Conservatives, in Canadian federal elections.

To everyone's surprise, the new party not only had sixty members elected, but one of the sixty was Agnes Campbell Macphail, the first woman to become a member of the federal House of Commons. Through five elections she continued to represent the people of her rural riding of Grey-Bruce.

The fiery Scottish orator claimed she inherited her flamboyant father's wit and her hard-working mother's tenacity. "I owed it to my father that I was elected to Parliament in the first place, but I owed it to my mother that I stuck it out once I got there."

As she walked down the long corridor to the opening of the Senate Chamber, she was so much aware of the fact that, as the first woman in Parliament, she was leading the way for others in the future, she claimed: "I could almost hear them coming."

Aggie was no ordinary member of parliament. The elected members had recently voted themselves an increase in pay, which meant they received $4 000 a year. She immediately turned back $1 500 of her salary into the public treasury, insisting $2 500 was enough income for anybody.

During her political career, Agnes was not only spokesperson for the farmers, she also became a champion of the underprivileged as she pushed the government to introduce welfare measures; an advocate of peace as she fought against introducing military training in the school cadet corps; and a defender of the industrial workers. When the miners of Glace Bay, Nova Scotia, went on strike against the British Empire Steel Corporation in 1925, she visited the area, returning to Ottawa to denounce the squalor and injustice she encountered there. Her fame spread to folk songs of the day:

"God give us more women like Agnes Macphail;
When the miners were hungry she never did fail."

In 1926, the Liberals had a minority government, the Conservatives were in opposition and the Progressives, headed by J. S. Woodsworth, held the balance of power. The Liberals, with bribes and offers of important positions in the government, enticed many of the Progressives to join their party, and the ranks of the third party dwindled to twelve members. Agnes was twice offered a position in MacKenzie King's cabinet if she would switch allegiance, but she refused to desert her party. Because the Liberals needed the support of the Progressives, Woodsworth was able to bargain with the government, and the first Old Age Pension Bill was passed.

Agnes also took advantage of the minority government regarding an unpopular cause: the plight of the prisoners in Canadian jails. It was she who first introduced the idea of reform rather than punishment. She visited many prisons and insisted on seeing conditions first hand. In those days, prisoners spent seventeen hours every day in their cells. Their heads were shaven, they were forbidden to talk to one another, and daily prison life was haunted by "the strap", "shackles", rats, vermin and sadistic guards. Agnes was responsible for penal reform in Canada; she forced the minority Liberal government to pass a bill that started work programs in the federal penitentiaries.

In February of 1954, Agnes Campbell Macphail died of a heart attack. Three years after her death, a special issue of *Telescope*, a magazine published by the inmates of the Kingston penitentiary, paid tribute to her:

"As inmates, most of us are prone to take for granted the privileges we have today, without remembering that it was not always so in this penitentiary. However, those of us who suffered from day to day and lifted our eyes to "Aggie", as she fought for

humane treatment of inmates, know that it was not always so and quietly revere and bless her memory, which the passing years have not dimmed.

"Aggie is dead, but lives on in the hearts of countless prison inmates who knew her and loved her. When the bell tolled for Aggie . . . it tolled for the inmates of every Canadian penitentiary."

TOPICS FOR DISCUSSION
1. Although the western provinces and Ontario gave women the right to participate in elections before 1920, the women of Quebec were not permitted to vote until 1948. Why would Quebec be different in this respect?
2. "Aggie" had to argue with her parents to allow her to remain in school. Do boys and girls today still have to argue with their parents for this reason?
3. There is no Progressive party today. Woodsworth later formed the C.C.F., which in turn became the New Democratic Party. Do you think it would be possible or wise for the farmers of Canada to have their own political party today?
4. Do you believe it would be better to return to the days when there were only two major political parties in Canada? Discuss the advantages and disadvantages of the two-party system.
5. What is a minority government? What are the advantages and disadvantages of a minority government?
6. Agnes claimed she inherited two qualities, one from each of her parents. What were they? What are

the main characteristics you have inherited from your parents or guardians? What characteristics would you like your children to inherit from you?
7. Agnes refused to accept her complete salary as a politician. Why? Are there politicians today who refuse part of their salary? What is the salary today of a federal politican in the House of Commons? What is the pension of a member of the House of Commons, and on what is it based? Who decides whether the members of the government should receive a raise?
8. Agnes was a strong supporter of welfare aid for the old, the unemployed, etc. Do you approve of the welfare that exists in Canada today? Should it be increased or decreased?
9. Are prisoners still treated badly? Should more be done to help them? What are conditions like in Canadian prisons today?
10. Are there any current politicans who are as popular as Agnes Macphail was? Would you have voted for her?

CREATIVE CHALLENGES
1. Write a description of a Canadian politician whom you admire.
2. Write a description of a Canadian politician whom you dislike.
3. Imagine you are forming a new political party in Canada today. Make a list of the policies that you would include in your platform.
4. Write a description of what you think would be "the perfect prison".

FREDERICK BANTING
The Doctor Who Discovered Insulin

Diabetes was a killer. The bodies of its victims for some reason would no longer burn sugar into energy, but instead consumed their own stored fats and proteins in a cannibal-like fashion. Thirst and hunger were the outward symptoms, and patients sometimes drank litres of water every day, only to lose it in a sugary urine. Before 1921, the only treatment known was to put the patient on a rigid diet to correct the disrupted chemical balance. And this was not a cure, it would only prolong the patient's life.

Very little was known about the cause of the disease. In 1889, a German scientist had removed a dog's pancreas in an experiment, to see if the animal could survive without it. The next day he observed flies buzzing around the puddles of sugary urine left by the dog, which, without its pancreas, had developed diabetes.

Scientists suspected that pancreatic juices might contain a factor that regulated the metabolism of sugar, but, when they tied off the ducts that carried those juices to the intestines, the pancreases in the dogs shriveled and degenerated *without* the animals getting diabetes. The shriveled pancreas was still producing the antibiotic factor.

Next, scientists began to investigate the thousands of tiny "islet" cells found in the pancreas, to discover if they secreted a mysterious "X" substance or hormone that regulated the burning of sugar. No one was successful.

Then a man from the small farming community of Alliston, Ontario,

J. G. Banting

joined the search. He had watched one of his classmates, a healthy, lively fifteen-year-old girl, dwindle and die of the dreaded disease.

As a medical student, Fred Banting had gotten only average grades; his attempts to start a medical practice in London, Ontario, had failed and his experience in research was non-existent. During World War I, he had served as a surgeon in the Canadian Army, where he was awarded the Military Cross for bravery. He also received a shrapnel wound in his right arm. Doctors wanted to amputate, but Banting refused and stubbornly nursed his arm back to health. Now, in 1921, the University of Toronto had agreed to give him a laboratory for eight weeks, together with ten dogs and an assistant, Charles Best, a twenty-two-year-old graduate stu-

dent working on his master's degree in physiology and biochemistry.

Banting's plan was simple: they would tie off the pancreatic ducts in their dogs. In seven to ten weeks, the pancreas would degenerate and stop producing digestive juices, so there would be nothing left to destroy the "X" substance. At that point, they could extract the pancreas and inject it into a diabetic dog, to discover if the sugar in the animal's blood and urine would be lowered.

The two men worked in a hot attic during the summer months, wearing little or nothing under their white lab coats and, since money was short, frying eggs and sausages over a Bunsen burner in their makeshift lab. When the experiments were threatened by a shortage of dogs, they jumped into Banting's Model T Ford, nicknamed "The Pancreas", and went hunting through the poorer parts of Toronto for fresh animals, which they bought from the owners for a dollar each.

As they came to the end of their eight-week time limit, they opened one of the dogs. Disaster! They had tied the ducts incorrectly. The pancreas was whole, and healthy, not shriveled up as they had expected. Many people would have given up at this point, but Banting decided to start over, since Professor Macleod, who had given them the use of the physiology department facilities, was still on vacation in Europe.

The second time, they tied off the ducts correctly. On July 27, 1921, they removed a degenerated organ, sliced it into chilled mortar contain-

Best (left) and Banting with a diabetic dog saved from death by insulin, 1921.

ing Ringer's solution, froze the mixture, allowed it to thaw slowly, ground it up and filtered it through paper. In the lab a dying diabetic dog waited, too weak to lift its head. Banting injected it with 5 cc of the filtrate. Blood tests over the next hours indicated that the dog's blood sugar level was decreasing steadily, until it reached the normal level. The dog, which had been close to death, was brought back to life, tail wagging.

The experiment was repeated again and again. Dog number thirty-three was Marjorie, a black-and-white collie mixture that learned to jump up on the bench and hold out her paw to give Dr. Banting a blood sample. For seventy days she was alive and healthy, until the supply of the extract, later to be known as insulin, ran out. That was a new problem. All of the extracted insulin from one pancreas kept only one dog alive for one day.

Fred Banting had been a farm boy. He remembered that the pancreas of an unborn animal consisted mainly of "islet" cells, since digestive juice wasn't needed in the womb. He knew, too, that farmers frequently bred cows to increase their mass and value before sending them to the slaughter house. The two men jumped into the Model T and headed for a slaughter house. Now they would have enough material to keep diabetic dogs alive as long as they wished to.

The all-important question was whether insulin would work on human beings. Leonard Thompson, fourteen years old, lay dying in the Toronto General Hospital. He had been suffering from diabetes for two years, and his mass had been reduced to twenty-seven kilograms. The boy could no longer lift his head from his pillow; he would be dead in two weeks.

Banting and Best had to be certain that their insulin would not be poisonous to a human being, so they rolled up their sleeves and injected each other with the extract. The next day they were both alive;

Leonard Thompson, age fourteen.

the only ill-effects were slightly sore arms. In January, 1922, the frail arm of little Leonard was injected. His blood sugar began to drop almost immediately. He ate normal meals and his sunken cheeks blossomed to life. Leonard lived another thirteen years, when he died of pneumonia following a motorcycle accident. He was the first of millions whose lives would be saved by the discovery of insulin.

Dr. Banting, who in one summer had discovered the answer that had eluded medical doctors for centuries, was given a Nobel Prize for his contribution to the world. In February of 1941, Major Banting was working on problems of aviation medicine when the two-engine bomber taking him to England crashed during a snowstorm. He died in the barren forests near Musgrove Harbour, Newfoundland.

TOPICS FOR DISCUSSION
1. **Who is the greatest hero to you, a doctor conducting research, a singing star, a superstar of sports, a soldier fighting for his country or none of the above? Explain your opinion.**
2. **In order to save millions of human lives, Banting had to delib-** erately give the dogs in his lab diabetes. Could you accept a job as a research doctor under such conditions? Do you agree that such experiments with animals are necessary?
3. **What diseases in the world today continue to kill people because medical science has not yet found the cure?**
4. **What, more than any other factor, do you believe allowed Dr. Banting to discover such an important medical breakthrough in such a short period of time? Do your classmates and friends agree with you?**
5. **Dr. Best, Banting's assistant, died in 1978. Should he be given as much credit for the discovery of insulin as Banting? Explain your viewpoint.**

RESEARCH CHALLENGES
1. **At least two other Canadian doctors are world famous: Dr. Wilder Penfield and Dr. William Osler. Investigate one of them or another Canadian doctor of your choice and report back to your classmates on his or her achievements.**
2. **Investigate which organizations are in need of financial support to aid in medical research. Perhaps you, your class, your friends, or your school could collect money to aid the one of your choice.**
3. **Gerhard Herzberg, became the third Canadian to win a Nobel Prize in 1971. What did he do to deserve world recognition?**

Gerhard Herzberg.

TOM THOMSON
The Case of the Dead Artist

Was Tom Thomson murdered? Did he commit suicide? Was his death accidental? The mystery is still unsolved today, although his body rose from the bottom of Canoe Lake in Algonquin Park, Ontario, on July 16, 1917, eight days after he had disappeared.

The legendary Canadian painter spent his youthful years hunting and fishing in the vast wilderness that surrounded Owen Sound, Ontario. As a restless young man, he tried several lines of work, but none satisfied him. He even tried to study at a business school, but, by 1905, was working in Toronto as a photo-engraver and within a few years joined a commercial art firm known as *GRIP*, which specialized in general artwork and design layout for stores such as the Thomas Eaton Company.

The large, mild-mannered Thomson was most at home in the woods among animals and trees. He shared a studio, actually an old shack in Toronto, with Arthur Lismer during the winter, where he painted from sketches collected during the summer months in the outdoors.

Although never formally educated in the techniques of oil painting, Thomson was an excellent self-taught colourist, copying accurately the emotions of the colourful scenes in nature. His two most famous paintings, "The West Wind" and "The Jack Pine", were completed in the last year of his life. He was already thirty-four when he bought his first real oil sketch box, and thirty-nine when he died. His final summers were spent exploring the wilderness of Algonquin Park, where he sketched, worked as a guide, fished, hunted and canoed in the unspoiled splendor he captured on canvas. He was a natural woodsman, who mashed potatoes with an empty bottle and stirred his coffee with his thumb.

"He lived humbly but passionately with the wild. It made him brother to all untamed things of nature. It drew him apart and revealed itself wonderfully to him. It sent him out from the woods only to show these revelations through his art and it took him to itself at last."

The mystery of how Tom Thomson died has been probed by many. It's been proved that he attended a rowdy party, not unusual for Thomson, at a cabin near Mowat Lodge on the evening of July 7, 1917. The following Sunday morning Thomson left the company of Shannon Fraser to go fishing. Later his empty canoe was found floating by itself, and after eight days, an unusually long time, his body finally came to the surface, with a large bruise on the right temporal area, blood in one ear, and a fishing line wrapped around his ankle.

One writer, David Silcox, suggested that Thomson had sprained his ankle and had wrapped fishing line around it for support. Then, when he tried to urinate from the canoe, he had slipped and hit his head on his craft as he fell over-

The Jack Pine, by Tom Thomson. The National Gallery of Canada.

board. The weakness with this theory is that an experienced woodsman like Thomson would have scarcely believed that tying fishing line around a sprained ankle would help it, nor would he have been clumsy enough to fall out of a canoe, managing to knock himself unconscious as he did so.

Another writer, Charles Plewman, talked of Thomson's secret engagement to Winnifred Trainor. Plewman claimed that Shannon Fraser, the proprietor of Mowat Lodge, had told him Thomson was under tremendous pressure to marry and had committed suicide instead. Some people suggested Winnie was pregnant, but no child was ever born. To believe the suicide theory, one has to accept the idea that marriage was a fate worse than death to Thomson, and that he couldn't simply say "no" to Winnie.

In his book *The Tom Thomson Mystery*, Judge William Little suggested that the artist was murdered by an American tourist, Martin Bletcher. According to Little, the two men had argued violently at the party, supposedly over the war, the night before Thomson disappeared. However, the author admits that the park ranger stationed at Canoe Lake, a good friend of Thomson's, saw the artist with Shannon Fraser the day after the party. To accept this theory, therefore, one has to believe that a drunken argument over the war in Europe led to murder on a sober Sunday, and that the American followed Thomson out into the wilderness to kill him. Shannon Fraser himself claimed he looked at his watch and that it was 12:50 p.m. when Thomson paddled away alone, never to be seen alive again.

The ranger's notes indicate that Tom's favourite paddle was missing and that numerous searches of the shoreline never brought it to light. His spare paddle was awkwardly strapped into portaging position, in

a manner very unlike Thomson's. There was no autopsy, for the coroner arrived after Thomson was buried, and his death was listed as "accidental drowning".

Roy MacGregor, yet another writer, described in an article in *The Canadian Magazine*, (October 15, 1977) an interview he had had with an eighty-nine-year-old woman, Mrs. Daphne Crombie, who had been a guest at Mowat Lodge during the winter of 1916-17. Mrs. Crombie said she had become friends with the only other woman there, gossipy Annie Fraser, the wife of Shannon Fraser. Annie had confided to her new friend the fact that her husband owed Thomson money, that Tom demanded the money from Shannon while at the party, that Shannon had lost his temper and had struck Tom, who fell and hit his head on a fire grate. If this account is true, Shannon panicked, dragged the unconscious artist out of the lodge, enlisted the aid of his wife to place Tom in his own canoe, towed him to Canoe Lake and dumped him overboard. To accept this last version, one has to accept that Fraser would kill rather than repay a debt, that his wife would aid him and later confess to Daphne Crombie, and that Daphne never felt obliged to tell anyone until she was almost ninety. There is also the fact that ranger Mark Robinson saw Thomson at a distance talking to Shannon Fraser the morning after the party!

The case of the dead artist still remains unsolved, but his valuable contribution to Canadian art is not in doubt.

TOPICS FOR DISCUSSION
1. Tom Thomson tried several lines of work during his life and began oil painting only when he was over thirty. Do you think you could one day become famous for a talent you have not yet developed?
2. Thomson's most famous art was

completed in the last year of his life. If he had lived, do you think he would have improved even more?
3. Have you ever been on a canoe trip in the wilderness? Would you like to go on one? If you went on one would you sketch, write poems, take photographs, hunt fish, or do something else?
4. Do you believe the death of Tom Thomson was accidental? suicidal? murder? Explain your viewpoint.
5. What is your favorite pastime? How could you best express it to the world?

RESEARCH CHALLENGES
1. Who were the Group of Seven? What did they have in common with Tom Thomson even though they were not formed until after his death?
2. Tom Thomson painted what he saw in front of him. Who was C. W. Jefferys? What kind of art did he create? How did it differ from Thomson's? Which illustrations of Jefferys' can you discover in this book?
3. Who are the best known Canadian artists today?
4. Who is Karsh? What is his art form?
5. Look up examples of Tom Thomson's art in your local library and prepare an oral opinion on them for your classmates.

CREATIVE CHALLENGE
Invent your own version of the death of Tom Thomson based on the information and personalities in this short description.

First make a rough list of the personalities involved. Second, indicate the known facts in point form. Third, invent your own theory of how Thomson died. Be certain that your theory explains the known facts. Write out your explanation clearly and then compare it with the opinions of your classmates.

PERCY PAGE
and the Edmonton Grads

Percy Page grew up in Bronte, Ontario, excelled at Hamilton Collegiate, graduated from Queen's University, and taught high school for two years in St. Thomas, Ontario, before he decided to head west for Alberta in 1912.

In Alberta, he introduced commercial subjects to McDougall Commercial High School in Edmonton and began to coach the girls in basketball, a game he had enjoyed during his own student days. In 1915, he established "The Edmon-

ton Commercial Graduates", a woman's basketball team that consisted solely of students or graduates from his Edmonton school. During the twenty-five years that the team existed, only two players who had not been students at McDougal were accepted on it — Gladys Fry and Mae Brown, who had both been excellent players on other Edmonton teams before joining "the Grads".

From 1915 until the team was disbanded in 1940, it won 96.2%

of its games, playing a total of 522 and losing only 20. At one point it won 147 consecutive games. In 1922, the Grads became Canadian champions, a title they never relinquished. In 1923, competing against an American team from Cleveland, the Canadian women won their first international series as well as the Underwood Challenge Trophy, which they retained against all challengers for seventeen years. When the Edmonton Grads disbanded in 1940, the trophy was given to them

World champions, the "Grads" of 1937 with coach Percy Page.

permanently.

The Edmonton Grads represented Canada at four Olympics: Paris 1924, Amsterdam 1928, Los Angeles 1932, and Berlin 1936. They won twenty-seven consecutive Olympic games, to make them the undisputed world champions of women's basketball.

Percy Page eventually became principal of McDougall Commercial High School, sat as a Conservative member of the Alberta House from 1952 to 1959, and was lieutenant-governor of Alberta from 1959 to 1966. He gave all the credit for his team's success to the players:

"They are champions because they are the most whole-hearted, sport-loving girls that it would be possible to find; they have won because the spirit of the Prairie is born and bred in them."

In 1925 in Guthrie, Oklahoma, as the Edmonton Grads were defeating their American competitors for the Underwood Trophy, a teacher at the University of Kansas stated that it was doubtful that any women's team had ever equalled the Canadian players "in all round strategy, brilliance of play and doggedness of attack". The teacher was none other than James Naismith, the Canadian who had invented the game of basketball.

TOPICS FOR DISCUSSION
1. Can you imagine a team from your school or your community being Canadian or world champions?
2. Can you think of any team in any sport that has had the winning record achieved by the Edmonton Grads?
3. The Edmonton grads existed as a team for twenty-five years. How much credit would you give to the coach for their continued success? Is a coach the most important member of a team?
4. Are Canadians regarded as world champion basketball players today?

CREATIVE CHALLENGE
1. Using either basketball or another sport of your choice, list the words used to describe it or the players. Separate the words into lists of nouns or verbs. For example, nouns would include: basket, key, centre, etc. while verbs would be: dribble, pass, pivot, etc. Some words such as "foul" might belong on both lists.

GEORGE YOUNG
"The Catalina Kid"

George Young, seventeen years old, and his buddy, Bill Hastings, climb onto Bill's battered motorbike in the east end of Toronto. The year is 1926, and the two boys are determined to travel across the continent to California, where over a hundred of the best swimmers in the world are gathering to attempt the long swim from Catalina Island to the mainland of California through treacherous currents and tides. No person has ever conquered the Catalina Channel; the only recorded crossing of the waters is by a fifteen-person relay team that took twenty-three hours in combined time, and William Wrigley, Jr., has recently offered $25 000 to the first swimmer to cross it alone. The youths reach Arkansas before their motorcycle breaks down, and then they hitch a ride to Los Angeles with a honeymoon couple who are driving that way. They arrive in early December, 1926.

Back in Toronto, George's mother works as a cleaning woman to support her family. The $25 000 in prize money looks attractive to the serious youth. He received his early swimming instruction at Toronto's west end Y.M.C.A., where, as a boy, he won the Toronto cross-the-bay swim four times and the Montreal bridge-to-bridge swim three times. The barrel-chested youngster is the Canadian champion for 200 m, but he is lost in the crowds of champions assembled for the highly publicized swim, among them conquerors of the English Channel and some of the world's best distance swimmers. The boy's dream, to reach the mainland ahead of the

Comic strip drawn by student Brendon Fox.

others, seems impossible.

On January 15, 1927, George stands in the cold wind, inconspicuous amid the 103 swimmers from around the world, and enters the water at noon. Once in the water, George attracts attention as he skims through the pack smoothly, in a steady rhythm of forty-four strokes per minute. His powerful strokes soon pull him ahead of the others, and by the late afternoon he is in the lead.

Darkness descends. The waters turn colder in the freezing January night. Now come the obstacles he never expected. First, the struggling youth fights his way through an oil slick, which seems determined to entrap him. Next, he feels bunches of kelp twinning around his vulnerable body as he continues to slash his way through the choppy waters. Then comes terror, as he realizes that he is not alone in the dark water — a shark is following him. Eventually, even the shark turns back.

Ahead, thousands of people line the mainland shore with lighted beacons. They shout encouragement, but the final obstacle is the strong ebb tide pulling against the weary swimmer. Two kilometres offshore, George battles against it for more than an hour until the tide passes and he steps triumphantly ashore to a hero's reception. He has conquered the channel in an unbelievable fifteen hours, forty-five minutes. Sports writers call him the "Catalina Kid", as newspapers across the continent carry the story under eight-column headlines, and editorials compare Young to the heroes of ancient Greece.

When George Young returns to Toronto, marathon fever hits the city. More than 150 000 people welcome him home in the crowded streets, and Prime Minister Mackenzie King sends a telegram assuring George that all Canada is rejoicing in the honour he has brought to his country.

TOPICS FOR DISCUSSION

1. What obstacles did George have to overcome in order to achieve his goal? What goals do you have in life? What obstacles do you have to overcome in order to attain them?

CREATIVE CHALLENGES

1. Write a description of George that one of the following people might have given to a newspaper reporter. Use your imagination.
a) His mother
b) William Wrigley Jr.
c) Bill Hastings
d) one of the other swimmers
e) Prime Minister Mackenzie King
2. The comic strip depicting the story of George was drawn by a student, Brendon Fox. Choose one of the heroes from this book and draw a comic strip that is based on his or her adventures.

BOBBIE ROSENFELD

Canada's Woman Athlete of the Half-Century

Bobbie Rosenfeld's favorite sport was hockey, which she learned on the corner lots playing with the boys. Constance Hennessey, founding member of the Toronto Ladies Athletics Club, described her abilities as follows:

"She was a fine hockey player – she checked hard and she had a shot like a bullet. On the basketball court she drove with the ball if she had it, she drove after it if someone else had it. She was just the complete athlete."

The wiry, aggressive woman had arrived in Canada as a baby in the arms of her Russian parents and grew up in Barrie, Ontario. She excelled in so many sports during her athletic career that she was selected as best Canadian woman athlete of the half-century.

Bobbie was unknown until the day she was playing with her girls' softball team at a picnic in Beaverton, Ontario. Her friends coaxed her to run in the ninety metre dash at the small track meet that was being held. She won. To her surprise, a gentleman introduced himself to her after the race as Elwood Hughes, manager of the Canadian National Exhibition, and informed her that she had just beaten Rosa Grosse, the champion Canadian sprinter.

Young Bobbie went on to play on several championship basketball teams in Ontario and Eastern Canada. In 1924, she was the champion tennis player at the Toronto grass courts. In 1925, she was the only entry representing the Patterson Athletic Club in the Ontario Ladies Track and Field Championship, yet she won the total-points title single-handedly for her club when she came first in the discus, the running broad jump, the 110 m low hurdles and the 200 m, as well as placing second in the javelin

Canada's Olympic relay team of 1928: Jane Bell, Myrtle Cook, Ethel Smith, and Fannie (Bobbie) Rosenfeld.

throw and the ninety metre dash.

During the Amsterdam Olympics in 1928, Bobbie was put in the 800 m race not because she had trained for the event, but to give moral support to seventeen-year-old Jean Thompson. On the stretch down the track, Bobbie sprinted from ninth position to run right on the heels of the younger girl from Canada. Jeannie began to falter, but Bobbie coaxed her on, refusing to pass her. The youngster finished fourth and Bobbie accepted fifth position for herself. In the ninety metre dash, Bobbie was neck and neck with the American runner, collecting a silver medal for her efforts, and in the relay team with Ethel Smith, Jane Ball, and Myrtle Cook, she helped win a gold medal for Canada.

Then, in 1929, arthritis struck, leaving her in bed for eight months and on crutches for a year afterward. By 1931, she was back in athletics, however, playing in the leading softball league as an outstanding hitter and fielder, and that winter she became the top Ontario hockey player in women's competition.

The career of Canada's best woman athlete ended sadly in 1933, when arthritis returned to retire her permanently from active sports.

TOPICS FOR DISCUSSION
1. Although Bobbie and her parents came from another country, she became Canada's best woman athlete. Most new Canadians contribue to our country in a positive fashion. Do you know of any others besides Bobbie Rosenfeld?
2. If you had been participating in an Olympic contest, would you have remained behind another contestant from your own team to encourage her or him?
3. Most people involved in sports retire at an early age and are forced to find another occupation. Bobbie became a journalist. Can you name some recent sports stars who have retired? What do they do now?
4. In your opinion, who is the best female athlete in Canada today? Who is the best male athlete?

CREATIVE CHALLENGE
1. Imagine it is the year 2000. Canadians have chosen the best male and female athletes of the entire century. Write a description of one of them, describing his or her accomplishments. What will be the records in various sports by the year 2000? What new sports will have been introduced to Canadians by that time? What will be the physical features of the athlete you are describing?

RESEARCH CHALLENGE
Etienne Desmarteau was the first Canadian to win a gold medal for his country. Each student could prepare a report on a Canadian who won a gold medal after 1905. Include in your report the event in which each person was acclaimed the best in the world, the age of the person, and the part of Canada from which he/she came.

Etienne Desmarteau.

ETHEL CATHERWOOD

"The Saskatoon Lily"

Six young women, decked out in cloth hats and bobbed hair, squeezed together on the platform of a railroad observation car to have their photographs taken. They were the greatest track and field team Canada ever sent to the Olympics. In Amsterdam in 1928, they triumphed over the United States women, twenty-six to twenty, to give the Canadian women's team an overall victory.

The tallest of the group was "The Saskatoon Lily". One Toronto sportswriter explained how she received her nickname:

*"From the instant this tall, slim, graceful girl from the prairies tossed aside her long flowing cloak of purple and made her first leap, the fans fell for her. A flower-like face of rare beauty above a long, slim body simply clad in pure white . . . she looked like a tall strange lily – and she was im-*mediately *christened by the crowd, "The Saskatoon Lily".*

Beautiful Ethel Catherwood, nineteen years old, had to face twenty-three jumpers, including Caroline Gisolf, a Dutch athlete and the world record holder, who was cheered on by a home-town crowd. Only competitors were allowed on the large field, which left Ethel, Canada's only entry in the high jump, alone. When the opportunity came, her co-ordinated body slipped gracefully over the bar at a height of 159 cm and Ethel had won an Olympic gold medal.

TOPICS FOR DISCUSSION
1. Canada has never done as well in Olympic competition as in 1928. Why? Are present-day Canadian athletes less accomplished?
2. How could we improve our athletic skills in the world competition?

RESEARCH ASSIGNMENTS
1. Who were the other members of Canada's women's team in 1928, and what medals did they win?
2. Canada's men also did well at the Ninth Olympiad, in Amsterdam in 1928. Percy Williams was a sensation with his double win in the sprints. Write a brief biography of Percy Williams, which describes his sports career.

CREATIVE CHALLENGES
1. Imagine you are a Canadian athlete at the next Olympics (choose the sport you like best) and describe how you would feel if you won a gold medal.
2. Write an exposition in which you state clearly your opinion of Olympic sports (you may approve or disapprove).

EMILE ST. GODARD

and Canada's Greatest Dog Hero, Toby

In records of his "Voyages" in 1577, Richard Hakluyt observed that the natives of the Labrador coast, "keepe certain dogs not much unlike wolves, which they yoke to a sled". Thus, dog teams and sleds were providing transportation across Canada's vast frozen northlands long before white people arrived on this continent, and they are still the most common vehicles in many isolated communities today in spite of the airplane and snowmobile.

As early as March, 1915, The Pas was holding dog sled races, although it is an American, Oliver B. Smith, who is officially credited with inventing dog derbies in 1919. By that later date, The Pas was hosting the Northern Trappers' Festival, with dog-sled racing as a high point in the events.

About this time a young boy, Emile St. Godard, moved to the isolated bush town of The Pas with his parents. In his early teens he saw his first dog-sled race, and from that moment his only ambition in life was to own a championship team.

He began collecting a team, preparing them and himself for the physical endurance necessary to conquer both elements and opponents. As he raced, Emile experimented with various combinations of dogs, reinvesting his prize money into the business of training and breeding. His experiments produced a half-huskie, half-greyhound named Toby, who became his lead dog.

In 1925, a well-known Alaskan musher originally from Norway won publicity and recognition when he and his team rushed

diphtheria serum to the isolated settlement of Nome. A challenge was issued, and St. Godard, who had won the annual 300 km race at The Pas in 1925 and 1926, beat the Alaskan team in a contest at Quebec City. It was the start of years of competition between the two teams — they returned to Quebec for the next six consecutive years, as well as racing in The Pas, Alaska, Minnesota, and New Hampshire. The slim French Canadian and Toby won the majority of the prizes. Their last encounter came in 1932, during an eighty kilometre race that was part of the Winter Olympics at Lake Placid, N.Y. There were twelve teams, including Canadian entries from Flin Flon, St. Jovite, Quebec, and Ottawa. After being defeated, the Alaskan agreed that St. Godard, who had won the race, was "the best".

At their peak, St. Godard and

Toby were racing 2 500 km a season. Emile's concern and kindness for his dogs became legend in racing circles. For example, in 1927, during a four-day race at Prince Albert, the dogs had to run forty laps a day. During the second day the weather turned colder, and what had been slush the day before turned to sharp, cutting crystals of ice. Emile's dogs were limping as he came across the finish line; Toby lay across the sleigh. Emile withdrew from the cruel contest with an emphatic statement: "I am not going to bleed my dogs to win a prize! There is blood every yard of that course!"

While dog-sled racing is becoming increasingly popular despite snowmobiles, no one has ever equalled the consistent record of Emile and Toby in winning the big races from 1925 to the mid-thirties. St. Godard is the only dog-sled racer in the Sports Hall of Fame, and

when Toby was too old to compete in the racing grind, Emile also retired with him from the sport.

TOPICS FOR DISCUSSION
1. If you had a choice, would you rather race on a snowmobile or with a team of huskies? Explain why.

CREATIVE CHALLENGES
1. Write a description of a dog-sled race from the point of view of one of the dogs.
2. Describe your favorite animal. If you are describing a type of animal, your description will be physical and factual. However, if you are describing a specific animal, such as your own pet, your description will not only include the physical appearance but will deal with the personal and emotional qualities of the animal.

HOWIE MORENZ
"Hockey's Martyr"

Thirteen-year-old Howie Morenz moved, along with his parents and five older children, from the small village of Mitchell, Ontario, to Stratford. His father worked in the Stratford railway shops and the youthful Howie, overflowing with energy, turned his enthusiasm to hockey, becoming the star of the Stratford entry in the Ontario Hockey Association junior competition.

Scouts from the Montreal Canadiens recognized his abilities, and, by the fall of 1923, he was the pride of Montreal fans. In 1924, his team won the Stanley Cup, capturing it again in 1930 and 1931. Howie's contribution to the team was obvious. He was the leading scorer in the league in 1927-28 and 1930-31 and the winner of the Hart Trophy as the most valuable player in 1928, 1931 and 1932. King Clancy described him:

> "Morenz was the best in his day, the best I ever played against and the best I've ever seen since. Nobody could dig in and get moving as fast as he could, he could start on a dime and leave you a nickel change."

The career of the man whom many consider to be the best hockey player to skate in the National Hockey League came to a sudden tragic conclusion in front of Montreal fans in January, 1937. Howie rushed into the corner, ready to turn quickly and streak back out with the puck, but his skate stuck in the boards. Big Earl Siebert, a defenseman, smashed into the struggling Morenz, snapping his vulnerable leg and sending the popular forward's head crashing into the ice. Six weeks later, due to the brain injury, Howie Morenz died.

Thousands of fans paid tribute to the gentle hero as they passed his bier at centre ice in the Montreal Forum. Writer Jim Coleman was to later sum up the memory of hockey's first superstar who died as a result of action on the ice:

> "Morenz was a dark-visaged, dashing knight. He was finely-tempered Toledo steel. When he picked up the puck, circled behind his own net and started for the opposing goal, he lifted you right out of your seat. His step was so light that he appeared to fly about two inches above the surface of the ice. . .he could skate faster than Davey Keon, he could shoot as hard as Bobby Hull and he was as strong as Gordie Howe."

TOPICS FOR DISCUSSION

1. Who do you consider to be the best hockey player?
2. Many people complain that hockey is too violent. Do you agree? Has it improved or become rougher since Howie's death in 1937?
3. Are Canadians the best hockey players in the world? Do they win the world championships?
4. Because American business controls hockey and because the support of American fans is so lucrative, the best Canadian hockey players belong to teams in the U.S.A. How could this situation be changed? Should it be changed?
5. Boys and girls are not usually allowed to play on the same hockey teams or in the same league. Do you think a person should be judged on his or her ability rather than sex? Do you think a woman could become a superstar on a mixed team in the N.H.L.?

CREATIVE CHALLENGES

1. Re-read the descriptions of Howie Morenze by King Clancy and Jim Coleman in this selection. Write a similar description of your favorite hockey player or athlete.
2. Write an exposition on violence in hockey in which you state clearly your own view point.
3. Imagine that the N.H.L. allows mixed teams in the future. Write a play by play description of a few moments of a game, as a radio or T.V. announcer would describe it, if both men and women were on the two teams.

RESEARCH CHALLENGE
Examine the photograph of men and women playing hockey in 1880 in northern Saskatchewan. This picture was taken five years before the North West Rebellion. What is the origin of hockey? Prepare a short radio show that informs the listeners of the history of hockey or some other sport that you chose. Place the radio show on a tape and play it for your classmates.

Be careful to speak clearly and smoothly. Try to use variety in tone, volume, and speed to emphasize your most important facts.

GREY OWL
The White Boy Who Became an Indian

Archie was sixteen. All his life he had waited for this moment – all the boring years in the rich English mansion where he had been raised by his grandmother and two elderly aunts, all the dull years at the snobbish Hastings Grammar School. Now at last he was waving good-bye to his tearful Aunt Ada and Aunt Carrie from the deck of his ship as it left the harbour and headed for Canada.

His father, the black sheep of the family, had scandalized the town when he married a barmaid, and the family had bought him an orange grove in Florida to ensure that he would not be around to embarrass them socially. The orange grove fell into ruin, the barmaid died, and the wayward George returned with a new wife, the barmaid's thirteen-year-old sister, who was already pregnant with Archie. The old ladies took custody of the baby and raised it like a gentleman.

And now, at last, Archie was headed for Canada, a vast, wild country where his father had disappeared into a new life. Archie had always been intrigued by stories of Indians and had spent most of his time at school or at home playing Indian games of tracking and hunting. His imagination had conjured up stories of how his father had become an Indian in the remote wilderness of Canada, and Archie's collection of wild animals, snakes, rabbits, frogs, birds, weasels, etc., had alarmed the sedate ladies of the house. With a dream in his heart of becoming an Indian, and with only five pounds sterling in his pocket, Archie arrived in Toronto in 1906.

He worked in a clothing store on King street for long enough to raise the train fare to Cobalt, Ontario, where silver had been discovered. As the train pulled out of Union Station, Archie tried to start a conversation with a dark, weather-beaten man. The stranger abruptly ended the brief encounter by telling Archie he would not last long in Cobalt with his fancy suit and upper-class British accent.

Archie Belaney at three years of age.

"I'd stay out of the north if I was you, kid. It's a dirty place for a greenhorn."

Eleven kilometres from Latchford the tracks were washed out, and the passengers had to walk. In his torn, mud-covered blue suit, Archie slept on the ground and ate nothing, because he didn't have any money. There were no jobs available for unskilled men; he could not bring himself to beg, and he had difficulty making friends because of his accent. One night he was in a fight, so a bystander took pity on him and gave him some "real clothes", worn overalls and a flannel shirt. The next day he tried to walk the last sixty-five kilometres to Cobalt.

Bitten by insects, breaking into a cold sweat, he was soon delirious with fever and was almost struck by a train that roared up behind him. Lying beside the tracks, with black flies settling in swarms on his face and body, he lost consciousness.

"Lucky we came across you when we did, or you'd be food for the wolves by now."

As Archie's eyes blinked open, he was amazed to see the dark man who wouldn't speak to him on the train. Behind him, in what was a log cabin, were two Indians. The man was Jesse Hood, a professional guide. Archie was given Indian medicine, and when he recovered was taught how to canoe by a young Ojibway Indian. On the beautiful northern lakes. surrounded by pine trees, Archie's dream came true. He learned trapping, snowshoeing and the Ojibway language. He got a job as a guide on Lakes Temiskaming and Temagami during the summer and carried mail by dog-sled through the winter. He was seventeen years old.

His darkened complexion and deerskin clothing made it increasingly difficult to distinguish Archie from the Indians at Bear Island as he lost his accent. He married an Indian girl, and in due course, the cabin which he built near his trapping grounds resounded with the cries of a baby daughter. But soon Archie grew bored with married life; he abandoned his family and moved westward to the Algoma district.

When war broke out, Archie joined the Canadian army and went back to Europe to fight. He enlisted as a "half-breed", was wounded in the foot, and had his lungs seared with mustard gas. In his hospital bed he concluded he was a fool to have gotten involved in the "white man's war". Recuperating in England at the home of his old aunts, he was visited by a childhood friend, Ivy, who was now a beautiful woman. They were married, but when she refused to return with him to the Canadian woods, Archie left her behind.

Back in Northern Ontario Archie seemed to go mad. He became known as the "wild man of the woods." No one would hire him, and if the Indians had not watched over him, he would have died. Instead, an old Ojibway trained him in manhood rituals, adopted him into the tribe and gave him his Indian name, Wa-Sha-Quon-Asin, or Grey Owl (literally, "Shining Beak"). He met and married a beau-

Grey Owl and Anahareo playing with beaver kittens.

tiful Indian girl, Anahareo, who was to have a greater influence on his life than any other person. They settled down to a life of trapping and guiding, always on the move through northern Quebec. Her sensitivity grew on him. He became disgusted by the cruelty of trapping — killing animals with broken limbs, discovering only a bloody paw in the steel teeth, noticing the silent tears in Anahareo's eyes. "You must stop this work," she urged; "It is killing your spirit as well as mine."

The next day they adopted two beaver kittens, the first of many wild pets, and Grey Owl, the conservationist, was born. As the baby beaver nuzzled under his chin and curled up on his chest to sleep, Grey Owl realized the total cruelty that was involved in the extermination of the animals. The Canadian nation had been built on beaver furs, and now it was time for someone to fight for the preservation of the industrious, friendly animals. "I am now the president, treasurer, and sole member of the Society of the Beaver People", declared Grey Owl, when Anahareo asked what he would do if he no longer hunted for a living.

Grey Owl's articles in magazines, his books on wildlife and his lecture tours of Europe and North America made the world aware of the slaughter taking place in the wilderness. The Canadian Indian who spoke compassionately for his forest friends became a celebrity. With the help of the Canadian National Parks Service, he set up conservation reserves for the beavers. A daughter, Dawn, was born to him and Anahareo, but the publicity and fame he was receiving depressed Grey Owl. Like his prevous marriages, this one also broke up.

Although Grey Owl continued his work and married a fourth time, he never seemed to rediscover the happiness he had once known with the woman who helped him to realize the truth about his own gentle nature.

He died of pneumonia on April 13, 1938, at Prince Albert, Saskatchewan. With his death came the revelation to the world that the famous Grey Owl was not an Indian but a white man, and newspaper headlines around the world read: "GREY OWL A FRAUD".

TOPICS FOR DISCUSSION
1. What is your opinion of hunting and trapping? Are they cruel pastimes? Is it necessary for some people to earn their living by killing animals? Have you ever killed an animal?
2. In your opinion, was Grey Owl a fraud? Explain.
3. What are some endangered species in the world today?
4. Grey Owl had four wives during his life, at a time when such a thing was unheard of. Does it affect your view of him? Do you expect to marry more than once during your life? Would you?
5. Would you have the courage at age sixteen to travel to a strange country about which you knew nothing? What countries in the world today or what parts of Canada are still primitive like the Canada Grey Owl loved?
6. Because he spoke and dressed differently than Canadians, Grey Owl was at first poorly treated and lonely in Canada. Do new Canadians arriving in this country still suffer from such persecution? Why do people resent those who are different? How could you help new Canadians to feel welcome?

7. It seemed impossible that an English-born youth could become world famous as a Canadian Indian, but it happened. Do you have a dream of what you would like to become even though it seems impossible?
8. Have you ever tried to adopt a wild animal as a friend? What problems are involved?
9. Grey Owl liked to live isolated from people, close to nature. What kind of person are you? Do you prefer isolation or society? Do you prefer the country or the city?
10. After one of his first public speaking experiences in front of an audience, Grey Owl described his fear: "like a snake that has swallowed an icicle, chilled from one end to the other". What simile would you use to describe the same fear of public speaking? Grey Owl became a famous public speaker despite his fear. Could you?

CREATIVE CHALLENGES
1. Plan a trip in the woods, with cameras, to see how close you can get to animals without hurting them.
2. Choose a subject you believe in as strongly as Grey Owl believed in conservation and give a short public speech on it to your classmates.
3. There are many groups in the world and in Canada today that are attempting to abolish various animal hunts. Write a report on one of them, in which you state clearly your own personal view either for or against what they represent.
4. Imagine you are each of Grey Owl's four wives and write a short description of him from each point of view.
5. Read one of the many books written by Grey Owl and report back to the class your opinion of it.

DR. NORMAN BETHUNE

"The White One Sent"

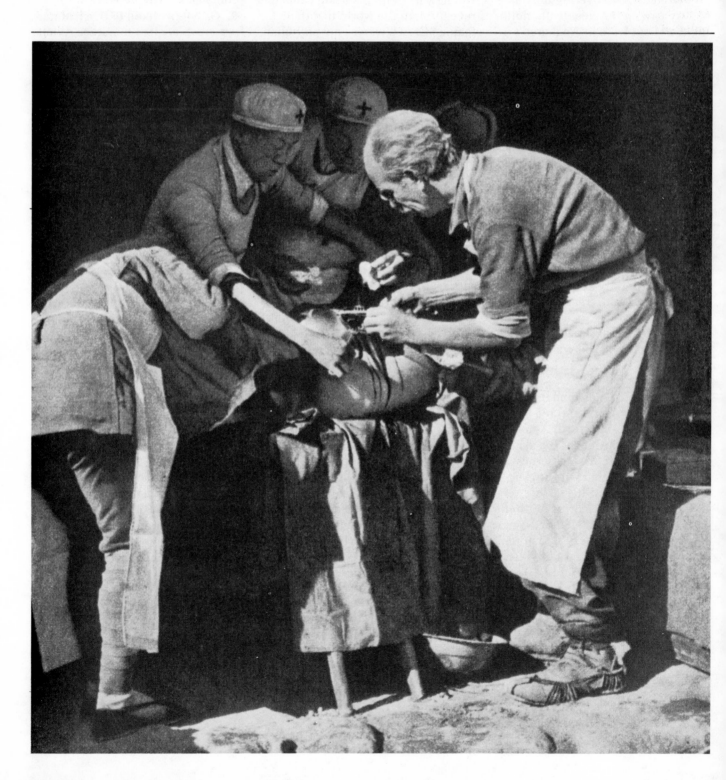

No one could have predicted that Norman Bethune, the boy from the small Ontario town of Gravenhurst, would become a hero to millions in far-off China. He led a highly active life full of violence and danger and, in the end, his vision of truth led to his own destruction.

When World War I broke out, Norman was still a student, but he immediately left medical school and enlisted in the army as a stretcher bearer. When he went to the aid of another Canadian during an artillery barrage, a piece of shrapnel ripped through his leg, and he spent six months in hospital.

Back in Toronto he finished the work for his medical degree and then enlisted again, this time as a medical officer aboard a war ship in the Atlantic.

After the war he led a wild, reckless life and met Frances Penny, whom he married. He was doctoring the poor in the slums when he learned of his own ill health. An X-ray indicated that he had pulmonary tuberculosis, for which there was no cure. Claiming that he did not want his wife to be tied to a dying invalid, he forced her to divorce him, and went to spend his final days at Trudeau Sanatorium in New York State. There he decided to go out partying, ignoring all the rules laid down by the doctors. He smoked and drank into the early morning with the other patients. At that time prohibition was in effect, which meant he was breaking the laws of society as well as ignoring the medical advice offered to him.

As the disease spread through his body, however, he read of a new theory in a medical book that proposed pneumothorax surgery — deliberately collapsing the diseased lung — which might prevent the tubercular growth from spreading. His choice was either to wait for a lingering death or to risk an immediate one by acting as a guinea pig for the untried theory. He gambled and won. Two months after the operation he left the sanatorium and returned to Montreal to specialize as a thoracic surgeon, saving the lives of hundreds of T.B. patients who, like himself, were merely waiting for death. He worked with distinction at the Royal Victoria Hospital in Montreal and at Sacre Coeur in Cartierville. His operating skill, his prodigious output of medical treatises, and his invention of many surgical instruments soon earned him a reputation as a world-famous thoracic surgeon. He explained his new outlook on life: "It is only the dull and unimaginative who can lie abed in a sanatorium for a year and fail to rise a better and finer person."

Bethune attempted to introduce socialized medicine to Canada in the 1930's, when the poor were dying because they could not afford the cures. His views were considered radical and communistic. He opened a free sick parade at the

Bethune in Canada working as a lumberjack. (centre)

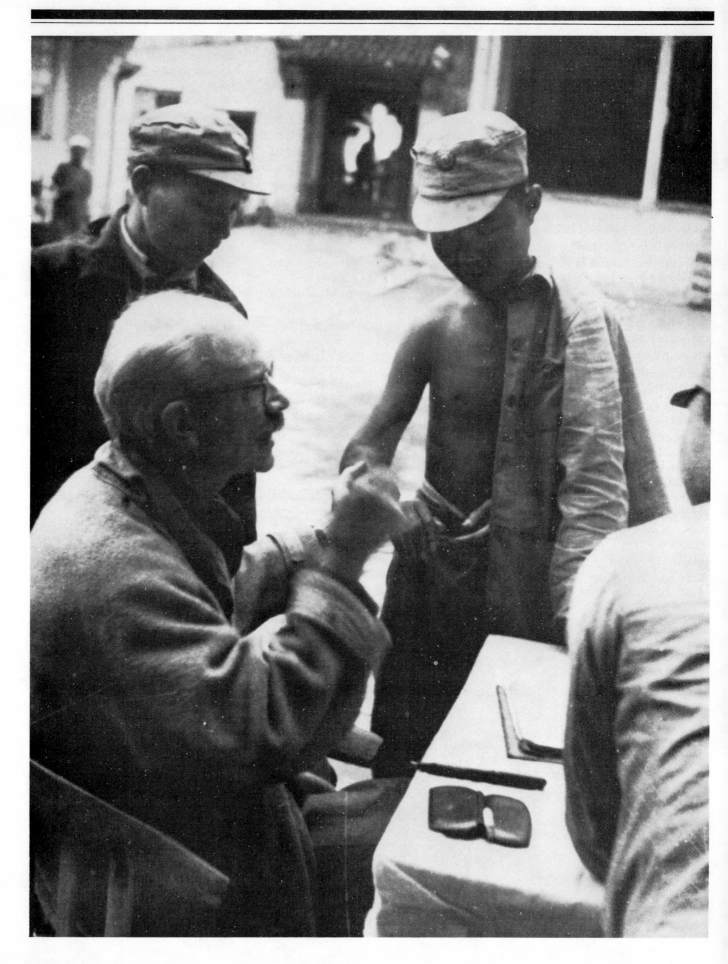

Verdun Y.M.C.A., but when civil war exploded in Spain he felt he should go to help the wounded.

In Spain he served with the losing side, the loyalists, as Franco's army, aided by Mussolini and Hitler, mercilessly slaughtered civilians. Bethune revolutionized battlefield medicine. With bombs dropping around him, he set up a mobile Canadian Blood Transfusion Service, which could take blood directly to the wounded, saving many lives which would otherwise have been lost if the patients had had to be taken all the way back to a hospital. His experiences in Spain made him angry and impatient with the politics of the democratic countries; he became a communist and travelled next to aid the Chinese army of Mao Tse-Tung in northern China.

In China he was welcomed by Mao, who made him Medical Chief of the Red Army. Medical knowledge and facilities were primitive. He worked without equipment, medicine, or finances to establish an entire medical corps from scratch. He trained thousands and improvised constantly, designing, for example, a compact field hospital capable of performing 100 operations and providing 500 dressings, which could be transported through narrow mountain passes on the backs of only two mules. He worked himself to death in his attempts to help the wounded Chinese.

> *"There is no morphine for their pain and when I hurt them, as sometimes I must, they weep the hopeless, overwhelming tears of little children. I have operated all day – ten cases, five of them very serious. I am tired, but I don't think I have been so happy for a long time."*

On November 13, 1939, Dr. Norman Bethune died. There were no surgical gloves available under the crude conditions, and a small cut from his own scalpel during an operation caused an infection to spread through his tired body. By that time his name had become a war cry used by the Chinese soldiers. Every November 13, a half-billion Chinese honour the heroic Canadian doctor whom they called "Pai Chu En".

TOPICS FOR DISCUSSION
1. Would you leave school to fight in a war as Norman Bethune did? Explain why or why not.

2. If you were wounded in a war, would you re-enlist as he did?
3. If you knew you were going to die, would you want to avoid your wife, husband, parents, children, friends?
Explain why or why not.
4. Would you risk immediate death with an untried operation as Bethune did or would you prefer to live a few certain years?
5. Is it possible to learn how to appreciate every day of life without first having to come close to death? If your life was saved by a miracle today, how would it affect your behaviour and attitude in the future?
6. Because he was a communist, Bethune was not recognized as a hero in Canada until recently. Do you think he should be considered a hero here? Explain.
7. Bethune went anywhere in the world where he felt his services were needed. Would you do the same?
8. Dr. Bethune could have lived a prosperous life in comfort as a surgeon. Why didn't he?
9, What does "Pai Chu En" mean in English?

SUGGESTION
Obtain and view the documentary film "Bethune" (B & W; one hour, National Film Board).

Bethune in Spain.

FILM CHALLENGE
Obtain and view the following short films which are available from the National Film Board of Canada. Your school or local library may also have copies of the films.

a) *Ride for Your Life.*

b) *Judoka*

1. Write a movie review on one of them. What was each film attempting to achieve? Were they successful? Did you enjoy them? Explain why or why not.

2. At the time each film was made, Mike Duff and Doug Rogers had only become the second best in the world in their chosen sports. Were they still heroes? Do you have to be first or the best to become a hero?

3. Just as a writer uses figures of speech, a film maker uses a variety of techniques to emphasize the main points. Define the following terms. Can you find examples of them in the two films? Choose a point in one of the descriptions found in this book that could be emphasized by each film technique.
a) slow motion b) close up c) high angle shot d) low angle shot
e) freeze frame f) pan shot g) fade in or fade out h) a rack focus.

Doug Rogers from Judoka

176

Mike Duff from Ride for Your Life.

"BUZZ" BEURLING
Spitfire Ace

As a boy in Verdun, Quebec, "Buzz" Beurling used to linger at the hangar door hoping for a friendly word from a passing pilot or an opportunity for a short flight above the Cartierville airport. At the age of fourteen, he began to fly. On one occasion he worked all month to earn ten dollars to pay for a single flying lesson. Later, Ernst Udet, a famous German ace in World War I, taught him aerobatics. By the time he was eighteen, lean and 183 cm tall, he competed against many veteran flyers, including two R.C.A.F. pilots at Edmonton, and beat them all.

Winning an aerobatics contest was not enough for Buzz. He wanted action; not just flying action but fighting action. He wanted to engage in the ultimate life or death struggle. First, he tried to get to China to fly against the Japanese, but he failed. When war broke out in Europe, he attempted to join the Royal Canadian Air Force. He didn't have enough education, however, so they rejected him. Next he learned that the Finnish Air Force was desperate for pilots in their war against Russia. They claimed he was acceptable provided his parents gave their permission, but his parents refused. Undaunted, he sailed to Scotland on a freighter and applied to join the Royal Air Force. They agreed to take him, but only if he produced a birth certificate. Buzz had to ship back across the Atlantic, pick up his birth certificate, and return to Britain before he was finally accepted as a fighter pilot with the R.A.F.

By May, 1942, Beurling shot

Buzz Beurling in Malta, painting crosses on his plane to indicate his victories in the air.

down his first enemy fighter over Calais, France. At that time Malta, a British island base, was being battered by the German Luftwaffe and the Italian Air Force. It was the only siege in history conducted entirely from the air, and it left the defenders exhausted and hungry against the more powerful enemy. It was the perfect challenge for the unusual skill and courage of Buzz Beurling, whose devotion, dedication, and daring mastery of deflective shooting were already recognized. He was sent to Malta.

For five months, day after day, from June to October of 1942, Buzz soared above the Mediterranean in his *Spitfire*, eliminating twenty-eight enemy aircraft and earning the Distinguished Service Order, the Distinguished Flying Cross, and the Distinguished Flying Medal and Bar. His brave exploits made him the greatest Canadian fighter pilot of World War II. Some called him "Screwball" Beurling, because that was a word he used repeatedly to indicate his opinion of life and the world.

The air force had fitted gyro gun sights on each plane to enable the pilot to calculate the angle of deflection, but Buzz's fellow pilots claimed that the Canadian ace carried his own gun sights in his head and that he was faster and more accurate without the help of technology. Beurling explained that he thought about angles at all times and claimed he enjoyed them as a musician enjoyed thinking about the notes of a symphony.

Up in the sky, alone in his *Spitfire*, Buzz was fearless and reckless. Once he charged into the midst of a formation of *Junkers 88* bombers and shot down one of the fighters escorting them. On another occasion, he took on ten enemy planes and destroyed two. One day he sent four enemy fighters to their deaths in the Mediterranean. On October 13, 1942, he shot down a *Junkers 88* and two *Messerchmitt 109's*, but it was the next day that he charged, in a head-on attack, against enemy bombers. After destroying a large bomber, Buzz saw his squadron leader being pursued by an enemy fighter. Although wounded from his first encounter, he flew to the rescue and sent the enemy to a flaming death. Not satisfied, he climbed again, to battle yet another adversary who was also destroyed. At this point, Buzz's bullet-ravaged *Spitfire* was in trouble, and he was forced to parachute into the sea below, from which he was later rescued.

After Malta, he came home, a wounded hero. The R.C.A.F., who had once rejected him, now accepted his transfer to their force, gave him a commission and a post as an instructor. But Buzz was an unorthodox loner: he didn't drink; he despised sloppiness; he didn't want to be an officer; he was insubordinate; he scorned the R.C.A.F. Within months he had transferred back to a fighting squadron, and he continued destroying the enemy until his total number of "kills" reached thirty-one. However, the new close-knit squadron fighting required team-work; so after repeated clashes with authorities, Buzz Beurling, the individualist, resigned from the R.C.A.F. in 1944.

In civilian life in Montreal, Buzz was restless. He wanted to fly for Chiang Kai-shek's nationalist air force against Mao Tse-tung, but Ottawa refused him a visa. He had the reputation of a trouble-maker. In 1948, he headed back to the Mediterranean to fly in the Israeli-Arab war. On May 20, 1948, he was making a routine take-off from the Rome airport to ferry a *Norseman* aircraft to Israel when the machine stalled and crashed. At twenty-six years of age, the Canadian Spitfire ace was dead.

TOPICS FOR DISCUSSION
1. Although the man who taught the young Buzz was a German, Beurling became famous as a man who destroyed German pilots. What does this suggest to you about the nature of war?

2. What do you think of Buzz's parents refusing to allow him to join the Finnish air force?
3. What do you think it would feel like to send an enemy plane into the sea below?
4. Buzz worked best on his own rather than with a team or a set of rules. What kind of a person are you? Do you work well with others? Are you more comfortable working by yourself?
5. After the war, Buzz Beurling, like many soldiers, sailors, and airmen returning from combat, felt restless. Do you think this was due to the war or to his own personality?

CREATIVE CHALLENGE
1. Imagine you are Buzz Beurling and the year is 1942. Write a letter home discribing your emotions after killing your first enemy pilot.
2. Imagine the classroom is a T.V. studio. (If the equipment is available turn it into a T.V. studio.) Appoint members of the class to play the following roles:
a) An interviewer.
b) A pilot who flew with Buzz Beurling at Malta.
c) A superior officer of Buzz Beurling who used to have problems with him in the R.C.A.F.
d) A German or Italian flyer who was an opponent of Buzz Beurling during the war.
If the interview is interesting, use the same concept to explore different viewpoints on other heroes or heroines in this book.

A Spitfire.

JOHNNY LONGDEN

"The Pumper"

Johnny Longden came from England to Canada at two years of age. His father, who settled the family at Taber in Southern Alberta, worked in the coal mines. The large family of six children was a poor one and, at the early age of ten, Johnny was working as a cowboy in the summer, riding herd on neighbours' cows that grazed on the unfenced plains of Western Canada. By thirteen he left school and went to work in the coal mines, digging from seven every morning until four in the afternoon for a dollar and a quarter per day.

It was at local fairs on the weekends that Johnny met an Alberta horseman, Spud Murphy, who hired him to ride quarter horses in the Roman races. The boy had to stand astride two horses, one foot on the bare back of each, and in the summer of 1924 he won fourteen races. His rodeo-like efforts won him a job on Spud's ranch, galloping horses for $35 per month plus room and board.

Johnny's family were devout Mormons, and in 1927, he decided to visit the mother city of the faith, Salt Lake City. He made certain his visit coincided with the thoroughbred racing season. It was there that the owner of a big black gelding, which didn't like to have a rider on its back, offered Johnny $5 to ride the animal in a race. Johnny accepted and won the race.

Back on the Prairie circuit in Canada, Sleepy Armstrong, a trainer, was looking for a regular jockey. Johnny claimed that meeting Sleepy was the best thing that ever happened to him, because Sleepy taught him everything he knew about riding. For example, he learned to be at the track every morning by 6:30 a.m., exercising his mounts and getting to know their individual personalities before riding them in the afternoon. It was a habit he continued all his life. Johnny's rapport with his horses became legend. He described it as "feel".

"I can talk to a horse and he can talk to me – through my hands. I can tell exactly how my horse feels, how he is striding, how much stamina he has left — through my hands."

Johnny Longden's style of riding was so unconventional it caused an Australian commentator to compare him to "a frog on a log". In racing circles he quickly gained the nickname "the pumper". Basil Smith, who became Longden's agent, described why he got that label.

"Longden has won more nose finishes than any other jockey because of his pumping style in the stretch. He has very short legs. His riding style is more of a stand-up than a sitting crouch. He raises and lowers his body in rhythm with the horse's stride and at the finish he rises up, pumping his arms vigorously in order to get more out of a horse, hand riding his mount for that last effort."

By the end of the 1930's, Johnny was winning the big races: the Brooklyn Handicap, the Champagne Stakes, the Louisiana Derby and the Arlington Handicap. But it was in 1943 that he rode Count Fleet to win the Triple Crown of racing in the Kentucky Derby, the Preakness, and the Belmont Stakes. At the San Juan Capistrano in 1950, on the back of Noor, he beat Citation and set a new American record for 2.8 km.

Five times doctors insisted that Johnny Longden's racing days were finished. He was kicked, thrown, and rolled on. He had his back broken, his collar bone broken, his legs broken, and he even won a race with two vertebrae broken. By 1955, arthritis almost forced him to stop racing, but Johnny's strong spirit and will allowed him to achieve one of his best years of racing in 1956. By the time he did retire in 1966 to become a trainer, he had ridden 6,032 winners, a record up to that time.

TOPICS FOR DISCUSSION
1. Have you ever ridden a horse? Do you appreciate what Johnny meant when he spoke of "feel"?
2. Johnny's early life was hard, but he developed his talents and became a millionaire. What talents or interests do you have? How could you develop them?
3. List Johnny's physical injuries. Would you continue in an occupation that is so hazardous?

CREATIVE CHALLENGES
1. There are many colourful personalities who have been associated with horses and racing in Canada. Investigate one of them and prepare a short narrative based on his or her life.

EARL McCREADY

Wrestling Champion

Although he was only fourteen years old, Earl McCready weighed ninety kilograms and he was all solid muscle. His dream was to fight and beat the world's greatest wrestlers.

The problem was that the boy didn't know how to make use of his strength. He grew up on an isolated farm in Saskatchewan, where there was no one to teach him how to wrestle. Then one day he spotted an advertisement in a magazine entitled "How to Handle Big Men with Ease" and he sent for the mail-order pamphlet.

Armed with the instructions, which had been prepared by two well-known wrestlers, Frank Gotch and "Farmer" Burns, Earl began to practice the variety of holds on the farm hands who came to work on the threshing teams. When he started high school in Regina, he signed up for the wrestling class at the Y.M.C.A., where he received his first instruction from coach Dan Matheson, a former Saskatchewan wrestling champion.

The inexperienced eighteen-year-old youth represented Regina at the Amateur Athletic Union meet at Westminster, B.C. in 1926, and won the Canadian heavyweight championship. He was immediately recruited by an American college,

the Oklahoma Agricultural and Mechanical College, to wrestle for their school. He won the national U.S. collegiate heavyweight championship in 1928, 1929 and 1930. In that last year he also became the U.S. national amateur champion. No one has ever equalled his record.

Meanwhile, McCready continued to defend his Canadian title successfully, and at the British Empire Games in Hamilton in 1930, he took the gold medal in the heavyweight division. Canada won every gold medal in all seven weight classes that year. Earl McCready is the only Canadian to be elected to both the American and Canadian Sports Halls of Fame.

After a twenty-five-year career as a professional wrestler, McCready retired, and with the degree he had obtained in physical education from the Oklahoma college, he became a masseur. When, in 1966, his left leg was amputated due to osteomyelitis, he did not allow it to affect his active life. Although he had an artificial leg, he continued to run his business and coached local high school wrestling and football teams.

TOPICS FOR DISCUSSION

1. Earl McCready achieved his boyhood dream. Do most people achieve their dreams? What are your dreams? Are you working toward achieving them?
2. Have you ever sent for an advertisement you saw in a newspaper? Were you happy with the product when it arrived?
3. Do you know any wrestling holds? Can you demonstrate them on your friends or classmates?
4. After becoming the best amateur wrestler in the U.S., Canada and the British Empire, Earl McCready turned professional. Is professional wrestling an honest sporting contest or an entertaining hoax?
5. If you lost one of your limbs, would you have the courage to continue despite the handicap?

CREATIVE CHALLENGE

1. Watch some professional wrestling on television. Listen to the interviews before and after the fights. Working with a partner, prepare an interview between a ringside commentator and a wrestler. Invent a name for the wrestler. Satirize the style of insulting and challenging your opponents. The verbs you use will have to be violent and aggressive. The adjectives used to describe your opponent should be insulting.

ARMAND BOMBARDIER

Inventor of the Snowmobile

The young French Canadian wanted to escape from his hometown of Valcourt. He felt confined by the snowdrifts that blocked roads to Sherbrooke and Montreal. Having a mechanical aptitude, he tackled the problem and the result was technology's answer to the dog-sled team, the snowmobile.

His first crude contraption, in 1921, included an airplane propeller that churned air and snow into a blizzard as the fourteen-year-old Armand tested it through the main street of Valcourt on a quiet Sunday. By 1936, after more than a decade of refinement, he produced his first successful machine.

Bombardier allowed Canadians and others throughout the northern countries of the world to surmount the snow barrier. He also introduced a new winter sport.

"He was an independent-thinking man, who was attracted to the things that other people couldn't do and one of those was to design a lightweight vehicle with extremely low ground pressures which would ride successfully on snow or muskeg swamp."

His inventor's imagination refused to rest. Rather than depending on sub-contractors or parts manufacturers, he made all the parts for his machines, including door locks and handles and even his own tires.

The independent Canadian also refused to sell out to large American companies, although he would have

been the richer for it. He stubbornly insisted on building his own business from scratch and soon was employing half the men in Valcourt as he exported his inventions throughout the world.

TOPICS FOR DISCUSSION

1. Make a list of things that could be invented to enhance your life or others. Just for fun, include some that are ridiculous or humorous.

2. Bombardier was not only an inventor, he was a businessman. What kind of a business would you like to open? What name would you give your business? What would be the best location for it?

3. Most Canadian students are encouraged either to go to university or to learn a trade. Does anyone encourage young people to open their own business, which, like Bombardier's, might one day employ people, rather than looking for someone who will employ them?

4. Why is there no such thing as a Canadian automobile, exported to other countries as an example of Canadian ingenuity and workmanship, as Bombardier did with the snowmobile?

5. Can you imagine yourself opening a business that might one day employ half your town or community?

CREATIVE CHALLENGE

1. Imagine that your class has been given the challenge of designing a Canadian automobile. Each student should be involved in one of the following activities. Perhaps the class could be divided into groups that compete against each other.

a) Design the automobile. Draw a picture of what it will look like and list the special features it will have. What kind of an engine will it have? How fast will it go? What safety features will it include?

b) Prepare a magazine advertisement which attempts to sell the product to the public. What name will you give it? What adjectives, verbs, and adverbs will you use to convince people to purchase it? Examine other car ads for ideas.

c) Prepare a radio or television advertisement for the automobile. How will you convince Canadians that this is the car made for them and their needs?

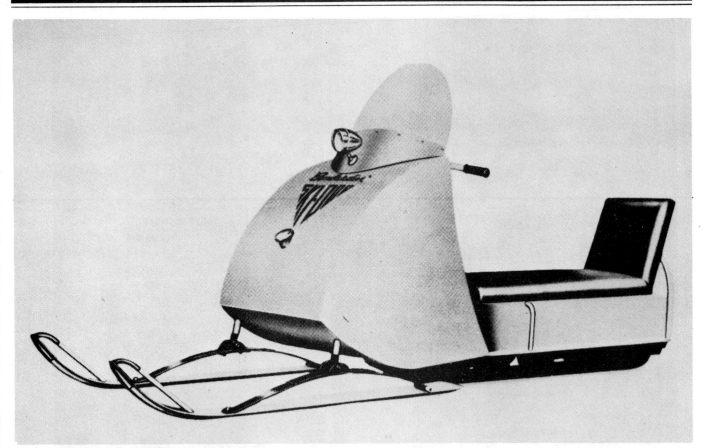

One of the original Bombardier snowmobiles.

A modern Bombardier snowmobile.

COLONEL DAN
"The Father of Harness Racing"

Dan MacKinnon was born in 1876 in Highland, Prince Edward Island, but at the age of ten he became an orphan and never continued in school. Instead he registered in a mail-order course in pharmacy and became Prince Edward Island's first registered pharmacist. At fourteen years of age he bought his first horse and drove in his first sulky race.

Dan was always interested in sports. He played football and, as a champion runner, won the Maritime title for 1.6 km in 1896, 1897 and 1898. Then he joined the 4th Regiment of Canadian Artillery in 1901 where, as a gunner, he was a member of the Canadian team that won the Londonderry Cup at Petawawa in 1907. As leader of the Canadian heavy artillery team, he beat the British competition in 1912. He was also a crack rifle shot.

When World War I broke out, he went overseas in 1916, where he was awarded the D.S.O. for outstanding service at the Somme, participated in the Canadian defence of Vimy Ridge, and for his gallantry at Passchendaele was awarded the French Croix de Guerre. When he retired from the military in 1923, he was appointed aide-de-camp to the governor-general.

Back in Canada, he opened a commercial fox farm and became one of the best breeders in the world. His school of silver fox farming in Charlottetown attracted students from around the world. He also owned the *Charlottetown Guardian* (the largest paper in the province) for over twenty years.

His childhood interest in harness racing, however, became Colonel Dan's main occupation. During his life he owned and trained seventy-eight horses, which he raced throughout Canada and the U.S.A. His victories on the tracks earned him the title of "father of harness racing" in the east and he was responsible for P.E.I. becoming "the Kentucky of Canada".

Even at the age of eighty-two, Colonel Dan was racing and winning with his trotter Windy June and his pacer Stalag Hanover.

***

TOPICS FOR DISCUSSION

1. Colonel Dan was successful in at least seven different areas of interest. Are you a versatile person? What are seven of your main interests?

2. At the age of eighty-two Colonel Dan was still active on the race track. What do most people do at eighty-two years of age? What do you think you will be doing when you are eighty-two?

3. What is your opinion of horse racing? Have you ever seen a horse race? Have you ever raced a horse? Have you ever seen a harness race?

CREATIVE CHALLENGE

1. Describe a senior citizen who you know and respect. Explain how the person's life was different than your own when he or she was your age.

2. Some people believe that the age of retirement should be extended or placed on a voluntary basis. Write an exposition in which you state clearly your own opinion. Give examples to support your viewpoint.

EMILY CARR
"Klee Wyck"

On December 13, 1871, Emily Carr was born in Victoria, British Columbia. She was to be a rebellious and eccentric individual most of her life.

Her mother died when Emily was only fourteen, and two years later her father died, also. To escape the strict discipline of her older sister and what she considered to be the hypocrisy of society in Victoria, she travelled to San Francisco when she was eighteen years old and studied art at the California School of Design.

Five years later she returned to Victoria and transformed the loft of a cow barn into a studio, where she painted and taught children's art classes. The courageous young artist suffered a lonely life when her work was not popularly accepted, but when the praise and recognition eventually came, she was embarrassed by it.

She travelled to France and England, where she encountered the "new art" at the turn of the century and adapted it to her own unique paintings of Indian forms and the vast British Columbia rain forests. She was a non-intellectual and learned intuitively, responding mainly to the spirit of things and people.

Emily loved birds and animals, and throughout her life felt strongly attracted to them. In fact, she seemed to prefer animals to people. Her collection of companions included dogs, cats, birds and even a pet monkey. In 1912, during visits to the wilderness areas of the Queen

Charlotte Islands and Skeena River, where there were no tourist accommodations, she was always accompanied by her big sheepdog as she slept in tents, toolsheds, missions, and Indian villages. From these rugged journeys she collected a wealth of sketches.

In the large cities of France and England Emily had become depressed and ill, but in the simple, open villages of northern B.C. she was given her Indian name, Klee Wyck, "the laughing one".

By 1927, acceptance by the Group of Seven and recognition in major art centres around the world established her as part of the international art stream. The cigar-smoking Emily expressed her happiness at succeeding in "making the

spirit of western places speak to westerners".

But then came a series of heart attacks that prevented her from continuing her excursions into the wilds. Undaunted, she turned her talents to writing, and in 1941 her book *Klee Wyck*, won the Governor General's Award, Canada's highest tribute to a writer. Although she published a second book, *The Book of Small*, in 1942, her writing career was cut short by illness, and she died on March 2, 1945.

TOPICS FOR DISCUSSION
1. Do you consider yourself rebellious or eccentric? Explain.
2. Are you embarrassed by praise? Why or why not?
3. Do you like Emily's paintings? Who is your favorite artist?
4. Do you find Emily's collection of pets strange, or do you understand how she felt?
5. When she could no longer travel, Emily developed a second skill, writing, and became equally famous as an author. What are your skills? Which ones will you develop?

CREATIVE CHALLENGES
1. If you are artistic, try to create a work of art that combines your talents and is a unique expression of Canada.
2. Write a description of your favorite artist explaining the main features of style represented in the artwork.

Zunoqua Of The Cat Village by Emily Carr.

BARBARA ANN SCOTT

The Youngest Ice Champion in History

From the moment her parents gave seven-year-old Barbara Ann her first pair of skates, she wanted to be a graceful figure on ice. By the time she was nine years old, skating was monopolizing her life to such a degree that she quit school and continued her studies with a private tutor. The flexible routine enabled her to spend eight or nine hours a day on the rink.

By 1939, her devotion to the sport began to reap its rewards as she won the Canadian Junior title, although she was only eleven years old. That was only the beginning. At sixteen she won the North American Championship, and became the youngest continental ice champion in history. International skating demanded two skills: the compulsory figures and free skating. Grueling practice ensured Barbara Ann's success in the first, and her natural talents were given an opportunity to shine in the second. After her North American victory, she expanded her practice schedule, looking ahead to European and world contests.

The World Championships at Stockholm in 1947 were her first opportunity, and she outskated the best to become the new world champion at only eighteen years of age. The victory was not won by luck. She proved it by adding to her conquests the European title in Davos, Switzerland. In their enthusiasm the home-town fans in Ottawa presented her with a new yellow convertible when they turned out by the thousands to cheer her home, but Barbara Ann refused the gift. To accept it might have damaged her amateur status, and that would have prevented her from attaining the one prize she had yet to win: an Olympic gold medal.

When Barbara Ann Scott returned to Europe the next year, she again took the European and world titles, but in addition she entered the Winter Olympics. The open-air ice conditions at St. Moritz were poor — the rink was bumpy — but Barbara Ann spun, leapt and

spiralled her way to a gold medal. She was an instant superstar. Fans mobbed her; crowds followed her; her country honoured her. Returning to Canada, she became the celebrity of the year. Her bashfulness and friendly charm won over the public.

Having collected every amateur title, Barbara Ann Scott turned professional and continued to amaze the millions of followers who flocked to see her dazzling displays around the world.

TOPICS FOR DISCUSSION

1. Is there anything to which you are so devoted that you are willing to spend eight or nine hours a day, working summer and winter, in order to excel at it?

2. Although Barbara Ann Scott was a Canadian champion at eleven years of age, Jean Wilson was being jeered by her schoolmates at fifteen for her awkward attempts to skate for the first time. Both became world champions. What does this suggest to you about what is necessary to become the best in the world in any achievement?

RESEARCH PROJECT

Research and write a short biography on one of the following women, who, like Barbara Ann Scott, became Canadian, and world, champion:

a) Lela Brooks, a speed skater from Toronto who, in 1926, became world champion.

b) Jean Wilson, another Toronto speed skater, who won world skating events during the Winter Olympics at Lake Placid, N.Y., in 1952. She set new speed records, but never collected the prize she had won because she died, after suffering from a rare muscular disease accompanied by progressive fatigue and paralysis.

c) Petra Burka, who arrived in Canada at four years of age from Amsterdam, and by eighteen had won the Women's Figure Skating Championship of the world for her-

self and her adopted country in 1965.

d) Karen Magnusson, a Vancouver figure skater who injured both legs during competition but recovered from wheelchair and leg casts to become the world champion figure skater in 1973.

RESEARCH CHALLENGE
QUIZ ON SKATERS

1. Speed skating is a popular sport in North America and Europe. Several Canadian men were world champions. Can you identify the following?

a) A youth from Winnipeg called "The Speed Skater of the Century", who set a world record for eight kilometres, a record which has never been equaled.

b) "The Toronto Flyer", who at nineteen broke three world speed records, and at the peak of his career held nine world records.

c) The world champion speed skater from Manitoba who, in the late 1800's became the first athlete from that province to win a world sporting title.

d) A speed skater from Bethany, Ontario, who challenged and beat the world champion when only sixteen, and who in old age, with both legs amputated, still gave skating lessons from a wheelchair.

2. Who were the three Canadian couples who won world Champion figure skating contests in the following years?

a) 1954, 1955
b) 1960
c) 1962

3. What do the following have in common?

a) Donald Jackson
b) Donald McPherson
c) Louis Rubenstein

If you wish to read more about any of the individuals in this quiz or to see photographs of them, obtain a copy of *Sporting Heroes of Canada* from your librarian.

191

LIONEL CONACHER
"The Big Train"

Lionel Conacher grew up in a poor family of ten children and had to survive on the rough streets of the Davenport Road area in Toronto. Like his brothers and sisters before him, he attended Jesse Ketchum Public School, where he became involved in sports at an early age, playing football in the Toronto City Rugby League. His father was a teamster and, with such a large family, couldn't afford to give his children a good education. Lionel dropped out of school in grade eight to help feed the family. He had con-

cluded even then that sports was the road he would take out of the poverty of his youth. His determination was to shape himself into the greatest all-round athlete in the history of Canada.

He mastered every sport he played. At the age of sixteen, he won the Ontario fifty-seven kilogram wrestling championship. Four years later, he fought his first competitive boxing match and took the Canadian light-heavyweight championship. In the meantime, he was playing middle wing for the Toronto Central Y's football team when they won the Ontario championship in 1918.

He had filled out to ninety kilo-

grams and over 183 cm of powerful solid muscle when he played for the Argos in the Grey Cup of 1921, leading them to a 23-0 victory over the Edmonton Eskimos by scoring fifteen points himself. In the same year he fought a three-round exhibition bout with the world heavyweight champion, Jack Dempsey.

One day, in 1922, he led the Toronto Hillcrest team to the Ontario baseball championship by hitting a triple in the final inning, then jumped into a car to rush across the city and join his lacrosse team, the

Maitlands, who were losing 0-3 in the Ontario lacrosse championship. Lionel scored four goals and assisted in another, helping to win the championship game 5-3.

Conacher explained why he got a slow start into hockey.

"The average kid starts skating at the age of seven or younger. I laced on skates for the first time at the age of sixteen, and you'll never know the humiliation and utter weariness of the long hours which I spent on the rinks with younger and much more skilled players before I won a post in junior circles."

He was on the Pittsburgh Pirates new team when it became part of the expanding National Hockey League. In 1934, playing for the Chicago Black Hawks, he lead his team to a Stanley Cup victory. The next year he was bought by the Montreal Maroons and helped them win the 1935 Stanley Cup. In eleven years as defenceman in the N.H.L., Conacher scored 80 goals and 105 assists. His nose was broken eight times and he collected over 600 stitches — 150 on his face and head.

Conacher finally retired from professional sports and entered politics as the Liberal MPP for Toronto Bracondale. He switched to federal politics in 1949, representing his Toronto Trinity riding. The "Big Train", so named because of the manner in which he charged through opponents, was chosen Canada's all-round athlete of the half century in 1950.

In May, 1954, he drove from Toronto to Ottawa to play for the MP's against the parliamentary press gallery in an annual softball contest. In the sixth inning he smashed a ball to left field, but as he rounded third base, he suffered a heart attack. He was dead in twenty minutes.

TOPICS FOR DISCUSSION

1. **Can you think of any Canadian athlete today who could compare to Lionel Conacher?**
2. **Although poor and uneducated, Conacher became famous and respected. Do young people in Canada still have the same opportunity to do well?**
3. **Many people from a family and social background similar to Conacher's might have ended up unknown. What determines a person's fate?**
4. **Would Conacher have made a good politician? Explain.**
5. **Does Conacher's death seem tragic, like that of Howie Morenz? What is tragedy?**

CREATIVE CHALLENGE

1. **Create a game based on famous Canadian athletes. The game should test the knowledge of the players. What equipment will your game involve? Will you use dice, cards, darts, etc? Write out the directions and rules. Keep in mind that instructions cannot be ambiguous. How many players will be involved? How will someone win the game?**

BROCK CHISHOLM
Soldier – Psychiatrist

Brock Chisholm, named after the military hero General Isaac Brock who died in the Battle of Queenston Heights during the war of 1812, was a contradiction in many ways. Brock was an outspoken strong-willed individual, as rugged in his viewpoints and determined in his convictions as any Canadian who has won world-wide recognition and acclaim.

In World War I he was a private in Canada's armed forces but by World War II he was head of the Royal Canadian Medical Corps, the only psychiatrist who ever had command of an army's medical services. His military life, like his public and private life, was controversial. Contrary to army tradition, he instituted a scientific system of "matching the man to the job", which won him world recognition and respect.

In Toronto in 1936, Brock was a practicing psychiatrist sadly realizing that his fight with the confused

psyches of his patients was a slow and painful one, caused by social evils. As he described it, "you can only cure retail but you can prevent wholesale". His concern for the health of the total community took him outside of Canada, and within ten years he was the executive secretary of the World Health Organization in Geneva. His dedication and visionary characteristics soon won for him the highest medical position in the world when he became the first director-general of the World Health Organization. For this reason the Canadian doctor's revolutionary viewpoint of health as "a state of complete physical, mental and social well-being and not merely the absence of disease and infirmity", became the corner stone of the World Health Organization's charter.

Under his guidance, United Nations teams warred against yaws in Indonesia, glaucoma in Africa and cholera in Egypt, but it was his abilities as an administrator which made it all possible. He initiated a world-wide epidemic warning system by short-wave radio as well as the global standardization of drugs and drug strengths. Even as a bureaucrat Brock was unique; he hated red tape and paper work. Like Napoleon, he allowed only six men to make reports to him, thereby avoiding hours of detailed conversations and enabling him to hear only the facts so he could make positive decisions quickly. On his wall hung a letter written by the Duke of Wellington, when in Spain, to the Secretary of War back in London. "My Lord, if I attempt to answer the mass of futile correspondence that surrounds me I should be debarred from all serious business of cam-

paign. I must remind your Lordship for the last time that so long as I retain an independent position I shall see to it that no officer under my command is debarred by attending to futile drivelling of mere quill-driving in your Lordship's office from attending to his first duty, which is, as always, to train the private men under his command."

Chisholm was more than just an international knight attempting to cure the world of its ills. He was also a thinker and philosopher, who predicted the population explosion and its consequences, as well as the dangers of nuclear war, long before such ideas were popular. His outspoken, careless nature, however, earned him a name as a villain rather than a prophet when, at a small, insignificant gathering of parents during a school meeting, he objected to the perpetuating of the Santa Claus myth. Newspapers magnified his observations beyond their importance, and one of the greatest medical heroes in the history of our country was branded as the man who hated Santa.

In 1953 Brock Chisholm retired from public office to a log cabin, which he built by himself on the rugged coast of Vancouver Island.

TOPICS FOR DISCUSSION
1. **Brock Chisholm was named after a Canadian hero. Which names, based on famous Canadians, would you give to a son or a daughter of your own?**
2. **What did Chisholm mean when he said "you can only cure retail but you can prevent wholesale"?**
3. **Both Chisholm and the Duke of Wellington hated "red tape". Describe your own experiences with red tape.**

4. **Do you object to perpetuating the Santa Claus myth? What are the psychological advantages or disadvantages of such a myth?**

CREATIVE CHALLENGES
1. **Imagine that you are a psychiatrist. Describe an interview with one of your patients.**
2. **Write a formal essay on the topic of psychology, the United Nations, or world health standards. First check with your teacher on the characteristics of a formal essay.**

Rosemary Brown M.L.A. —(Vancouver-Burrard) This psychological counselor from Simon Fraser University become ombudswoman for the B.C. Status of Women Council, entered politics, fought discrimination as a representative of the National Black Coalition of Canada, and became the first Canadian to be awarded a coveted United Nations Human Rights Fellowship.

DOUG HEPBURN

"The Crippled Giant"

Doug Hepburn hated school, because the other students made his life miserable by mocking his physical deformities. The skinny youth was born with crossed eyes and a clubfoot. Doctors who operated on his foot bungled the job, leaving him with a withered leg and a permanently weak ankle. To add to his problems, his parents were divorced when Doug was only five years old, and he went to live with his grandmother. He turned to weightlifting to gain the muscle necessary to beat the school bullies, but he became so involved in lifting barbells and increasing his weight from a weak 66 kg to a powerful 102 kg, he dropped out of school and left home to become a bouncer in a beer parlour.

Doug learned several years later about competitive weightlifting, and without coaching he mastered the three Olympic lifts, the press, the clean-and-jerk, and the snatch, until he felt confident enough to enter a Vancouver competition. He pressed ninety-one kilograms — a new Canadian record. When word of his accomplishment reached the weightlifting headquarters in Montreal, the national officers would not believe it. Doug Hepburn was an unknown name.

In 1949 he went to Los Angeles, entered the United States national open championship, and beat John Davis with a press of 157 kg. The weightlifting authorities in Canada still ignored him; he was not even invited to join their team in the 1952 Olympics at Helsinki. Ironically, the gold medal was won by the American, John Davis, who

Hepburn had defeated three years before in California.

Friends of Doug had to raise the money themselves to send him to the Stockholm world championships in 1953. In a stadium packed with thousands of fans, men from twenty nations vied for the weightlifting championship of the world. The favourite with the crowd was the giant with the withered leg from Canada, limping on a sprained ankle. Without a coach or even a companion he beat the best in the world, to win the championship with a total lift of just over 467 kg.

Canada finally recognized its unknown hero. The *Toronto Star* voted him Canada's athlete of the year, and the B.C. Newsman's Club elected him British Columbian of the year. The mayor of Vancouver gave him a salary of $150 a month, calling him a personal bodyguard to assure his amateur status in sports, during the period of time he was in training for the British Common-

wealth games, which were to be held in Vancouver in 1954. Hepburn did not let down his friends and supporters. He won the gold medal and established new games records, with lifts of 168 kg in the clean-and-jerk, 168 kg in the press, and 130 kg in the snatch.

However, Canada did let Doug Hepburn down as it has done for many of its heroes and heroines. When the Commonwealth games finished, his salary with the city ended. No one raised the funds he needed to defend his world title in Germany. After unsuccessful careers pro-wrestling and running a gymnasia chain, Doug started drinking. Finally he was forced to enter Hollywood Hospital in Vancouver, where he received L.S.D. treatments for his alcoholism.

TOPICS FOR DISCUSSION
1. **Doug was different from the other students in school, so they made his life miserable. Are there**
students in your school whom others mock? What can you do to make life more pleasant for such people?
2. Through exercise and determination, Doug built up his physical strength. Could you improve your physical condition? Why don't you?
3. Hepburn had to support himself to a large degree. Do you believe that anyone who has an exceptional talent should be aided by the Canadian government and people? Is it possible that many Canadian athletes remain unknown despite their talents?
4. Which other heroes or heroines did Canada "let down"? Explain how.
5. Which other heroes or heroines of Canada developed drinking problems?

CREATIVE CHALLENGE
Invent an imaginary ending of your own to conclude the story of Doug Hepburn.

MARILYN BELL
The Girl Who Conquered Lake Ontario

Just before midnight on September 7, 1954, sixteen-year-old Marilyn kisses her parents and slips into Lake Ontario at Youngstown, N.Y. For the first few hours she sprints toward her destination, Toronto, which is on the other side of Lake Ontario. The lake has never been swum across, and although this is not a race, young Marilyn is overshadowed by two older, more experienced women swimmers: Winnie Roach Leuszler, twenty-eight, who, like Marilyn, is attempting the long swim because she feels a Canadian swimmer can conquer a Canadian lake as easily as an American, and Florence Chadwick, thirty-four, the American who is considered the world's best woman swimmer.

Of the three contestants, Ms. Chadwick is the only one who has been offered the prize money of $10 000 if she makes it across the lake to the Canadian National Exhibition grounds. Ironically, although the money is offered by the Canadian National Exhibition in Toronto as a part of its tradition in marathon swims, the two Canadian swimmers were not invited to take part and will not be given the prize even if they beat the American swimmer imported for the occasion. The swim will be an all-night ordeal; the C.N.E. sponsors hope Chadwick will arrive in Toronto by mid-afternoon the next day.

Chadwick is pulled sick and exhausted from the cold grip of Lake Ontario twenty kilometres from the start. Leuszler lasts thirty kilometres before the lake defeats her. Only Marilyn Bell continues the struggle.

Radio and newspapers alert the public, and people begin to gather at the waterfront. The news flashes across the country. The world's best swimmer is out. A young Canadian girl is still swimming. The hopes and hearts of millions battle the cold waves with Marilyn. The same question is asked by all, can she make it?

Through the day, offers of prizes

and gifts pour in. After sixty-five kilometres and twenty-one grueling hours, she reaches the breakwater west of the exhibition grounds, which are overflowing with cheering spectators. The C.N.E. announces that Marilyn will be given the $10 000 posted for Chadwick's swim.

TOPICS FOR DISCUSSION
1. What is the longest distance you have ever swum?
2. Many young swimmers have followed Marilyn's lead and crossed Lake Ontario since that time. Many have drowned trying. Why would people like Marilyn risk their lives to swim a lake?
3. Are there young Canadians today who have become famous as distance swimmers?

CREATIVE CHALLENGES
1. Many famous people are hired by businesses to promote products. What products do you think Marilyn Bell could advertise? i.e. bathing suits, swimming pools, etc. Write a script for her that might be used to promote the product.

Using other famous Canadians found in this book, pick an appropriate product and write similar endorsements. The choice of words is an important part of any advertisement. Underline the adverbs and adjectives you used.

TWO FAMOUS CANADIAN SHIPS
and Their Captains

Bluenose was one of the finest fishing schooners ever built and a symbol of Nova Scotian skill. She beat every American ship that challenged her for the International Fisherman's Trophy and today can still be seen on each Canadian ten cent coin. Her skipper, Captain Angus Walters, was a colourful character who first went to sea at the age of thirteen.

Miss Supertest III was built in a former chicken house and driven by an Ontario chicken farmer, Bob Hayward. She won the Harmsworth trophy, the highest prize for international powerboat racing, in 1959, 1960, and 1961. In September, 1961, Hayward was killed during a race and the designer, Jim Thompson of London, Ontario, retired the craft from competition, explaining:

> "With the untimely death of Bob Hayward, the members of our racing team would derive little satisfaction from further success."

Captain Angus Walters.

Bob Hayward.

RESEARCH CHALLENGES

1. **Choose either the *Bluenose* or *Miss Supertest III* and research the story of how each became a world champion.**
2. **Write a biography on either Captain Angus Walters or Bob Hayward.**
3. **George Herrick Duggan was known as the dean of Canadian yachting. Who was he and what did he do to earn his title?**
4. **Walter Windeyer brought Canada its first world championship in the international Dragon Class in 1959. What is the "Dragon Class" and how did Windeyer win it for Canada?**
5. **Write a physical description of either the *Bluenose* or *Miss Supertest III*.**

The Bluenose.

Miss Supertest III.

NANCY GREENE
"Tiger"

"I can't remember not being able to ski", explained Nancy, who, from the age of three in Rossland, British Columbia, accompanied her parents and five siblings skiing on Red Mountain. From the beginning, her natural ability was obvious, but it was not until she joined her high school team that she began to race. When only fifteen years old, she competed in the Canadian junior championships and, within two years, had won a place on the Canadian Olympic team.

It was then that competitive skiing took over her life, both winter and summer. Her fighting spirit won her the nickname "Tiger", as the sport that had once been merely a pleasure became the centre of her existence. During the winter Olympics in 1960 at Squaw Valley, she was 22nd in the downhill race, but by the 1964 Innsbruck Olympics she was 7th in the downhill and 15th in the slalom.

In 1967, the first World Cup competition was instigated, the sport at the time being dominated by skiers from France. Points would be given on performances in nine different meets, to be held in Europe as well as North America. After the first three meets in Europe, Nancy held an overall lead, but she left the competitions to return to Canada and promote races on Canadian slopes. She felt it was more important to develop Canadian talent than to pursue her personal career. By the time Nancy returned to the World Cup competition, she had missed three of the meets and had fallen behind Marielle Goitschel and Annie Famose, both from France.

By the final meet, held at Jackson Hole, Wyoming, Nancy was still twenty-one points behind Goitschel. She easily won both heats of the giant slalom, and in the women's slalom she edged out the French skier to win the world title for Canada by seven hundredths of a second.

The next year the pressure was on Nancy to retain her World Cup title and to win an Olympic gold medal to prove herself the best skier in the world. She sprained her ankle in competition before the Olympics at Grenoble, France, and was discouraged when she placed tenth in the downhill. However, in the slalom she came back with a beautiful second run, to place second and win a silver medal, watching her French rival Goitschel take the gold.

Only the grand slalom was left. Nancy got tough, and her determination won her a gold medal. She described her victory enthusiastically; "I feel great. It is the best race I've ever skied."

Her time was four seconds under that of her closest competitor, the widest margin in recent Olympics. In the same year, 1968, on the slopes of Red Mountain, British Columbia, where she had learned to ski, she ensured her second win of the World Cup competition in front of a home-town audience. It was her last skiing victory. She retired that year, although named Canada's outstanding female athlete for the second year in a row. France was displaced as the dominant power in women's skiing, as Nancy Greene proved to all Canadians that we can produce world champions.

TOPICS FOR DISCUSSION
1. At the time this book was published Canada had never had a male world champion skier. Why do you think this is the case in a country of mountains and snow?
2. Is a feeling of nationalism in sports competition beneficial? Is nationalism in areas outside sports beneficial? Is nationalism always beneficial? Are Canadians too nationalistic?
3. There are fewer women in this book than men. Is this because women are less heroic or because they have not been given an equal opportunity in the past? Do you expect to see more heroines in the future?

RESEARCH CHALLENGES

1. Write a brief biography on one of the following women who became world champion skiers.

a) Betsy Clifford, from Quebec, who at sixteen was the youngest skier to win a world title in the history of the sport when she won the giant slalom at Val Gardena on February 14, 1970.

b) Anne Heggtveit, from Ottawa, who at twenty-one years of age won a gold medal during the Winter Olympics at Squaw Valley in 1960.

c) Lucile Wheeler, from St. Jovite, Quebec, who won Canada's first Olympic medal in skiing in 1956.

2. Make a list of the men and women in Canada today who you would consider heroic. Compare them with the personalities chosen by your classmates. Conduct a survey in your school or neighbourhood. When listing the people consider areas such as medicine, entertainment, sports, politics, military, business, etc.

George Athans, Jr., Canadian water skier and the world champion in 1971, 1972, and 1973.

LESTER B. PEARSON
A Man of Peace

Lester was born in Toronto on April 23, 1897 and, when a teen-ager, fought with the Canadian army during the war of 1914. He held the rank of captain until he transferred in 1917 to the R.F.C. as a pilot with the rank of flight-lieutenant.

After the war, he taught history for four years at the University of Toronto before joining the Department of External Affairs in 1928. After a successful diplomatic career, which included being Canada's ambassador to the U.S.A., he left the civil service and became a politician. Prime Minister St. Laurent appointed him Secretary of State for External Affairs.

It was as Canada's representative at the United Nations that he built a world-wide reputation as a man dedicated to keeping world peace. There he initiated the U.N. Emergency Force in the Middle East, a force that was later expanded to other troubled regions around the world and whose objective was to keep peace. In recognition of his work, he was awarded the Nobel Peace Prize in 1957.

In January, 1958, he became leader of the Liberal Party and on April 22, 1963, was elected Prime Minister of Canada.

TOPICS FOR DISCUSSION
1. How many different occupations did Lester B. Pearson participate in during his life? How many occupations do you expect to have? Do you have any idea what they might be? Do you think Pearson knew ahead of time what he would become or achieve?

2. **What skills would be involved in the following jobs?**
a) **Fighter pilot**
b) **University professor**
c) **Ambassador in a foreign country**
d) **Politician**
e) **Secretary of State for External Affairs**

f) **Prime Minister of Canada**
4. **Is the U.N. Emergency Force still active in the Middle East? To what other countries have Canadians been sent to maintain peace?**
5. **Who was Prime Minister of Canada before Pearson? Who was Prime Minister after him?**
6. **Lester B. Pearson also signed the**

North Atlantic Treaty for Canada in 1949. What is N.A.T.O.? Why is it a cornerstone of Canadian Foreign policy?

7. What is your personal opinion of Lester B. Pearson? Explain clearly your reasons for reaching such a conclusion.

8. What is the Nobel Peace Prize?

CREATIVE CHALLENGES

1. Write a comparison showing the similarities between the roles of the U.N. Force and the original North West Mounted Police Force that went to western Canada. What characteristics would the members of both forces have to have in common?

2. Research and write a report on the history of the U.N. Force. Conclude with your own personal opinion of it.

3. Imagine yourself to be a member of the U.N. Force and describe an adventure you have while working as a soldier in a foreign country, where the language and customs are different from your own.

4. Write a science-fiction story describing the formation of an "Inter-Planetary Peace Force", established by a Canadian in the year 2100.

Canadian soldier serving as a member of the United Nations Peace Force in Cyprus.